Autogen

MCFARLAND HEALTH TOPICS SERIES

Living with Multiple Chemical Sensitivity: Narratives of Coping.
Gail McCormick. 2001

Graves' Disease: A Practical Guide.
Elaine A. Moore with Lisa Moore. 2001

Autoimmune Diseases and Their Environmental Triggers.
Elaine A. Moore. 2002

Hepatitis: Causes, Treatments and Resources.
Elaine A. Moore. 2006

Arthritis: A Patient's Guide.
Sharon E. Hohler, RN. 2008

*The Promise of Low Dose Naltrexone Therapy: Potential Benefits
in Cancer, Autoimmune, Neurological and Infectious Disorders.*
Elaine A. Moore and Samantha Wilkinson. 2009

Living with HIV: A Patient's Guide.
Mark Cichocki, RN. 2009

*Understanding Multiple Chemical Sensitivity:
Causes, Effects, Personal Experiences and Resources.*
Els Valkenburg. 2010

*Type 2 Diabetes: Social and Scientific Origins, Medical
Complications and Implications for Patients and Others.*
Andrew Kagan, M.D. 2010

*The Amphetamine Debate: The Use of Adderall,
Ritalin and Related Drugs for Behavior Modification,
Neuroenhancement and Anti-Aging Purposes.*
Elaine A. Moore. 2011

*CCSVI as the Cause of Multiple Sclerosis: The Science
Behind the Controversial Theory.* Marie A. Rhodes. 2011

*Coping with Post-Traumatic Stress Disorder: A Guide
for Families,* 2d ed. Cheryl A. Roberts. 2011

*Living with Insomnia: A Guide to Causes, Effects
and Management, with Personal Accounts.*
Phyllis L. Brodsky and Allen Brodsky. 2011

*Caregiver's Guide: Care for Yourself While You Care
for Your Loved Ones.* Sharon E. Hohler. 2012

*You and Your Doctor: A Guide to a Healing Relationship,
with Physicians' Insights.* Tania Heller, M.D. 2012

*Autogenic Training: A Mind-Body Approach to the
Treatment of Chronic Pain Syndrome and
Stress-Related Disorders,* 2d ed. Micah R. Sadigh. 2012

Autogenic Training

*A Mind-Body Approach to the
Treatment of Chronic Pain Syndrome
and Stress-Related Disorders*

Second Edition

MICAH R. SADIGH

MCFARLAND HEALTH TOPICS SERIES
Elaine A. Moore, *Series Editor*

McFarland & Company, Inc., Publishers
Jefferson, North Carolina, and London

LIBRARY OF CONGRESS CATALOGUING-IN-PUBLICATION DATA

Sadigh, Micah R.
    Autogenic training : a mind-body approach to the
treatment of chronic pain syndrome and stress-related
disorders / Micah R. Sadigh — 2nd ed.
        p.   cm — (McFarland health topics series).
    [Elaine A. Moore, series editor]
    Includes bibliographical references and index.

    ISBN 978-0-7864-7073-0
    softcover : acid free paper ∞

    I. Title.   II. Series: McFarland health topics.
    [DNLM: 1. Autogenic Training — methods.   2. Chronic
Pain — therapy.   3. Pain Management.   4. Stress Disorders,
Post-Traumatic — therapy. WM 415]
    616'.0472 — dc23   2012018738

BRITISH LIBRARY CATALOGUING DATA ARE AVAILABLE

Cover photograph © 2012 Shutterstock

Manufactured in the United States of America

McFarland & Company, Inc., Publishers
  Box 611, Jefferson, North Carolina 28640
  www.mcfarlandpub.com

For El Elyon

Contents

Acknowledgments

This is a tremendous opportunity to express my gratitude to my teachers and friends without whom the writing and publication of this book would not have been possible. I am indebted to the late Dr. Richmond Johnson, who introduced me to the wondrous world of psychology and psychophysiology during my undergraduate training at Moravian College. It was in his course in applied psychophysiology that I was introduced to autogenic therapies. Dr. Johnson also supervised my first scientific study on the treatment of migraine headaches with autogenic training. I was also blessed with wonderful mentors while I was completing my graduate work at Lehigh University. I am especially grateful to my amazing mentor Dr. Debra Finnegan-Suler who introduced me to the world of psychoanalysis. So much of what I know about psychotherapy I learned from her. I will forever cherish my memories of learning from and interacting with my two dear professors, the late Drs. John Mierzwa and William Stafford. It was an honor to be one of their students.

My clinical training in pain management would not have been complete without the privilege of working with my teacher and friend, the respected surgeon, Dr. Peter Kozicky, who has been tirelessly involved in helping those who are suffering from recalcitrant pain. His vision of a multidisciplinary pain center was decades ahead of its time.

I have been blessed to have met two remarkable pain and sleep medicine experts, Dr. Barry Glassman and Dr. Don Malizia, with whom I have had the pleasure of presenting at many conferences. My thanks to both of them for their friendship and professional association.

I want to extend heartfelt gratitude to my good friends and

dedicated clinicians Anne Schubert, Dr. Marcus Weber and Dr. Rick Schall for their helpful comments and encouragement during the preparation of the manuscript.

I am grateful to my colleagues at Cedar Crest College for their continued support. Special thanks to my friends and colleagues in psychology: Drs. Kerrie Baker, Diane Moyer, Sharon Himmenan, James Scepansky, and Jane Tyler-Ward. My thanks to my friend and colleague Dr. Allen Richardson, for suggesting such a wonderful publisher of scholarly books. To my students at Cedar Crest College, I owe special thanks for their enthusiasm, dedication, and their inspiring desire to learn.

My thanks and appreciation to Ms. Elaine Moore, the series editor. It has been a pleasure.

Finally, this book would not have been possible without the ever-steady support, love, and encouragement of my dear wife Michelle, who sacrificed much to give me the time for researching and writing. I promise that one of these days we will go on vacation without my bringing along books, articles, notes, and the aging laptop!

Micah R. Sadigh, Ph.D. • Bethlehem, Pennsylvania

Preface

Nearly ten years have passed since the publication of the first edition of this book. During these years, I have received a large amount of correspondence from patients and clinicians throughout the world with comments and questions. In this second edition I have provided additional information, examples, and case studies with regard to autogenic training, which address many, if not all, of the questions that were sent to me. After decades of using autogenic training to reestablish self-regulation, both in research and clinical settings, I am convinced that it remains one of the most powerful treatments for stress-related disorders, chronic pain, and other chronic conditions that require psychophysiological methods of symptom management.

My exploration of autogenic training began when I was completing my undergraduate studies at Moravian College and decided to take a class in psychophysiology and biofeedback. After reading dozens of papers about this technique and its medical and psychological applications, I became so intrigued that I decided to make a major investment and purchased the six "classic" volumes on autogenic therapy. These volumes consisted of autogenic methods, medical applications, applications in psychotherapy, research and theory, dynamics of autogenic neutralization, and treatment with autogenic neutralization. The wealth of clinical and empirical knowledge contained in these volumes was so vast that it took several years to read them.

It has been more than twenty years since those days, and autogenic training has continued to be a steady and important part of my professional life. After years of conducting research with this technique, I began using it to treat patients with chronic pain, anxiety disorders, and stress-related conditions, particularly cardiovascular disorders. In addition, I found the technique to be of immense value in treating recalcitrant insomnia and some of the more complex forms of sleep disorders, namely post-traumatic nightmares, night terrors, and the like.

As I mentioned above, throughout the years I have found the autogenic

1

technique to be a superior psychophysiological intervention, especially when used in the context of a multidisciplinary approach to pain management. Most patients not only report an improvement in their ability to cope with persistent pain, they almost invariably notice cognitive and emotional changes that are consistent with a replenishment of their physical and psychological resources. A steady improvement in sleep quality is a consistent result and without a doubt a hallmark of autogenic training. Because sleep loss is one of the main complaints of most chronic pain sufferers, the clinical benefits of this intervention cannot be overemphasized.

Thousands of published studies attest to the therapeutic effects of autogenic training. However, except for the six classic volumes mentioned previously, few books have been written on this topic, and none about its use in treatment of chronic conditions. Unfortunately, the coverage of autogenic training in books on relaxation therapy is so basic (usually one or two pages on heavy and warm phrases) that it is unlikely to produce any therapeutic results. Even worse, such overly general instructions may potentially bring about paradoxical and adverse therapeutic results.

The main purpose of writing this book is to present practitioners with a concise exploration of autogenic technique and its clinical use, especially in treating those suffering from chronic pain syndrome. Furthermore, the training principles presented here can be effectively used to treat a variety of stress-related conditions. As it will be emphasized throughout the book, patients who will be receiving autogenic training need to be under close medical supervision, mainly because of its potent and dynamic therapeutic nature. Various medication dosages may need to be adjusted as in many cases, lower doses of certain medication may become sufficient in symptom management. Changes in medications must remain under the purview of physicians. To further assist with appropriate uses of autogenic training in the treatment of particular disorders, a chapter has been dedicated to medical and psychological screening, which I highly recommend that practitioners review prior to assessing patients for this training.

Organization of the Book

The book is divided into three sections. The first section consists of chapters that address theoretical aspects of the treatment of chronic pain. Here special attention is paid to the connection between stress and chronic pain. A chapter is dedicated to the review of the literature on chronic pain disorder and its treatments. In addition to autogenic training, a variety of established mind-body techniques which purport to affect pain are also discussed.

In the second section, detailed information is provided about autogenic training, including its history and clinical formulations. Chapters are dedicated to requirements for effective training and medical and psychological screening. This section highlights the breadth, depth, and the multidimensional aspects of this training.

Finally, the third section consists of a detailed, step-by-step manual for autogenic training. The rationale for each component of training is provided prior to instructions for each exercise. At the close of each chapter in this section, detailed case studies are provided to act as examples of how autogenic training may be used in the treatment of various conditions. A total of six new case studies has been added to these chapters.

Several chapters are dedicated to advanced autogenic training, autogenic biofeedback, and the treatment of insomnia. Three new chapters have been added to this section. A comprehensive chapter on autogenic neutralization explores the use of this technique as a powerful form of psychophysiological psychotherapy. Detailed case presentations demonstrate the principles of autogenic abreaction and autogenic verbalization. A chapter has been added on the treatment of post-traumatic nightmares. This is followed by a final chapter on the use of autogenic training as palliative care. This section concludes with some of the most commonly asked questions about autogenic training and their answers. Additional questions and answers were added to this section.

I hope that practitioners and students will find the book helpful in exploring the many benefits of autogenic training as an effective treatment for chronic pain and stress-related disorders. Ultimately, it is our task to help our patients gain greater control over their symptoms and to assist them with tools to improve coping with the hope of reducing suffering whenever possible. A time-tested technique such as this should prove to be of significant therapeutic value.

Once again to those friends and colleagues who encouraged me and have incessantly reminded me of the benefits of writing this book, I owe my gratitude. Finally, I wish to quote a tribute originally given to the great Dr. Paul Ehrlich. This sentiment applies to the father of autogenic training, Dr. Johannes Schultz, and his tireless protégé, Dr. Wolfgang Luthe, as well.

Was vergangen kehrt nicht wieder,
Aber ging es leuchtend neider,
Leuchtet's lange noch Zuruck.

What has passed will never return,
But if it sank in dazzling flame,
Flashes of light will still remain.
[as quoted in Martha Marquardt, 1949].

The science of mind-body medicine owes much to the dedication and tireless empirical explorations of the pioneers of autogenic training and its adjunctive, therapeutic interventions. May this volume encourage further study of its clinical benefits, and inspire researchers to design and implement new investigations to the mechanisms of self-regulation.

Introduction

"So neither ought you to attempt to cure the body without the soul; and this...is the reason why the cure of many diseases is unknown to the physicians of Hellas, because they are ignorant of the whole, which ought to be studied also; *for the part can never be well unless the whole is well*"* [Plato's Charmides].

The history of medicine can be traced to the practices of the earliest civilization on the planet in Mesopotamia. Nearly 6,000 years ago, the priests of that ancient world assumed the role of physician-healer. The conceptualization of disease was based on a spiritual notion that disease was from the gods. Hence, prayer played a significant role in the process of healing. In addition to prayer, the proper use of water was emphasized, as water also came from above and had spiritual properties. A few centuries later, the Egyptians and the Hebrews developed their own practices of healing, which were multifaceted and life centered. That is to say, their initial focus was on preventative methods to enhance life and to avoid disease. The letters *Ankh* (Egyptian for life) and *Chai* (Hebrew for life) almost always appear in healing instructions of both of these cultures, a notion that was far in advance of how we view healing even to this day. Once again, both the Egyptian and Hebrew cultures emphasized prayer as a critical aspect in enhancing the body's recuperative properties. They had their own version of a mind-body medicine.

With the advent of Greek medicine, less emphasis was placed on spirituality as greater knowledge about anatomy led to a better understating of how disease progressed within the body. This brought about an explosion in the material understanding of disease and the role of bodily fluids in various sicknesses. One central method of treatment became that of finding ways to balance the bodily humors. Finally, the nineteenth-century revolution in medicine brought about significant changes in the conceptualization of causes of

*Emphasis was added.

5

disease and the search for effective treatments. Louis Pasteur's *Germ Theory* placed emphasis on the invisible, microorganismic causes of sickness and death. One key to disease prevention was, hence, the eradication of such microorganisms.

Other great scientists such as Rudolf Virchow asserted that disease was ultimately caused by defects in cells and organs of the body. *Omnis cellula e cellula,* or all cells come from cells, became a convincing argument to explore tissue pathology to understand the cause of disease. Such linear and mechanistic views about the nature of sickness became the very core of the revolution in medical science and persist with some degree of determination to this day (Weiner, 1977). The biomedical model came to view the human as a mechanical system that required a variety of interventions when it broke down or failed to function properly. As a result, this model did not incorporate any psychological and social variables that could potentially contribute to disease or recovery from disease.

Among the great minds of nineteenth and early twentieth century medicine was Paul Ehrlich, a man who has been viewed by many as the father of chemotherapy. He introduced the curative medical model based on the infectious and the cellular pathology models. Ehrlich believed that if the pathogenic origin of a disease was known, then the effective cure was only a matter of discovering the right chemical combination to eradicate the disease-generating pathogens. He referred to such curative chemical substances as magic bullets. After years of tireless work, his idealistic views became a reality as he developed the compound 606, an arsenic derivative which was used effectively to treat and cure the dreadful epidemic of neurosyphilis. The ingenious magic bullet concept has resulted in the discovery of innumerable compounds that have saved millions of lives. At the same time, it has plagued the Western world with the idea that for every disease there must be a "magic bullet," a curative pill, treatment, or injection. While Ehrlich's model has proven its effectiveness in the treatment of many diseases, it has serious limitations, especially when applied to the treatment of chronic and disabling conditions. It also fails to account for psychological, environmental, and stress-related contributors to the development of disease and physical breakdown. When it comes to the treatment of chronic conditions, unfortunately, there are no magic bullets.

These significant changes in the field of medicine brought about changes in the conceptualization of disease that were, at least theoretically, open to scientific scrutiny. To be sick meant that the physiology was compromised, and to be well again meant that the defect was repaired. This linear formulation was impressive, and worked in many cases, but often failed. A patient who was physiologically intact was manifesting symptoms of a disease, a disease which was unknown to the astute minds of the physicians of the time.

With the advent of psychoanalysis in the late 19th century, it was demonstrated that thoughts, feelings and internal, intrapsychic conflicts played a significant role in the manifestation of certain disorders. In the early days of psychoanalysis, much emphasis was placed on the neurological disorders that emerged from unconscious sources that resulted in a breakdown in the proper functioning of the nervous system. Such contributions gave birth to the development of a new branch in medicine, psychosomatic medicine. This branch of medicine grew as a result of remarkable empirical studies that were conducted by some of the pioneers of this field such as Helen Flanders Dunbar and Franz Alexander. Sickness was not simply a matter of a broken body but also an overwhelmed, conflicted mind. The re-introduction of the "mind factor" (thoughts and emotions) to the practice of medicine was not an easy one, nonetheless it was a necessary one. Alexander (1950) remarked on this development, saying, "Progress in every field requires a reorientation with the introduction of new principles. Although these new principles may actually be contradictory to the old ones, they are often rejected or accepted only after much struggle for recognition" (p. 19). The critical development of psychosomatic medicine was one critical step in developing a better understanding of health and disease, a long overdue development that had finally arrived.

After decades of research, Engel (1977) introduced the biopsychosocial model of medicine, which has gained much recognition since its inception. It has an integrated model of combining the time-tested biomedical model with the psychosomatic model, adding to it additional components, which were at one point left out of the equation of treatment and disease prevention. Let us further elaborate on this point. The biopsychosocial model, that is, a non-linear model, emphasizes that to understand the nature of disease and illness one must recognize the intimate interdependence and interactions among genetic, biological, psycho-emotional, cognitive, behavioral, and sociocultural variables and processes. "The biopsychosocial model is a scientific model constructed to take into account the missing dimensions of the biomedical model" (Engel, 1980, p. 535).

For example, persistent and recalcitrant conditions such as chronic pain syndrome, fibromyalgia pain syndrome, and chronic fatigue immune deficiency syndrome, as well as myriad of stress-related disorders, can best be understood from a biopsychosocial perspective since these conditions are multifactorial in nature and involve many complex variables. The traditional biomedical model with its focus on microorganismic and pathophysiological concepts is too limiting when it comes to the assessment, evaluation, and treatment of the aforementioned clinical entities. These system-wide conditions require a multidisciplinary approach with focus on coping and effective symptom management.

Haddox (1997) suggested that since the traditional, biomedical approach is not sufficient in effectively treating patients with chronic pain, the biopsychosocial model may be more applicable when addressing the needs of this population. This point was further highlighted in the works of Goldenberg, Burckhardt, and Crofford (2004) who emphasized the limitations of the biomedical model when it comes to the proper treatment of conditions such as fibromyalgia pain disorder. Since one of the most important goals of pain management is to improve quality of life, rather than a one-dimensional goal of pain erasure, a more integrated treatment approach is required. Again this echoes the intentions of Engel's biopsychosocial perspective. This model explores "physical (biomedical) aspects, psychological characteristics (e.g., behaviors, personality traits, coping styles, cognition, affective disturbances), and social features (e.g., employment history, job satisfaction, compensation status, role reversal) [of the patient]" (Haddox, 1997, p. 189). For instance, in recent years, a number of studies have suggested that when it comes to the assessment and treatment of chronic conditions, it is critical to consider how personality styles and disorders may affect coping (Sadigh, 1998; Sadigh, 2003). A study by Polatin and colleagues (1993) found a high prevalence of personality disorders (over 51 percent) in a population of chronic back sufferers. Hence, by recognizing personality factors, clinicians can more effectively design treatment packages and programs that can be most beneficial to the patient (Sadigh, 2003; Taylor, 2012).

Clearly, any chronic condition poses a challenge to clinicians who attempt to provide a treatment strategy with the hope that it will reduce anguish and help those affected live with fewer limitations. One of the most critical dimensions of chronic pain, and, for that matter, any other persistent condition, is the experience of suffering, which often evolves from the realization that there may be no relief in sight. Suffering can result in the experience of anxiety, depression, and learned helplessness, especially when the cause of the persistent symptoms, such as pain, is uncertain. Leshan (1964) stated that chronic pain patients live their waking hours in a nightmare because of the continual experience of having no control and helplessly wondering what may happen next. This is the type of a nightmare from which one cannot easily wake. Tollison (1998) further emphasizes this point by stating that "no one dies from benign [chronic] pain, but many victims suffer a disabled and pleasureless existence. In addition, an alarming percentage of severely afflicted chronic pain patients have no interest in longevity and instead await death and its end to suffering with anticipation" (p. 3).

When people recognize that their attempts at relieving suffering have failed, they begin to withdraw and isolate themselves as their very sense of self begins to fragment. According to Seligman (1975), the experience of learned helplessness is likely to have motivational, cognitive, and emotional consequences that may threaten the very integrity of the person. Reestablishing some sense of control over the persistent symptoms becomes of paramount importance in reducing suffering. Current studies suggest that by improving coping skills, it may be possible to reestablish the lost sense of control and to ameliorate reactive depression (Blanks & Kerns, 1996; Brannon & Feist, 2010).

Within the context of the biopsychosocial model of pain management, psychophysiological techniques play an important role in the treatment process, and once combined with other interventions, they can bring about significant changes in the overall functioning of the patient, reduce helplessness, and increase self-efficacy. Gallagher (1997) suggested that such techniques can significantly affect pain perception by reducing biomechanical strain, and by significantly affecting neuropathic pain generators. Taylor (2012) emphasized that in addition to pharmacological and surgical interventions methods of pain management, there is a great deal of support for the use of other clinical treatments such as relaxation training, biofeedback hypnosis, guided imagery, and cognitive therapy. A panel of the National Institute of Health that explored the efficacy of relaxation techniques in the treatment of chronic pain concluded that "there is strong evidence that relaxation techniques (e.g., deep and brief autogenic training, meditation, progressive muscle relaxation) are effective for the treatment of a variety of medical conditions, including chronic pain.... Relaxation techniques as a group generally relieve pain by altering sympathetic nervous system activity as indicated by decreases in oxygen consumption, respiration, heart rate and blood pressure" (Berman, 1997, p. 172).

Among the various psychophysiological therapies for pain management is a well-recognized, empirically based technique, autogenic training, which was developed by the respected neuropsychiatrist, Johannes Schultz. For over eighty years, autogenic training has been used throughout the world, especially in the treatment of chronic and stress-related conditions. Literally thousands of published studies support the effectiveness of this technique in enhancing the body's self-recuperative mechanisms.

Perhaps one of the most concise descriptions of autogenic training was stated by Wolfgang Luthe, Schultz's most prominent protégé.

> One of the most important assumptions of autogenic training is that nature has provided man with homeostatic mechanisms not only to regulate fluid and electrolyte balance, blood pressure, heart rate, wound healing and so on, but also to readjust to more complicated functional disorders that are of a psychophysiological nature. In autogenic training the term "homeostatic self-regulatory brain mechanism" is often used. This concept assumes that

when a person is exposed to excessive, disturbing stimulation (either physical, or emotional), the brain has the potential to utilize natural biological processes to reduce the disturbing consequences of the stimulation (i.e., neutralization). At the mental level, some of this self-regulatory neutralization or recuperation occurs naturally during sleep and dreams. The techniques developed and used in autogenic training have been designed to support and facilitate the natural self-healing mechanism that already exists [Luthe, 1977, p. 2].

In a sense, this technique simply activates, supports, and enhances the body's inherent repair mechanism duplicating what happens in the deeper stages of sleep when the body is provided with a chance to renew its resources. Also, as it will be explored in the chapter on sleep (Chapter 16), most people with chronic conditions suffer from a lack of quality sleep, i.e., they are sleep deprived. Since we cannot simply induce entry into deeper stages of sleep and hope that patients will receive the needed rest, we need to rely on techniques such as autogenic training that promote a state of repair. Interestingly, as the body's resources are replenished, a greater likelihood for entering deeper sleep and benefiting from quality rest is observed.

Autogenic training not only has the potential to assist individuals in coping with persistent pain, it also improves their emotional, cognitive, and psychological functioning (Luthe, 1973). Also, as mentioned, one of the most devastating concomitants of any chronic condition, the state of "helplessness," can be addressed through this technique by empowering individuals to gain greater control over their symptoms with greater efficiency. Hence, suffering and depression are reduced as a greater sense of self-mastery begins to emerge.

As I shall note throughout the book, autogenic training is a most potent treatment for chronic conditions primarily because it is based on a sound theoretical formulation that emphasizes activating the body's potential for repair and regeneration. Clinical and experimental data collected from years of research have supported the many theoretical and clinical premises of this technique.

One of the greatest values of the autogenic technique is that once it is mastered, its therapeutic effects can be summoned relatively quickly. Once individuals realize that through regular practice they can effectively reduce their suffering, the recovered sense of hope will, by itself, help them to improve their coping abilities and is likely to remind them that they have at least some control over their pain and suffering. As this sense of control begins to evolve, other physiological, psychological, and interpersonal changes are apt to occur.

At this point it needs to be emphasized that autogenic training is only one intervention within a multidisciplinary approach to pain management — it is by no means a panacea and it cannot replace other therapeutic approaches such as pharmacotherapy, physical therapy, and psychotherapy. As will be discussed, there are certain conditions for which autogenic training is not indicated. For example, in the case of severe depression, psychopharmacologic agents combined with psychotherapy are more appropriate interventions. Once the depression is more effectively managed, the training may commence in conjunction with other therapies.

The great Swiss physician, Paracelsus, often reminded his students that the greatest medicine a physician could offer his patients was hope. Therefore, as practitioners, we need to do whatever is necessary to renew a sense of hope within those we treat. In pages to come, the autogenic technique and its adjunctive methods will be discussed in detail. The most potent therapeutic techniques, however, can only make a difference if they are practiced with consistency and perseverance. Perhaps one of the most effective methods of motivating others is to be a good role model. I recommend that the readers of this text begin regular practice of the technique as a way of learning its intricacies and benefits to more effectively engender a sense of motivation within their patients.

If the experience of helplessness can bring with it changes in motivation, cognition, and physiology, is it possible that by improving the patient's sense of self-efficacy such "symptoms" can be reversed? Perhaps one of the most important benefits of treatment methods that attempt to improve self-regulation through the practice of various psychophysiological techniques is that they empower patients; while at the same time they demonstrate to them that they can be active participants in their own process of healing. An empowered patient is a motivated patient, who may gain access to resources from within and without which may far surpass any technological advancements.

1

The Dimensions of Chronic Pain Syndrome: A Brief Review of the Literature

"No one on the planet is a stranger to pain. It wears many disguises. There is the physical pain we are all subject to from the pain of teething to the pain experienced in acute and chronic illness. There is the psychological pain born of the disappointments of life; the pain of interpersonal conflicts; betrayal of trust; the pain of goals not reached; anguish of loneliness; the agony of victimization; the loss of meaningful work. There is also spiritual pain that stalks us in the form of doubts..." [Graber, 2004, pp. 127–128].

Chronic pain is a complex phenomenon that can have profound physical, emotional, psychological, interpersonal, and even societal implications. It is a multidimensional phenomenon, at times a puzzle, which requires ongoing scientific scrutiny and analysis (Kulich & Loeser, 2011; Sadigh, 2003). One of the basic characteristics of chronic pain is that in most cases, it does not serve a biological purpose, as opposed to acute pain which may be considered a survival mechanism, often signaling tissue damage, and/or a need for rest and convalescence (Taylor, 2012). Chronic pain, on the other hand, remains elusive, while it affects every aspect of the patient's life, especially as it persists, especially when it remains refractory to a variety of interventions.

According to the data from the Institute of Medicine (2011), more than 116 million Americans are affected by chronic and intractable pain, which by far exceeds the total number of those adults who are diagnosed with cancer and diabetes. It costs the United States up to 630 billion dollars each year to treat chronic pain. Recent data from the Institute of Medicine continue to suggest the dollars spent annually to treat chronic pain by far exceed the costs of treating heart disease, cancer, and AIDS. These staggering figures appear to be on the rise as the medical science struggles to better understand the enigma of chronic pain.

In reality, chronic pain should be viewed as a powerful source of stress with its unrelenting demands on the body, the mind, as well as interpersonal connections (Seaward, 2011). Indeed, it may be viewed as a source of inescapable, often uncontrollable, stress. While we may be able to leave behind a stressful situation, even for a short while, that is not an option with chronic and persistent pain, as there is no physical escape from pain. Pain becomes an aspect of the life of the sufferer and consumes a great deal of physical and emotional energy. It is there when the patient is awake, and it interferes with her sleep when she falls asleep. It seems to demand everything and it offers little in return.

A highly useful model that depicts the dynamics of how an initial injury evolves into significant changes in a person's life is that of Loeser's (1982). In this model (Figure 1.1), pain often starts with an injury, a painful stimulus (nociception). However, if pain persists and remains refractory to treatment, the patient enters the next level, what Loeser refers to as suffering. This is a very germane conceptualization as suffering denotes a level of helplessness with regard to an inescapable source of stress. Frankl (2006), who had a profound understanding of the nature of suffering, suggested that it is meaningless suffering that threatens an individual's very sense of self. Often times, chronic pain patients grapple with the meaningless of their pain, which further devastates them, leaving them in a state of total bewildered confusion. According to Cassell (1991), "Suffering occurs when an impending destruction of the person is perceived; it continues until the threat of disintegration has passed or until the integrity of the person can be restored in some other manner" (p. 33). Therefore, unless some restoration of self is achieved, the person goes on living in a fragmented state, struggling often helplessly to achieve some semblance of wholeness.

The dynamics of suffering require close examination, as it affects every aspect of a person's life. It cannot be medicated, nor can it be meditated away. It may not have any visible manifestations, nor can suffering be measured in an objective manner. This makes it very difficult to communicate the magnitude of the distress that the sufferer is experiencing. All at once, he or she becomes alone — disconnected from others — while resorting solely to desperate attempts at finding a way out of its grips. Meanwhile, statements such as "But you look fine" contribute to further emotional injury. Even though the intention behind making such statements may be pure and supportive, they are often viewed as insensitive at best, or often accusatory. Social isolation may become a way of avoiding such injurious interactions. In reality, such an inclination is likely to bring about greater complications. That is, the sense of selfhood is further damaged as the social aspect of what it means to be a person begins to disintegrate.

Unrelenting suffering leads to the final stage of this model, termed "pain behavior." As pain becomes protracted and unyielding to treatment, people begin to resort to behaviors that promise to bring about at least some temporary relief, even distraction from the gnawing pain. Such behaviors are oftentimes maladaptive in nature. That is, they produce some favorable results initially, while in the long run they result in more complications. For example, a person in unretractable pain may discover that by drinking alcohol he is able to fall asleep faster. This behavior appears to work, at first, as he falls asleep with very little diffi-

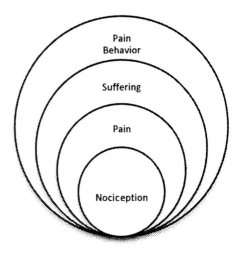

Figure 1.1. Loeser's model of chronic pain

culty. However, as the alcohol metabolizes in his body, and turns into sugar, it begins to significantly interfere with his sleep cycles. Either he is awakened by this surge of sugar in his bloodstream, or he wakes up un-refreshed. In time, the maladaptive behavior of drinking may create more complications in the patient's health than he suspected, his cardiovascular system and his digestive system begin to pay the price. New sets of symptoms begin to emerge, new strategies must be devised, which may potentially result in the development of more maladaptive behaviors. Another common maladaptive behavior is that of avoiding physical activity so as to prevent the worsening of the pain. This may actually result in a weakening of the muscles, a gradual deterioration of the cardiovascular activities, and a general decline in overall health. It is, therefore, imperative to view persistent pain as phenomenon that reaches far beyond a localized phenomenon (i.e., an injured knee), but reaches out to every aspect of the person's life as manifested in a variety of often desperate, maladaptive behaviors.

As it was mentioned, it is essential to view chronic pain as a dynamic, multifaceted, phenomenon that has grave consequences as far as the patient's health is concerned. Pain often affects a person at physical, physiological, cognitive, emotional, interpersonal, behavioral, biochemical levels, while it threatens any semblance of meaning in his or her life (Sadigh, 2006) (see Table 1.1). Most people view pain as mainly a physical phenomenon and dismiss its other dimensions. For example, pain can have significant effects on interpersonal relationships. At the same time, those in pain may lose their sense of meaning and purpose in life. The dimension of meaning, which falls under the spiritual dimension, requires close attention as the lack of meaning can directly contribute to loss of motivation, and may result in self-destructive tendencies (Karren, Smith, Hafen, & Jenkins, 2010).

Table 1.1. The multifaceted nature of chronic pain.

Dimension of Pain	Examples of Potential Manifestations
Physical	Tension, physical atrophy
Physiological	Increased cardiac output
Cognitive	Obsessive thinking, anxiety
Behavioral	Overeating
Interpersonal	Avoiding social contact
Biochemical	Endocrine changes
Spiritual	Loss of meaning

A few examples of chronic pain include migraine headaches, arthritis, fibromyalgia, irritable bowel syndrome, low back pain, temporomandibular joint disorder, and cancer pain (Institute of Medicine, 2011). In the past few decades, clinicians and researchers alike have been involved in further exploring, understanding, and treating a chronic form of muscular pain often referred to as fibromyalgia (previously referred to as fibrositis), whose etiology remains poorly understood. While fibromyalgia is a relatively new term and a recent diagnostic concept, the condition itself has been recognized by physicians and medical researchers for some time. It has been estimated that well over six million Americans suffer from fibromyalgia pain syndrome (FMS) and the most conservative estimates suggest that the cost of the management of this and other forms of chronic pain to the economy exceeds billions of dollars annually (Brannon & Feist, 2010; Weitz, 2007).

Wilke (2009) stated that fibromyalgia is considered as one of the most widely treated conditions in a rheumatology practice. According to Goldenberg, Burckhardt, and Crofford (2004), approximately 12 percent of the general population is diagnosed with generalized musculoskeletal pain that is idiopathic in nature, with no indications of discernable pathology, which is often referred to as complex musculoskeletal pain syndrome (that is, FMS). In exploring the most effective means for the treatment of FMS, these authors concluded that a combination of pharmaco-therapy, education, cognitive therapy, as well as physical exercise seemed helpful in ameliorating the symptoms of this disorder. These suggestions apply not only to FMS but all forms of chronic pain. Fibromyalgia is a form of chronic pain with additional features, but refractory pain remains its most central ingredient; therefore its treatment requires comprehensive pain management.

Sometime between 1850 and 1900, German physicians began describing a peculiar musculoskeletal condition that due to a lack of a proper descriptive medical term they referred to as "Muskel-harten" or hard muscles (see Simons, 1975). A few years later, in 1904, the respected physician William Gowers introduced the concept of fibrositis which suggested that the enigmatic musculoskeletal symptoms were due to an inflammation of the fibrous tissue, hence the term fibrositis. Although this term has been used by physicians, and especially rheumatologists, for nearly a century, medical researchers have found little use for its clinical applications due to the absence of a true inflammatory condition that could explain the nature of the muscular symptoms. In recent years, this diagnosis has fallen out of favor within the medical community and is rarely used as a diagnosis for widespread, non-inflammatory muscle pain (Goldenberg, 1992).

It is helpful to note that on many occasions, both among researchers and medical practitioners, fibrositis became synonymous with "psychogenic rheumatism," an erroneous formulation which took years to shed. Semble and Wise (1988) defined psychogenic rheumatism as a psychiatric condition with significant emotional and psychological difficulties and bizarre and inconsistent symptoms. People with this condition were observed to have almost a startle response to mild touch or pressure when it was applied to certain body parts. Even today, there are still those who continue to espouse a psychiatric approach in the treatment of FMS.

Thieme, Turk, and Flor (2004) conducted one of the most comprehensive studies on the connection between FMS and other psychiatric disorders. The findings of their study were consistent with previous studies and clinical impressions, although it provided a better understating of the complex nature of this disorder, particularly from psychiatric and psychosocial perspectives. If one were to capture the key conclusion of their study, such a conclusion must be based on the diversity of people of different psychosocial backgrounds who suffer from fibromyalgia. Hence, "FMS appears to be a heterogeneous diagnosis comprised of subgroups of patients. [It] is characterized by significant levels of pain and fatigue along with a host of distressing co-morbid symptoms" (Thieme et al., 2004). The co-morbidities that these authors refer to range from: various forms of anxiety disorders, mood disorders, to symptoms of post-traumatic stress disorder. Some or all of the above symptoms seem to be present in most if not all chronic pain sufferers.

Although patients suffering from FMS, at times, show above average levels of anxiety and may present with clinical depression, these are naturally expected symptoms when one considers the profound changes that any chronic condition can bring about in the life and the psychological state of the sufferer. Depression, for example, is often experienced by chronic pain patients and is the result of both neurohormonal changes as well as the experience of helplessness when dealing with a condition that does not readily respond to common, medical interventions (Weitz, 2007). Current studies have failed to show a strong link between fibromyalgia and predisposing psychiatric conditions. There is clearly a need for longitudinal studies to fully explore such possible links.

Neurasthenia was another term used at times to describe what we refer to as fibromyalgia. This term has also been used extensively in the literature regarding chronic fatigue syndrome. However, since the majority of patients with fibromyalgia present with symptoms of fatigue, it may be helpful to explore the historical origins of neurasthenia and its clinical features. The American physician George Beard (1869) coined the term "neurasthenia," which means nervous exhaustion or a lack of nerve strength, as a way of describing a peculiar disease of the industrial world which was the result of exposure to prolonged stress and environmental toxins. According to Beard, regardless of rest and sleep, the neurasthenic was unable to regain his strength and vitality. Almost fifty years before the diagnosis of chronic fatigue was introduced by the Centers for Disease Control (Holmes et al., 1988), the respected physician and author William Sadler wrote, "In the last analysis, neurasthenia is to be defined as a state of accumulated chronic fatigue" (p. 114). Here are some of the symptoms of neurasthenia as cataloged by Gray (1978): "Persistent musculoskeletal pain, tenderness of the entire body, insomnia, fatigue, irritability, abnormal dryness of the skin, vertigo and dizziness, memory and concentration problems, lack of decision making in trifling matters, numbness, tenderness of the entire body, difficulty swallowing, noises in the ear, and sweating hands and feet" (p. 206).

It is interesting to note that during the 1930s and 1940s a large number of explanations for the possible causes of neurasthenia emerged from fields of medicine, psychology, psychiatry, and sociology. These explanations ranged from unresolved intrapsychic conflicts, unknown microorganismic infections, food that was devoid of essential nutrients, to cultural and religious changes. It was believed that certain cultural and religious beliefs that once served to suppress some of the day-to-day anxieties and worries were less relied upon, which made people more vulnerable to life's uncertainties. Too much brain activity and too little time for rest and recuperation was one prevailing formulation for this condition. Even today many fibromyalgia and chronic fatigue patients attest to an inability to "shut down" or quiet their thinking, especially late at night as their hope to gain some rest from the nightly slumber eludes them. Some of the most common treatments that were prescribed for nervous exhaustion included better nutrition, better air, relaxation, recreational activities, and one that was endorsed by many physicians and which solely relied on the patient: lifestyle changes.

Although American physicians have abandoned the use of the term neurasthenia as a valid diagnosis, many European and especially Chinese physicians find the concept quite helpful both for diagnostic and treatment purposes. "Nervous exhaustion" makes a great deal of sense to the practitioners of oriental medicine who view symptom manifestation as a result of a drop in the vital bodily energy. In Eastern countries, a combination of herbal remedies and acupuncture are used to restore the body's resources.

As mentioned earlier, while musculoskeletal pain, both widespread and diffuse, is an integral part of fibromyalgia syndrome, it seems to be accompanied by a number of other specific conditions such as fatigue, headaches, malaise, gastrointestinal distress, sleep disorder, and oversensitivity to weather conditions (e.g., heat and cold) (Goldenberg, Burckhardt, & Crofford, 2004; Semble & Wise, 1988). Clauw (1995) pointed out that patients may also present with symptoms such as abnormal movements of the eyes (ocular dysmotility) and sensitivity to noise and light, as well as difficulties with balance due to vestibular abnormalities. In addition, a large number of fibromyalgia patients (approximately 70 to 80 percent) appear to have indications of mitral valve abnormalities which are supported by echocardiography studies (Pellegrino et al., 1989), as well as other problems related to cardiovascular regulation (Del Paso, Garrido, Pulgar, & Vazquez, 2010). Simons (1976) asserted that the presence of specific tender points constituted a major diagnostic feature of this syndrome (then called fibrositis). A major study undertaken by Campbell and his colleagues (1983) clearly demonstrated that fibromyalgia patients had significantly more distinguishable tender points than those in the control group.

In another study, Leavitt, Kantz, and Golden (1986) investigated the presence of tender points in both fibromyalgia and rheumatoid arthritis patients. Their study confirmed that pain affected multiple sites in both groups with fibromyalgia pain being more widespread and less localized than in the arthritis group. In the same study, the investigators used a modified version of the McGill Pain Questionnaire to further evaluate differences between the two groups. Their findings suggested that the fibromyalgia subjects were more likely to use more diverse descriptors of pain to define and characterize their pain as compared to patients with rheumatoid arthritis. However, during the past 10 years, many researchers have expressed concern about the overemphasis on the tender points as the key aspect of the diagnosis of fibromyalgia (Wilke, 2009).

Based on the review of a number of studies, Adams and Sim (1998) listed other symptoms of fibromyalgia, such as "a sensation of muscle tension and morning stiffness, chronic headaches (tension or migraine), irritable bowel syndrome, ... jaw pain, microcirculatory disorders such as Raynaud's syndrome, and post-exertional muscle pain, etc." (p. 307). Yunus (1994a) stated that over 50 percent of fibromyalgia patients complain of a swollen feeling, mostly in the upper extremities, and paraesthesia in both the upper and the lower extremities. Such sensations are primarily subjective in nature and often are not substantiated by neurological studies, while at the same time they do not appear to have a psychological origin either. Unknown, underlying biochemical changes may be contributing to the experience of such sensations. Finally, significant premenstrual symptoms and distressing urinary difficulties are also reported by these patients (Yunus, 1994a).

Yunus, Masi, and Calabro (1981) discovered that fatigue was one of the most prevalent symptoms of fibromyalgia. Their study showed that over 90 percent of their sample of fifty-two fibromyalgia patients suffered from fatigue, whereas this symptom was predominant only in 10 percent of the normal subjects (Yunus, 1994a). The question of the nature of fatigue in FMS patients was further highlighted in the works of Hauser, Hermann, Nutzinger, Schiltenwolf, and Henningsen (2009), who emphasized the impact of this symptom alone as a major source of distress in patients' lives.

Other studies have also hinted that gender may play a role in this disorder. According to Goldenberg (1992) and Goldenberg, Burckardt, and Crofford (2004), fibromyalgia appears to be more prevalent in women than in men. A greater understanding of gender as a possible contributing variable is necessary to allow a better formulation of the etiology and the pathophysiology of fibromyalgia. The literature on this topic is very inconclusive. A number of researchers have suggested that generally speaking, women may be more aware of their somatic symptoms and are more willing to report them. This observation may be very accurate but lacks any substantial empirical support.

Depression and Anxiety as Concomitants of Chronic Pain Syndrome

As it was mentioned earlier, depression is often a concomitant of chronic pain. This appears to be especially true with widespread pain. Several studies have documented a higher prevalence of depression in patients suffering from fibromyalgia and rheumatoid arthritis than in controls (Goldenberg, 1989a; Goldenberg, 2008; Wolfe, Cathey, & Klienheskel, 1984). Similarly, patients with fibromyalgia showed higher rates of anxiety disorder and significantly higher rates of major depression when compared with a rheumatoid arthritis group (Arnold, 2008; Hudson, Hudson, and Pliner, 1985).

As mentioned before, many researchers despite the prevalence of mood and anxiety disorders in chronic pain patients refrain from suggesting that there is a direct cause and effect relationship between these factors in the pathogenesis of pain. The experience of depression and anxiety in any chronic condition may be attributed to a growing state of learned helplessness, which is often exaggerated by the patients' desperate attempts at conquering the pain (Goldenberg, 1989; Thieme et al., 2004).

Furthermore, stress appears to play an important role in worsening the perception as well as the intensity of pain, regardless of its cause. Sapolsky (2004) suggested that while acute stress may induce an analgesic effect, such is not the case with chronic stress. Indeed, chronic stress seems to render the body vulnerable to pain. From an evolutionary point of view, the physiological changes that occur during the stress response are meant to take the person out of the environment in which a threat may exist. Hence, it makes sense to provide the body with all the resources necessary to make such an escape possible, such as reducing the severity of pain due to an injury. When stress persists, on the other hand, the adaptive resources may not be as readily available. This will inevitably result in the breakdown of the various systems of the body. As we shall see in the next chapter, excessive stress may result in a significant reduction in the body's natural pain modulating biochemicals.

Arnold (2008) stated that the experience of chronic widespread pain may be related to a chronic dysfunction in the hypothalamic-pituitary-adrenal (HPA) axis, which may be brought on as a result of exposure to chronic stress. In this manner, "chronic stress may induce pro-inflammatory cytokines expression in the brain, and cytokines, in turn, may contribute to symptoms of both depression and pain enhancement. Cytokines might cause depressive symptoms through modulation of HPA axis — for example, through glucocorticoid resistance — or they may cause down-regulation of the synthesis of serotonin; both of these effects might contribute to the development of depression and enhanced pain perception" (Arnold, 2008, p. 14). Hence, depression may be a manifestation of disturbances in the neurohormonal mechanism as a result of exposure to excessive and unrelenting stress. Stress in addition to other pre-disposing variables may shed some light as to the pathophysiology of this condition. However, we are far from defining such variables. There are many individuals who are exposed to excessive stress but they do not necessarily experience symptoms of fibromyalgia.

Chronic Pain and Sleep Disturbance

Another common complaint of patients suffering from this syndrome is sleep disturbance and a lack of quality sleep. Several studies have documented that those suffering from chronic musculoskeletal pain tend to have abnormal non-rapid eye movement (NREM) sleep, usually consisting of alpha wave intrusion or reduced Stage 4 sleep (delta sleep), a condition which is particularly present in some FMS patients (Moldofsky et al., 1975). In a pioneering study, Moldofsky and colleagues (1975) were able to induce increased muscle stiffness and aching in normal volunteers by depriving them of delta sleep. Although the biochemical changes occurring during Stage 4 sleep remain poorly understood, a serotonergic connection does appear to be a key factor that promotes a restorative process in this stage of sleep (Moldofsky & Lue, 1980). This is perhaps why tricyclic antidepressants such as doxepin and amitriptyline, which promote an increase in the serotonin levels within the brain, have shown therapeutic promise in the treatment of this syndrome (Jouvet, 1969; Goldenberg, 1992).

From an intrapsychic standpoint, much happens during the nightly slumber. For one thing, the ego defense mechanisms that protect us from the experience of disturbing, internal events begin to lose their effectiveness. Hence, unresolved and painful thoughts and affect have an opportunity to manifest themselves. This process in and of itself can generate much unwanted anxiety, which is likely to result in an unconscious resistance to submit to the state of rest. This may also be viewed by the ego as a state of profound vulnerability (Fosshage, 1983). With the ego defenses largely put to rest, only a chronic state of arousal can protect the self from exposure to unwanted images tainted with affective material that may be overwhelming and possibly quite threatening. Sloan (1990) suggested that the censorship of the ego is not entirely dismantled during sleep and continues to interfere with the emergence of especially distressing affect. This formulation may explain the reason chronic pain sufferers so often complain of disturbed, non-restorative sleep.

Can we then propose that one function of such disruption in sleep activity is to maintain a state of hypervigilance? If this is the case, the consequences of such hypervigilance are quite obvious: impaired rest, limited recuperation and replenishment with potential disregulatory ramifications. The overly driven, perfectionistic, and even obsessive-compulsive tendencies that are observed in fibromyalgia patients serve as powerful distraction and unconscious tendencies. However, these same characteristics cause disruptions of sleep cycles through arousal, and perhaps even hyperarousal to the point of exhaustion. Confronted by the experience of an inner state of emotional turmoil, the patient seeks constant stimulation and distraction even during sleep. It is important to note that sleep brought on through exhaustion does not possess the recuperative ingredients of normal sleep. One study clearly demonstrated that exhausted subjects were deficient in slow wave or delta sleep, which suggests that initiating sleep through the means of merely exhausting one's self will result in impaired sleep (van Diest & Apples, 1994). This once again suggests that prolonged deficiency in restorative sleep has the obvious and deleterious consequences that have been reported in the literature.

Russell (1989) found that serum levels of serotonin were significantly lower in chronic pain sufferers than in healthy controls. As Clauw (1995) has pointed out, the serotonin connection deserves further investigation because abnormalities in this hormone are also seen in patients with migraine headaches, those suffering from depression, and also in patients with colitis. Also, an increase in serotonin levels can bring about an improvement in the digestive tract, weight loss through a decrease in a desire for consumption of foods rich in carbohydrates (Courmel, 1996), and as mentioned earlier, sleep latency and sleep maintenance are substantially enhanced with increased serotonin availability.

Deficiencies in neurotransmitters, such as serotonin and nor-epinephrine, have also been shown to bring about a drop in the pain threshold and consequently may result in a greater sensitivity to pain. These findings further suggest the potential importance of various neurotransmitters in fibromyalgia and the chronic pain syndrome.

Bennett and colleagues (1992) found abnormalities in other hormones such as somatotropin (growth hormone) and somatotropin C in chronic pain patients. The growth hormone, which seems to reach its peak production in deep sleep, is necessary for repair and regeneration of muscles and joints. Somatomedin C (produced in the liver), whose production is intimately linked to somatotropin and is similar to insulin, plays a critical role in metabolic functions. Current studies are further exploring the abnormally low levels of these hormones in some FMS patients and possible causes of such changes.

Finally, it should be emphasized that sleep deficiency alone does not appear to be the cause of this condition. Some of the abnormal sleep patterns seen in fibromyalgia patients have also been documented in patients with other conditions who did not seem to suffer from persistent musculoskeletal pain. This clearly suggests the need for more detailed studies which explore the connection between sleep abnormalities and pain.

Treatment Interventions

Pharmacological Interventions

The pharmacological treatment for chronic pain often requires the combination of several classes of medication. These include antidepressants, hypnotics, anticonvulsives, and a variety of analgesic medications (Clauw, 2008).

Goldenberg, Burckhardt, and Crofford (2004) reported that among the various antidepressants, there was a consistent and strong support for the tricyclics, particularly reasonably low doses of amitriptyline (Elevil) (25–50 mg), which can be used for pain management as well as a treatment for sleep disorders. Other antidepressants include the selective serotonin reuptake inhibitors (SSRIs) such as fluoxetine (Prozac), and the more recent selective serotonin, nor-epinephrine reuptake inhibitors (SSNRIs, or more commonly known as SNRIs) such as venlafaxine (Effexor), duloxetine (Cymbalta), and milnacipran (Savella) (Boomershine & Crofford, 2009; Goldenberg et al., 2004).

Most people in pain rely heavily on non-steroidal anti-inflammatory agents (NSAIDs) such as naprosyn and ibuprofen and analgesics such as acetaminophen to manage their pain. Russell et al. (1991) in a double-blind study found the combination of alprazolam (Xanex, an anti-anxiety agent) and Ibuprofen to result in a significant decrease in subjective levels of pain and objective assessment of trigger points as compared to a placebo group. Such findings, however, have been the subject of much debate and scrutiny in recent years. Although many anti-anxiety agents may promote a relaxed state, they should not be used for extended periods of time because they tend to interfere with entry into deeper stages of sleep. Because of difficulties with sleep quality and sleep maintenance in chronic pain patients, the use of such medications should be minimized. Some patients with disturbing and persistent symptoms of "restless legs" have reported some relief from these nocturnal symptoms when they were prescribed low doses of clonazepam (Klonopin). Again, long-term use of this medication is not recommended nor warranted. McIwain and Bruce (1996) also cautioned against the long-term use of NSAIDs and again questioned their appropriateness in treating symptoms of musculoskeletal pain. They listed nearly forty side effects of these medications, especially when used for an extended time. These side effects include gastrointestinal irritation (which may become severe at times, such as peptic ulcers and intestinal bleeding), liver and kidney damage, dizziness and disorientation, dermatological disorders, tinnitus, fatigue, and other symptoms.

As it was indicated, antidepressants have been used rather consistently in the treatment of persistent pain. Tricyclics (such as amitriptyline), heterocyclics (such as Trazodone), and SSRIs (such as Paroxetine) have been helpful in the treatment of this condition for perhaps two reasons. First, they tend to increase the availability of serotonin in the brain, which by itself has analgesic properties. Second, antidepressants have been shown to reduce rapid eye movement (REM) sleep which may indirectly improve the potential for an increase in Stage 4 or delta sleep — a stage of sleep which appears to be deficient in FMS patients. These antidepressants are used at significantly lower doses in the treatment of fibromyalgia and chronic pain than when they are prescribed for the treatment of depressive disorders, such as major depression, and dysthymia.

To date, amitriptyline appears to be one of the tried-and-true drugs of choice in the treatment of chronic pain (Goldenberg et al., 2004). Carette and colleagues (1986), in a double-blind, placebo-controlled study, found amitriptyline to result in significant changes associated with improvements in morning stiffness, sleep quality, and subjective levels of pain. Stein and colleagues (1996) found amitriptyline to be a superior intervention for the treatment of acute low back pain when compared against the effectiveness of acetaminophen. The authors went on to say that "the present study suggests, however, that the efficacy of Amitriptyline in acute LBP [low back pain] is not related to its antidepressant properties.... Acute pain has been associated with increased anxiety in this as well as in other studies. Any maneuver that decreases anxiety may reduce the subjective intensity of acute pain. Amitriptyline has been found to possess an anxiolytic activity that can be achieved relatively quickly" (p. 68). Even though the dynamics and the psychophysiology of acute and chronic pain may differ in many ways, the above statement may apply to both conditions. Pain, particularly when it is idiopathic, results in the experience of anxiety as it presents itself as an unknown, the core element of what anxiety is all about. It is important that the presence of depression may actually reduce the effectiveness of amitriptyline as far as its analgesic properties are concerns, specifically as such effects relate to those with low back pain (Stein et al., 1996).

Elsewhere, Treadwell (1981) found amitriptyline to be beneficial in improving tenderness in soft tissue and quality or restful sleep. In a more recent meta-analytic study of the effects of antidepressants in the treatment of fibromyalgia, it was found that tricyclic antidepressants resulted in clinically significant changes in sleep quality, overall bodily aches, and tenderness in fibromyalgia patients (Arnold, Keck, & Welge, 2000). The authors also suggested that based on their findings, patients with a history of depression, anxiety, and fibromyalgia seemed to especially benefit from therapeutic doses of tricyclic agents. In addition to effective dosing, one must also consider sufficient period of treatment for achieving desired therapeutic effects.

Recently, a number of studies have documented the effectiveness of a relatively new medication, duloxetine (Cymbalta), an SNRI, in the treatment of fibromyalgia with some very promising results. Russell et al. (2008) found that compared to the placebo, the group that received duloxetine reported significant changes in reported pain levels as well as impressions of improvements. The medication was most effective at 60 and 120 milligrams per day, with the latter dose showing even more immediate and consistent improvements. The authors concluded that this medication may be an effective choice of treatment for fibromyalgia patients with or without major depressive disorder.

Arnold et al. (2009) in their pooled analysis of four placebo-controlled clinical trials found duloxetine to be an effective treatment for widespread pain. More specifically, based on the pooled analysis of the four studies, the authors concluded that after 12 weeks of treatment, patients who took duloxetine showed a significant reduction in pain, improvement in mood, and reported positive changes in quality of life and overall function when compared to the placebo groups.

Non-Pharmacological Treatments of Chronic Pain Syndrome

Acute pain often times signals two messages that need to be heeded. The first message is that there is an injury that needs to be addressed; otherwise, there may be biological consequences. The second message, which is directly related to the first, is that there may be a need for convalescence so as to promote healing while avoiding further injury. Hence, one of the most prudent responses to acute injuries is to reduce physical activity at least for a period of time.

In case of pain that has persisted for a while and there are no longer discernable indications of pathology, physical activity is actually required to improve the body's healing of the once injured area. Sadly, many chronic pain patients who are determined to avoid further injury tend to reduce activity, which leads to de-conditioning and further complications. Most chronic pain patients tend to lean toward a sedentary lifestyle, a tendency that will have serious mind-body consequences. Due to the complex set of symptoms and widespread muscle pain or arthritic pain, many patients may avoid physical activities altogether. A number of studies have shown that a systematic, pre-planned, paced approach to regular physical exercise may bring about noticeable changes in pain levels in chronic pain sufferers. According to Mannerkorpi and Iversen (2003) a low intensity aerobic exercise regiment at least twice a week may bring about positive changes in FMS patients' function and decrease levels of muscular tenderness. These authors highlighted the importance of developing individualized exercises for each patient as each may have specific needs that must be considered when introducing physical exercises.

Herring, O'Connor, and Dishman (2010) reviewed articles regarding the benefits of exercise from 1995 to 2007 and found that exercise consistently brought about positive changes in patients who were suffering from chronic illnesses. Additionally, exercise training programs that lasted for at least 12 weeks seemed to effectively reduce symptoms of anxiety in patients who had become sedentary due to a chronic illness. Hence, exercise by itself may have anxiolytic properties. This makes a great deal of sense as exercise may improve self-efficacy, reduce the sense of helplessness that is common in pain patients, and at the very least acts as a distracter. These psychological improvements in addition to increased circulation, modulation of stress biochemicals, and improved mobility are important changes that can take place in patients who are in persistent pain, so as to enhance the quality of their lives and overall functioning.

Stress management strategies such as biofeedback and relaxation techniques have been widely used in the treatment of chronic pain and stress-related disorders (Chou & Huffman, 2007; Gallagher, 1997; Taylor 2012). These modalities may be of special value in the treatment of fibromyalgia. Ferraccioli, Ghirelli, and Scita (1987) found significant improvements in fifteen fibromyalgia patients after fifteen sessions of electromyographic (EMG) biofeedback. The subjects showed improvements in pain ratings, morning stiffness, and in tender point counts. These same subjects had previously responded poorly to NSAIDs. The second part of the study evaluated the effects of pseudo–EMG biofeedback versus true biofeedback. Subjects in the true biofeedback group showed significant improvements whereas the pseudo-biofeedback subjects experienced little or no change. Sadigh (1997) reported two successful single-subject case studies in which fibromyalgia patients were provided with twelve sessions of autogenic biofeedback. Significant changes were noted regarding patients' subjective levels of pain, depression, and somatization as measured by the Symptom Checklist, 90 Revised (SCL-90-R) (Derogotis, 1983). A six-month follow-up showed both subjects had maintained their improvements. The obvious limitation of the study is the small sample size, and consequently a lack of generalizability.

Grossman, Tiefenthaler-Gimer, Raysz, and Kesper (2007) studied the use of mindfulness stress management in the treatment of women with fibromyalgia. The eight-week program of mindfulness training resulted in significant improvements in pain intensity, quality of life, anxiety, depression, and general physical complaints, when compared to the control group. The results of the study were maintained at a three-year follow up. Even though the study suffered from some methodological limitations, such as a small sample size, etc., the findings of the study were rather impressive. The study needs to be replicated with a larger sample size and better controlled for follow up data that includes the experimental group members as well as those in the control group as a way of gaining a better understanding of the continual effects of mindfulness training.

Banks and colleagues (1998) explored the use of autogenic relaxation training in affecting muscle activity, especially in myofascial trigger points, in fibromyalgia patients. This study was conducted on the growing support for a connection between trigger point activities, psychological stress, tension, etc. While specific muscle groups may not show much electrical activity in FMS patients, trigger points often do. Hence, the researchers used needle EMG sensors to assess trigger point activity before, during, and after the practice of autogenic (relaxation) training. Their findings showed that autogenic training had a significant effect in reducing the trigger point activity in FMS patients. This is a most promising study which may suggest that a combination of this technique with other important therapeutic interventions (for example, physical therapy) may bring about lasting relief from very painful myofascial trigger points that may be resistant to other forms of treatments.

A variety of physical therapy modalities have been shown to bring about some positive changes in fibromyalgia patients. These include heat, massage, stretching exercises, ultrasound, and transcutaneous electrical nerve stimulation (TENS) (Hench & Mitler, 1986). Massage therapy is one of the oldest forms of medical intervention and is increasingly being recognized (perhaps rediscovered is a better word) for its therapeutic value. In addition to making sore muscles feel better, when properly administered, massage can improve circulation, alleviate pain, and reduce physical as well as mental tension. When combined with other therapeutic modalities such as heat, transcutaneous electrical nerve stimulation (TENS), and microcurrent electrical nerve stimulation (MENS), massage therapy can prove to be of significant benefit to fibromyalgia and chronic pain sufferers.

Whereas in the treatment of myofascial pain syndrome specific physical therapy modalities have been shown to play an important therapeutic role (e.g., the spray and stretch technique) and may have lasting effects, their long-term effectiveness in the treatment of fibromyalgia requires further investigation (Goldenberg, 1989b). Meanwhile, manual and gentle physical therapy, because of its profound psychophysiological implications, is likely to become a highly promising area of research. Also, there are strong suggestions that medically supervised physical exercises such as cardiovascular fitness training do bring about desirable changes in some of the symptoms of fibromyalgia.

Danish (1997) developed a comprehensive physical therapy approach to the treatment of fibromyalgia pain syndrome. This approach combines gentle, manual physical therapy (craniosacral therapies, gentle massage, myofascial release), and applications of micro-current therapies, with active stretching exercises and education. He summarizes his approach in the acronym PACE which stands for: Pain (modulating pain via some of the above mentioned modalities); Activity (stretching, flexibility, and movement exercises); Conditioning (aerobic, aquatic, and light resistance training); and Education (mechanisms of pain, lifestyle changes, etc.).

Russell (2006) highlights the importance of helping pain patients set realistic goals for themselves and to maintain a positive attitude regarding their diagnosis. Cognitive-behavior therapy is a very useful approach that can assist patients in confronting distorted cognitions with regards to their symptoms while maintaining a more realistic view of what they can or cannot do. It is not uncommon for such cognitive distortions to contribute to the experiences of anxiety and depression in those suffering from persistent pain. In addition to addressing negative ideations, patients are encouraged to remain physically active, set goals for their progress, and reinforce positive changes in behavior. Cognitive-behavioral therapies, for example can bring about significant changes in sleep habits, a major source of distress in nearly all chronic pain patients.

In addition to implementing interventions that promote positive cognitive and behavioral changes, it is important to emphasize the importance of effective social support when dealing with chronic illnesses, as it can play a critical role in promoting better coping abilities in patients (Karren, Smith, Hafen, & Jenkins, 2010; Russell, 2006). Nearly twenty years of research has consistently demonstrated that those with a strong social support tend to live longer and cope better with a variety of chronic illnesses.

2

Stress and Pain

Stress is a fact of life. It is a term that has increasingly become a part of the lexicon of the physician, the mental health professional, and the layperson. Scientific research in the field of mind-body medicine suggests that there is a significant, positive correlation between stress levels and a variety of psychological and physical symptoms that may drastically affect a person's well-being as well as overall functioning (Girdano, Everly, & Dusek, 2009). Indeed, the medical literature is replete with reliable data that demonstrate the relationship between excessive, unrelenting stress levels and a worsening of symptoms in conditions such as chronic pain syndrome, musculoskeletal pain syndrome, various forms of skin disorder, chronic gastrointestinal disorders, rheumatic pain as well as other chronic conditions. Stress is now also known to be a major contributor to coronary heart disease, cancer, lung ailments, accidental injuries, and suicide (Taylor, 2012). It should come as no great surprise that some of the best-selling medications in the United States are prescribed for stress-related conditions. Other symptoms related to excessive stress include the experience of fatigue, panic attacks, and addictive tendencies. None of these statements suggest a cause and effect relationship. Stress is a powerful contributor to these conditions, but is not the cause of them as far as scientific studies can verify.

The physiological, emotional, and cognitive changes that are brought on by chronic pain are almost identical to those experienced as a result of exposure to prolonged stress. Therefore, we may conclude that the experience of chronic pain is potentially the most damaging form of stress. As it was discussed before, while people can, at least temporarily, get away from a stressful job environment or a stressful relationship, chronic pain sufferers cannot simply leave their pain behind even for a short while. To effectively survive persistent pain, one needs to learn to manage it and its concomitant stress. For this reason, a thorough knowledge of the mechanisms of stress and the rationale for useful coping techniques is in order.

30

In an elaborate discussion of the effects of stress on pain perception, Sapolsky (2004) presented several models based on laboratory and clinical data. He asserted that while acute stress may induce a state of reduced pain perception, that is, "stress-induced analgesia," such is not the case with pervasive, recalcitrant pain. In fact, evidence suggests that in chronic stress, it is likely for us to become more sensitive to pain. One explanation for such sensitivity may rely on the observation that chronic stress does, indeed, deplete the natural opioids that reduce pain sensitivity. Once these natural pain killers have been exhausted, we are likely to experience more pain just as we will have more difficulty managing such pain.

The connection between stress and pain is, therefore, extremely critical when it comes to pain management. By reducing stress levels in those who are suffering from chronic pain, we may be able to allow the body to once again replenish its opioid levels so as to bring about better pain relief. But this is not an easy endeavor to undertake. As it was discussed above, pain by itself is a powerful stressor and cannot be easily abandoned. However, we now have access to powerful techniques that if and when used properly should assist with stress and pain reduction. First, let us explore the various conceptualizations of stress as such understanding will provide us with a better formulation of what is needed to combat its deleterious effects.

The Concept of Stress

Stress is derived from the Latin "stringere" which means to strangle or tightly bind (Jencks, 1977). Before entering the psychophysiological and the medical vocabulary, the term was primarily used by engineers. For example, in metallurgy, when significant force is placed upon a piece of metal until it fractures, it is said that the metal has reached its "stress point." Now, the word has become commonplace and is viewed by many as a detrimental state which can bring about a host of psychological, emotional, and physical complications.

Research on stress is so extensive that virtually a month does not go by without the word finding its way into the medical and the psychological literature. There is, however, a lack of consensus about a precise definition of the word. Girdano, Dusek, and Everly (2009) defined stress as "a mind-body arousal that can on the one hand save our lives and, on the other, fatigue body systems to the point of malfunction and disease. Stress is both a physical response that protects us and a natural defense mechanism that has allowed our species to survive" (p. 1). This is a very helpful definition as it emphasizes the importance of stress as a natural, adaptive response, while at the same time it highlights the potential damaging effects of excessive stress.

Others view stress as any kind of demand that depletes a person's adaptive resources, regardless of whether such demands are physical, emotional, social, or a combination of them (Olpin & Hesson, 2010). From this vantage point, the initial reaction to stress is believed to bring about adaptive changes needed to meet situational demands placed upon the person. If these demands, such as seen in chronic medical conditions, are severe, persistent, and prolonged, the coping mechanisms may not be able to prevent the eventual tissue breakdown with life-threatening consequences.

When exposed to excessive stress, one may experience psychological states such as anxiety, feelings of distress, and heightened arousal. Physiologically, one experiences increased heart rate, elevated blood pressure, higher electrodermal (skin) activity, and changes in electroencephalic (brain wave) activity. Finally, on the behavioral level one experiences trembling, stuttering, and physical avoidance of the stressor. Given the above dimensions of the stress response, a comprehensive definition of stress must attempt to incorporate these three dimensions.

Convincing evidence suggests that a strong positive correlation exists between elevated, unyielding stress levels and the development of degenerative illnesses such as rheumatoid arthritis, hypertension, and cardiac disease. Low, Salomon, and Mathews (2009) in their study of a group of adolescents observed the potentially damaging effects of exposure to excessive stress, especially early in life and particularly in terms of cardiovascular reactivity. In their words, "Chronic stress early in life demands that developing physiological systems adapt repeatedly to stressful circumstances. It has been proposed that exposure to chronic stress leads to repeated, exaggerated cardiovascular responses to acute stressors and that this cardiovascular reactivity may be pathogenic, representing a mechanism by which chronic life stress influences cardiovascular health" (p. 927). Hence, early exposure to unremitting stress may lay the foundation for future, debilitating conditions. There is now ample evidence to suggest that exposure to unpredictable and uncontrollable stress, a concomitant of chronic pain, is followed by a decrease in sensitivity to others. This may include a decrease in helping behavior and an increase in aggression toward self and others (Taylor, 2012).

In the past few decades there has been a growing interest in the development of the field of psychoneuroimmunology — a field that is primarily concerned with the immune system and how it is affected by stressful, psychological, and emotional events. It has been documented that any stressful process which alters the normal physiology of the body will naturally have an impact on the immune system. This may result in susceptibility to colds, infections, arthritic changes, and even various forms of cancer. Also, Sklar and Anisman (1981), in their study of the relationship between stress and cancer, found that tumor growth is intensified after long exposure to uncontrollable stress.

Models of Stress

There are four models of stress which represent several dominant schools of thought in this field: the stimulus (life events) model, the response model, the interactional model, and the conservation of resources model.

The Stimulus Model

Stress considered as stimulus has been used to describe social and/or environmental events characterized as sudden, unexpected, new, or rapidly changing. Lazarus (2006) adds additional psychological and social variables to such events by including threat of failure, isolation, bereavement, and rapid social change to the above list. In other words, from this vantage point, stress is viewed in terms of external variables or stimuli that bring about internal changes.

Stress as stimulus has resulted in much research in the area of life events and their impact on physical and psychological health. Based on this model, Holmes and Rahe (1967) developed the Social Readjustment Rating Scale (SRRS) to determine the relationship between life changes, the onset of illness, and its severity. They discovered a strong positive correlation between major health changes and life crises, such as death of a spouse, divorce, marital separation, and death of a close family member. Furthermore, they demonstrated that even certain positive events could be viewed as a cause of stress with potential health-threatening effects. In other words, any event in the life of a person that requires him or her to make certain adjustments is considered a source of stress. Too many adjustments in too short of a time should become cause for concern with regard to the person's physical and psychological well-being.

For many years, the SRRS became one of the most popular instruments for measuring stress. Many investigators used the Holmes and Rahe scale in their exploration of the impact of life events on the health and well-being of people in different walks of life. It is true that not too many years ago, some insurance companies used to use the SRRS to help people better plan for appropriate insurance coverage. Table 2.1 is the instrument in its entirety as it appeared in the *Journal of Psychosomatic Research* in 1967. As one may note, some of the items are clearly dated as compared to the way of life in the 1960s (most mortgages today are ten times more than the example in the table).

Based on the initial studies, the interpretation of the results of the instrument are quite straightforward. Those individuals with scores between 200 to 300 have a 50 percent likelihood of developing a serious condition which would require medical intervention. On the other hand, those with scores of

300 and above have an 80 percent likelihood of suffering from a serious medical illness within the subsequent twelve months. The chances of developing clinical depression also rise with scores above 300. Although the instrument was not as accurate as it was hoped to be, it clearly showed that the experience of certain social and environmental sources of stress contributes to the development of medical conditions.

In recent years, there has been abundant criticism of the stimulus model of stress. Several researchers have argued that this model does not consider other important variables such as coping resources, anticipatory reactions, and individual differences. Furthermore, others have stated that the SRRS, which was constructed based on the stimulus model, is not an appropriate instrument for all populations such as chronic pain patients. For example, the instrument does not reflect stressors such as powerlessness, helplessness, and hopelessness. Other special issues that chronic pain patients experience that are not reflected in the SRRS are constant physical discomfort, adjustments to pain, making career decisions, and difficulties with achieving quality sleep.

Lazarus (2006) further criticizes the stimulus model by stating that focusing solely on life changes may be a very narrow way of conceptualizing stress. He stated, "Our daily lives are filled with experiences that are stressful but rather than representing major life changes, as emphasized in the Holmes and Rahe approach, many of these daily experiences arise from chronic or recurrent conditions of our lives, some of them seemingly minor irritants or daily hassles" (p. 56). Even though such minor, day-to-day "irritants" may never make it to the list of significant life events, nevertheless they have the potential for acting as significant stress stimuli, especially if they are persistent and unyielding.

Table 2.1. The social readjustment rating scale.

Life Events	*Point Value*
Death of a spouse	100
Divorce	73
Marital separation	65
Jail term	63
Death of a close family member	63
Personal injury or illness	53
Marriage	50
Fired at work	47
Marital reconciliation	45
Retirement	45
Changes in health of family member	44
Pregnancy	40
Sex difficulties	39
Gain of new family member	39

Life Events	Point Value
Business readjustment	39
Changes in financial state	38
Death of close friend	37
Change to different line of work	36
Change in number of arguments with spouse	35
Mortgage or loan over $10,000	31
Foreclosure of mortgage or loan	30
Changes in responsibilities at work	29
Son or daughter leaving home	29
Trouble with in-laws	29
Outstanding personal achievement	28
Spouse begin or stop work	26
Begin or stop work	26
Change in living conditions	25
Revision of personal habits	24
Trouble with boss	23
Changes in work hours or conditions	20
Changes in residence	20
Change in schools	20
Change in recreation	19
Changes in church activities	19
Changes in social activities	18
Mortgage or loan less than $10,000	17
Changes in sleeping habits	16
Changes in the number of family get-togethers	15
Changes in eating habits	15
Vacation	13
Christmas	12
Minor violations of the law	11
Total Score	____

Source: Holmes and Rahe (1967). Reprinted by permission.

The Response Model

One of the most detailed, and, for a long time, very popular, models of stress is the response model. This model was proposed by Hans Selye (1950), perhaps the most respected pioneer in stress research. According to Selye (1984), stress is a generalized bodily response to a demand that is placed upon the body. That is, when the homeostasis of the body is disturbed, certain internal processes begin to take place as a form of preparation for dealing with the disruption. This loss of a state of balance, if prolonged, can result in the development of certain illnesses and even death.

After studying pathological changes in sick humans and over-stressed animals, Selye (1950) proposed the existence of a stress syndrome made up of the physiological changes that spontaneously occur and stimulate the body's defensive reactions in response to any stressor, physical or psychological. The syndrome is known as the general adaptation syndrome or GAS, and consists of three stages. The first stage of GAS is termed the alarm reaction. This reaction consists of activation of the body's defenses to combat the stressor and in turn secretes bio-chemicals, which bring about an increase in heart rate, higher oxygen consumption, and a drastic increase in the metabolic activity. This powerful activation of the body's energy resources can only be maintained for a short time.

Eventually the body adjusts to the stressor and the second stage of GAS, called adaptation or resistance, ensues. During this second stage, levels of resistance that promote coping rise above normal. However, the adaptive energy of the body is finite and after prolonged exposure to the stressor, the body becomes depleted of its resources. This depletion results in exhaustion, which is the third and final stage of GAS. During this stage, the body's resistance is diminished and symptoms of varying intensity are experienced. If the stressor is severe enough, irreparable damage may occur to the body. Although the body normally resists and adapts to various stressors, its coping mechanisms can become derailed, and the individual may suffer from the harmful and even life-threatening effects of stress. Too much of this undue stress or distress (also known as "bad" stress) may result in what Selye called the disease of adaptation or stress diseases (Selye, 1982). A list of distress symptoms (Selye, 1976, pp. 174–177) includes the following:

1. General irritability
2. Pounding of the heart
3. Dryness of the throat and mouth
4. Impulsive behavior
5. Inability to concentrate
6. Weakness or dizziness
7. Floating anxiety
8. Insomnia
9. Loss of or excessive appetite
10. Queasiness of the stomach
11. Alcohol and drug addiction
12. Neurotic behavior
13. Psychosis

Selye (1984) considered stress from a variety of perspectives, suggesting that it does not always result in deleterious effects, especially when the exposure to the stressor is limited. Here we encounter the word, "eustress," which is defined as good stress; distress, which suggests bad stress; hyperstress, which is when we are exposed to relentless stress; and finally hypostress, which may come about as a result of a lack of stimulation (Cooper & Dewe, 2004).

The response model of stress as proposed by Selye has also been criticized in recent years. Perhaps one of the most important limitations of the model has to do with the fact that it does not include psychological variables in the experience of stress. For the most part, Selye's model is a physiological model. Another major criticism is directed at Selye's conceptualization that the stress reaction is a uniform process. This notion has been effectively challenged by studies that have explored the role of perception in the stress response. That is, two people may have significantly different responses to an identical stressor depending on their perceptions of the stressor. This has necessitated the development of other models of stress such as the one proposed by Lazarus.

The Interactional Model

Lazarus and Folkman (1984) and Lazarus (2006) proposed an interactional or transactional model of stress. This model, which has gained a great deal of popularity in recent years, suggested that it is the combination or interaction of situations and inherited tendencies that control the person's reaction to stressful situations. This model places greater emphasis on individual differences, both in terms of physical and emotional makeup. This suggests that an individual's stress responses cannot be easily anticipated, nor is it accurate to make conclusions about the person's response to stress simply by assessing environmental and/or life events.

When either the internal or environmental demands (or both) exceed a person's resources for coping, the person begins to experience the adverse effects of stress. As noted, some people may be exposed to an identical source of stress and may respond quite differently. As we will discuss later, some may respond with little agitation when they begin to experience another "bad pain day," while another person may feel quite overwhelmed and may find it exceptionally difficult to cope with her pain.

Based on this model, stress is defined as any event in which environmental or internal demands or both surpass the adaptive resources of the person. In this view, stress involves a transaction, a give and take, in which the availability of resources must be determined before expending them. Another way of looking at this model is to say that the person assesses or appraises the nature of the demand and available resources for coping with it, and then engages in a response (Lazarus, 2006). How an individual responds to stressful experiences, therefore, is a function of both personal factors and the situation.

After reflecting on the description of this model, it is important to educate patients that just because others can handle certain stressful situations, it does not mean that they should be able to do the same. If the patient's resources are depleted or are near depletion, a "simple" task such as getting dressed and going to the corner store may seem so enormous that the mere thought of it may make him or her feel tired. There are days when many chronic pain patients find it difficult to get out of bed. Unfortunately, most of them continue to further deplete their energies by becoming upset or giving up altogether and by spending hours in bed, which is likely to further result in stiffness and additional pain.

Conservation of Resources Model

The conservation of resources model was originally introduced by Hobfoll in 1989. It is an intuitive, empirically sound, and testable model that defines stress in terms of loss of resources, whether these resources are from internal or external resources. Hence, anything that threatens to take away a person's physical or psychological resources may be viewed as a source of stress. Hobfoll defines resources as "those objects, personal characteristics, conditions or energies that are valued by the individual or that serve as a means for attainment of those objects, personal characteristics, conditions or energies" (p. 516). In other words, the loss of these "resources" constitutes the very nature of stress. From this vantage point, our resources give us a sense of integrity and wholeness; hence, it is only natural to preserve them, or to invest them with the hope that they will be replenished or multiplied. Chronic stress (as in chronic pain) tends to seriously threaten an individual's well being by depleting her resources in a persistent fashion, often without any promise of full restoration.

Hobfoll (1989) makes a distinction between this model and the interactional model which was previously discussed in this chapter. Even though both models emphasize the importance of resources, the conservation model provides a conceptual framework for a tendency in people who are not under stress to build "resource surpluses" so as to prepare themselves for potential exposure to sources of stress. Such surpluses will promote a sense of protection within the person that will result in an improved perception of health. However, when such surpluses are no longer available, vulnerability to the deleterious effects of stress may begin to increase.

The implications of this model have tremendous clinical value. First and foremost, in the chronically stressed we often observe behaviors that suggest almost helpless attempts at conservation of resources, which if not executed properly may potentially have negative consequences, especially as far as interpersonal relationships are concerned. Secondly, based on this model, a major goal of stress management should not simply focus on reducing or avoiding stress, but the preservation, conservation and replenishment of resources, with the ideal scenario of building a surplus of resources. This model not only attempts to explain the psychology of stress, it can also be applied to its psychophysiology.

Psychophysiology of Stress

During the last few decades, much knowledge has been gained with regard to the biochemistry and the psychophysiology of stress. The two systems that are primarily responsible for the stress response are the sympathetic-adrenal medullary system (SAM) and the hypothalamic-pituitary-adrenocortical system (HPAC) (Girdano, Everly, & Dusek, 2009). Because of their central role in understanding the stress phenomenon and how pain can bring about significant biochemical changes, these two systems and their functions will be briefly discussed in this section.

The Sympathetic-Adrenal Medullary System (SAM)

The autonomic nervous system (ANS) is that branch of the peripheral nervous system that is responsible for regulating the functions of all the visceral systems in the body (e.g., the cardiovascular system, the respiratory system, the gastrointestinal system, and the excretory system), as well as the smooth muscles. The ANS operates beyond conscious awareness and as a result was once, erroneously, referred to as the involuntary nervous system. With the advent of applied psycho-physiology, namely biofeedback, it is possible to gain some conscious control over the activity of this branch of the nervous system, hence the term autonomic is a far more accurate term to describe the activities of this branch of the nervous system.

The ANS is composed of two subsystems or branches which are: the sympathetic nervous system (SNS) and the parasympathetic nervous system (PNS). Whereas the SNS is generally responsible for increasing the activities of various organs, such as increasing the heart rate and constricting blood vessels (for the most part), the PNS reduces their activities, such as lowering the respiratory rate, decreasing the heart rate, while stimulating digestion, and allowing bodily repair to take place.

The sympathetic nervous system has a catabolic function, that is utilizing resources to increase energy expenditure. On the other hand, the function of the parasympathetic nervous system is to reduce energy expenditure and to replenish the bodily resources. The sympathetic nervous system is activated during a stress response, such as when a certain source of threat is perceived, and the parasympathetic nervous system is activated during the regeneration response, when the lost resources are replenished.

The scientific interest in the impact of the sympathetic activation in stressful situations may be traced back to the observations of the prominent physiologist Walter B. Cannon (1932), who introduced the concept of the fight-or-flight response. Since Cannon's early studies of the fight-or-flight response, a large body of evidence has suggested that the sympathetic activity plays a major role in the stress response. The sympathetic-adrenal medullary (SAM) axis of the stress response functions in the following fashion. When a person encounters a threatening and/or stressful situation, the SNS stimulates the adrenal glands which are located on top of the kidneys. More specifically, this activation is focused on the inner layer of the adrenal glands, known as the adrenal medulla. The adrenal medulla will then initiate the production of powerful catecholamines, known as adrenaline (epinephrine), and nor-adrenaline (nor-epinephrine). These catabolic, energy-generating hormones prepare the body to either fight the source of threat or to flee it, hence the "fight or flight" syndrome (Jones & Bright, 2001). The activation of these hormones and their secretion into the bloodstream occur with great rapidity as the system is controlled through the nerve impulses via the sympathetic nervous system.

It has been documented that over-activation of the sympathetic-adreno-medullary system may result in a chain of reactions that could eventually result in physical and psychological complications. For example, excessive catecholamine secretion is believed to cause many of the illnesses associated with stress such as hypertension, increased cardiac output, disorders of the digestive tract such as indigestion and irritable bowel syndrome, constriction of peripheral (arms, hands, legs, and feet) blood vessels, and dilation of blood vessels within the internal organs (Selye, 1984). The constriction of peripheral blood vessels has also been implicated in conditions such as Raynaud's disease, in which sufferers experience extremely cold hands and feet even to the point that their hands actually turn blue. This extremely painful condition is especially aggravated by prolonged exposure to stress. Many chronic pain patients, especially those with chronic migraine headaches, often complain of similar symptoms, although they may not meet the specific criteria for the diagnosis of Raynaud's disease.

Prolonged activation of the sympathetic adreno-medullary system due to stress and pain may also result in a condition known as dysautonomia, which results in fluctuations and even at times an abrupt drop in blood pressure. Sudden dizziness and fatigue are some of the most common symptoms of this condition. Problems with depression and sleep disorders may also be attributed to states of dysfunction and depletion in this system. That is why certain antidepressants (for example, Effexor) are used to help some of the symptoms of chronic pain because they help to replenish and make more available the needed levels of nor-epinephrine in the central nervous system.

The Hypothalamic Pituitary-Adrenocortical System (HPAC)

Another system which plays an important role in the stress response is the hypothalamic pituitary-adrenocortical system (HPAC). This system begins with the hypothalamus, a major regulatory mechanism in the brain which closely interacts with the master hormonal regulator, the pituitary gland, located at the base of the brain. The hypothalamus interacts with the pituitary gland via the production of the corticotropin releasing hormone (CRH). Once a stressful stimulus (e.g., physical, psychological, environmental) is perceived and CRH is released, the pituitary gland stimulates the outer layer of the adrenal gland (the adrenal cortex) through the secretion of the adrenocorti-cotrophic hormone (ACTH). As a result of the stimulation of the adrenal cortex, specialized hormones known as glucocorticoids (such as cortisol and corticosterone) are poured into the bloodstream. Cortisol is primarily involved in the metabolic function through the process of gluconeogenesis, which provides the body with the needed source of energy. Cortisol also plays an important role in reducing inflammation and inhibiting fluid loss (Goldstein, 1998). Prolonged secretion of cortisol may result in structural damage (tissue degeneration), muscle wasting, and suppression of the body's immune system (Selye, 1982). Some studies have shown that the secretion of cortisol appeared to be especially high among people who were struggling with emotional stress and felt ineffective in managing their situation (Schneiderman & Tapp, 1985).

A significant decrease in cortisol levels may bring about a phenomenon which sometimes is seen in those who have been exposed to excessive stress, known as adrenal insufficiency syndrome. Symptoms of this condition include fatigue, weakness, diabetic-like symptoms, and immune dysfunction. Indeed, one of the most common symptoms of cortisol insufficiency is debilitating fatigue, followed by joint pain, muscle tenderness and pain, swollen glands, allergic responses, and finally disturbances in mood and sleep (Sapolsky, 2004). Griep, Boersma, and de Kloet (1993), in their study of patients with primary fibromyalgia, concluded that these patients suffered from adrenal insufficiency, which may be due to exposure to prolonged stress. The authors also suggested that the reduced cortisol levels may explain changes in aerobic capacity and the consequent impairment in muscle activity. Such findings may be applied to many chronic pain sufferers or those grappling with incessant, unremitting stress.

The other hormone produced by the adrenal cortex is aldosterone. Aldosterone affects the availability of certain minerals which are crucial for proper heart and muscle functioning. This mineralocorticoid is responsible for intercellular retention of sodium, and water, as well as the excretion of intercellular potassium, magnesium, and calcium. It is important to note that many chronic pain and chronic fatigue patients are found to be deficient in magnesium, which plays an important role in metabolic functions (Cox, Campbell & Dowson, 1991; Eisinger et al., 1994). In chronic exposure to stress, the retention of additional sodium may result in edema, bloating, and significant changes in the blood pressure.

A number of studies have suggested that during the experience of constant stress, such as in chronic conditions, the activities of the adrenals can become chaotic and quite problematic. For example, a person's neurochemical system may begin to respond in a haphazard, unnecessary fashion to a minor stressor that may be quite harmless but is perceived as threatening. Again, such inappropriate stress responses are especially seen in those who feel helpless and "victims" of a chronic condition. An increase in a sense of mastery over the situation appears to gradually rectify this problem.

In summary, both the SAM and the HPAC axes play important functions in the stress response. Prolonged activation of the two systems appears to be responsible for potentially deleterious effects, particularly as far as the cardiovascular system is concerned (Cooper & Dewe, 2004). Chronic conditions, such as chronic pain, if not managed properly, can in time bring about a breakdown in various body systems. I can easily recall at least a dozen chronic pain patients who reported that they always had low blood pressure only to realize that after a few years of grappling with pain, "all of a sudden," they were diagnosed with hypertension. There are also those who "suddenly" discover that they have diabetes or a bleeding ulcer.

Again, it is important to note that it is not pain that causes these conditions, but prolonged stress in addition to some hereditary vulnerability. Since stress inevitably tends to increase the body's rate of wear and tear, dormant conditions that are often genetically linked can become visible in time — often surprising the person by the sudden appearance of unexpected symptoms. A detailed study of the presence of specific, persistent stressors, however, will reveal that the exhaustion of psychophysiological resources contributed to the surfacing of such dormant conditions. The nature of recent and uncontrollable stressors must always be examined while planning proper treatment protocols.

In conclusion, stress reduction and management play important roles in treating patients who are suffering from chronic pain and other chronic, stress related conditions. In the next chapter we will review several techniques that purport to accomplish this task. Once patients have an adequate knowledge of such approaches, they can then begin incorporating them into their daily activities.

3
Methods of Stress Management

In recent years, concern over the stress epidemic has promoted much research and investigations in the areas of stress management and stress reduction. Several stress management interventions that have been advocated by different practitioners and researchers include relaxation training, psychotherapy, assertiveness training, biofeedback, and cognitive restructuring.

Among these, relaxation strategies have shown strong empirical support for their ability to result in physical, psychological, and emotional improvements. It has been suggested that some of the most effective and non-intrusive methods of managing pain and stress are relaxation therapies which are often combined with psychophysiological methods such as biofeedback modalities (Jones & Bright, 2001; Gallagher, 1997). Stoyva and Anderson (1982) suggested that the major reason relaxation techniques have shown superiority over other stress reduction procedures is because they bring about psychophysiological changes which are diametrically opposed to the active/striving (stressed) mode.

Well-designed studies that have incorporated cognitive and behavioral techniques for pain and stress management have been shown to be superior to routine medical interventions (see Goldenberg, Burckhardt, & Crofford, 2004; Keefe & Van Horn, 1993). These relatively inexpensive procedures tend to bring about physical and psychological improvements that have a lasting effect. Such effects may be related to at least two contributing factors. First and foremost, stress management approaches have shown to promote a hypometabolic state, during which the body repairs itself as well as replenishes its resources (Benson, 2000). Second, they provide the person with tools that are likely to increase his or her sense of control over the environment or the source of stress. Even if such control is not all encompassing, the resulting increase in self-efficacy is likely to encourage more effective and adaptive behaviors to emerge.

Stress Management Techniques

The widespread prevalence and harmful effects of stress have resulted in the development of a variety of stress-management techniques and strategies. The most widely used stress management techniques are cognitive restructuring, biofeedback, stress inoculation, and relaxation training. These techniques and approaches will be discussed briefly in this section.

Cognitive Restructuring

One of the most powerful and empirically supported forms of stress management is that of cognitive restructuring. People often are unaware that there is an intimate interaction between thoughts, feelings, and behaviors. A negative thought can almost instantly have emotional manifestations, which may in turn influence the way one behaves. This is especially important to keep in mind when we are experiencing persistent pain. At times a simple twinge of pain may result in the experience of anxiety, fear, frustration, and even helplessness. This may result in behaviors that may actually worsen the pain. The behavior may in turn cause more negative thoughts and feelings, which makes one feel trapped in a vicious cycle with no end in sight.

The major task of cognitive restructuring is to assist people to become aware of their faulty thoughts (cognition) and to teach them ways of modifying or replacing these thoughts with more constructive ones, which will bring about a change in feelings and behaviors. In a clinical setting, and with the help of a trained therapist, this is accomplished through exploratory interviews, visualization techniques, and self-monitoring homework (Beck, 2008). After exploring the nature of the faulty thinking (for example, "This is going to be a terrible day because I woke up with pain"), the individual is provided with specific techniques and homework assignments to develop a new cognitive repertoire (more positive and helpful thoughts) with which to counteract stress-provoking thoughts, feelings and behaviors (Beck & Alford, 2009). During a cognitive-restructuring session, the therapist may ask the patient to think of different stressful situations when negative thoughts may arise. Such thoughts are then replaced with more realistic or positive ones, for example, "Just because I woke up with pain it does not mean that my day is ruined. Perhaps instead of staying in bed I should take a hot bath which has helped me in the past."

According to Pretzer and Beck (2007), it is the cognitive conceptualization of a situation (the way one thinks or views the situation) that contributes to a stress response. Therefore, cognitive restructuring (or revising) lowers physiological arousal and counteracts the deleterious effects of stress. Cognitive restructuring has shown to be effective in reducing specific stress reactions due to chronic pain and other chronic conditions, especially those that may be judged as uncontrollable and outside one's domain of influence (Meichenbaum, 2006). This approach has also been used successfully and effectively in reducing stress connected with coping with anxiety and anger (Meichenbaum, 1977). Many researchers have found cognitive restructuring and a modified form of systematic desensitization to be equally effective in treating chronic stress.

Biofeedback

Biofeedback, or, more accurately, psychophysiological feedback, is the use of sensitive instrumentation (often electronic) to provide psychophysiological (mind-body) information about activities and processes that the person is not normally aware of and which may be brought under conscious control. One such example would be learning to increase one's circulation in the hands and the feet. To achieve this, the person is provided with immediate and continuous information (feedback) about his or her biological conditions, such as muscular tension, peripheral temperature, and blood pressure. This "returned" information or feedback helps the person become an active participant in reducing tension, managing stress, and enhancing his or her health maintenance (Fuller, 1986). The key here is active participation in symptom management and health enhancement. Patients quickly discover that they are capable of modifying those behaviors that may further damage their health. The biofeedback instruments simply act as a mirror that provides an accurate picture of internal processes and how they are affected through volitional interventions.

One of the most important aspects of biofeedback is that it tends to increase the patient's self-efficacy, which reverses the perception of helplessness that emerges from grappling with chronic conditions. Such instruments can immediately demonstrate to the patient that he or she is making a difference. Cognitive, behavioral, and psychophysiological changes, hence, can be promoted through the use of biofeedback instrumentations. When a patient who has suffered from Raynaud's disease for years realizes that she can raise her hand temperature, which can be monitored in the office or at home, she gains the confidence that she can do something to make a difference. In this process, she is all at once empowered, motivated, and learns that she can directly contribute to her health.

The most common biofeedback technique that has shown to be highly effective in counteracting the harmful effects of stress is electromyographic feedback (EMG), which provides individuals with immediate information about their muscular tension. Muscular relaxation has long been noted as an important treatment factor for a variety of psychophysiological and stress-related disorders. After conducting a comprehensive meta-analytic study, Crider and Glaros (1999) concluded that there was enough data to suggest that EMG biofeedback was an effective treatment for temporomandibular joint disorder (TMJD). The studies that were reviewed provided consistent support for long-term effects of this intervention even after extended follow-ups, which suggested that effective learning and reconditioning had taken place.

In another study, Bendtsen and Fernández-de-la-Peñas (2011) found EMG feedback to be an effective treatment intervention for tension-type headaches, which are some of the most common forms of headaches in all ages. This is consistent with studies for the past 30 years that have shown superior tension reduction in these types of headaches. (Autogenic-biofeedback will be discussed in greater detail in Chapter 15.)

Stress Inoculation

Stress inoculation training may be viewed as a form of cognitive restructuring and behavior modification. It is a systematic program of providing coping responses to more effectively cope with a wide range of stressful situations including chronic pain and headaches (Meichenbaum, 2007). Stress inoculation has been referred to as a form of "psychological vaccination" that helps the individual more effectively handle difficult situations. In other words, it provides the individual with "a prospective defense or set of skills to deal with future stressful situations. As in medical inoculation, a person's resistance is enhanced by exposure to a stimulus strong enough to arouse defenses without being so powerful that it overcomes them" (Meichenbaum & Turk, 1976, p. 3). This approach provides coping strategies that can be used with sources of stress on the cognitive, physiological, and behavioral levels.

Meichenbaum (2007) developed a systematic approach to stress inoculation that consists of three "interlocking and overlapping" stages. The application of these stages not only will help with stress reduction, they will also promote changes in thoughts and behavior that will assist in exhibiting more proper and adaptive responses to stressful situation. These stages begin with an educational component, where various concepts of the training are explained. It is also an important time for data gathering. This is followed by an intensive rehearsal stage followed by an application stage. These stages will be explained in more detail below.

THE EDUCATION STAGE

The first stage of stress inoculation is based on information gathering and is essentially instructional in nature. The therapist and the patient briefly discuss the nature and sources of stress, such as pain, anxiety or anger. Special attention is placed upon the patient's thinking patterns when he or she experiences a source of stress. Furthermore, patients are asked to discuss coping strategies that they are currently using.

After gathering this information, the therapist will provide the patient with an examination of his or her emotional responses based on certain thoughts and how a stressor brings on such responses. It is believed that as a result of the information gathering educational phase, the patient becomes aware of his or her maladaptive thoughts and behaviors. Such awareness will allow him or her to pay particular attention to thoughts, feelings, and behaviors that need to be changed (Meichenbaum, 1977).

THE REHEARSAL STAGE

The second step of stress inoculation is rehearsal. During this step, patients are provided with specific coping techniques to change their thoughts and behaviors. For example, relaxation techniques may be taught to reduce physiological reactivity to stressful situations. Behavioral skills may also be taught to enlarge one's repertoire of responses. The main focus of this phase of treatment is to provide appropriate and more effective coping skills that can be used with greater flexibility. Furthermore, the training involves mastery of an assortment of techniques that can be used to combat the negative effects of stress. Special attention is paid to the development of a collection of positively phrased coping self-statements. This allows the individual to more rationally estimate a stressful or threatening situation and utilize appropriate coping skills.

THE APPLICATION STAGE

During the final step of stress inoculation, the application stage, the therapist helps the patient to apply the techniques and the skills that have been taught into proactive, daily use. The individual may be asked to imagine or visualize certain situations and to put to use some of the acquired techniques (in vitro training). From mental images, one then moves to applying these skills in real situations (in vivo training). As coping skills are rehearsed and a greater sense of self-mastery is achieved, the patient begins to move away from a preoccupation with avoiding stress and demands and is likely to begin considering more positive and constructive options. From time to time, it may be necessary to review one's repertoire of skills and if necessary add new responses to them. Also, "booster" sessions are often recommended to help avoid setbacks.

Relaxation Training

Relaxation techniques are widely used strategies to manage and reduce pain and stress. It is believed that practices similar to relaxation methods have been used in medical treatment of a variety of conditions in some cultures for thousands of years. Some have estimated that over 5,000 years ago, the Egyptian priests frequently treated disease through various forms of imagery relaxation, while other cultures mastered various forms of meditative-relaxation through the use of mantras and breathing techniques (Lavey & Taylor, 1985; Benson, 2000).

In recent years, the growing concern over the deleterious effects of exposure to prolonged and uncontrollable stress has prompted scientists and clinicians to explore the effectiveness of a variety of stress reduction techniques and interventions. Among various stress management approaches, relaxation procedures have provided strong empirical support for bringing about positive physiological, psychological, and emotional changes.

It has been shown that relaxation may provide three therapeutic gains: balancing and reconditioning of the central nervous system; desensitization of distressing thoughts; and insight into ongoing, damaging, and ineffectual patterns of behavior. Regular practice of relaxation techniques has shown to be of considerable psychological and emotional value in dealing with stressful situations — a value that is difficult to ignore when the overall safety and cost-effectiveness of this training is considered.

Stoyva and Anderson (1982) conducted a study in which patients who were suffering from stress-linked disorders were closely watched and many of their psychophysiological activities monitored. They found that these patients showed signs of high autonomic arousal even when they were not placed in stressful situations. Hence, it was concluded that such people lacked the ability to shift to a rest condition — a condition that can be helped by various relaxation techniques.

Relaxation therapy was introduced into the modern Western world by Johannes Schultz in Germany (autogenic training), and Edmund Jacobson in the United States (progressive relaxation). Pelletier (1979) stated that almost all meditative-relaxation techniques result in a decrease in sympathetic activity and an increase in parasympathetic activity. The increase in parasympathetic activity results in cellular repair as well as decreased blood pressure, lower respiratory rate, and relaxation of the skeletal muscle. Perhaps that is why relaxation approaches have been shown to counteract the harmful and damaging effects of stress and result in improved health.

Carson and colleagues (1988) examined the effect of meditative-relaxation on systolic blood pressure, plasma lipids, and blood glucose of a group of highly stressed patients. Subjects were assigned to either a placebo/control group or relaxation treatment group. Subjects' blood pressure and cholesterol levels were closely monitored throughout treatment. After an eight-week period of treatment, those subjects who practiced relaxation showed a significant decrease in their systolic blood pressure, and a significant reduction in plasma lipids and cholesterol. The placebo-control group remained unchanged. The authors suggested that evidence supports that relaxation can be used as a strong preventative modality in reducing cardiac disease. Also, a large number of well-controlled studies have clearly documented that relaxation exercises can be effectively used to reduce pain, reduce the use of pain medications, and finally reduce the frequency of visits to the emergency room (Schwartz, 1984). A study by Turner (1982), showed that patients who practiced muscle relaxation techniques were able to significantly reduce their need for medication and felt less depressed when compared to those patients who did not receive relaxation training. What is important to note is that after a two-year follow-up, the relaxation group was still showing signs of improvement.

Even when pain is chronic and extremely severe, relaxation techniques seem to make a substantial difference in improving patients' coping abilities. Syrjala and colleagues (1995) in a controlled clinical trial found relaxation and imagery interventions to bring about significant reduction in pain levels in a group of cancer patients. The study also suggested that adding cognitive-behavioral elements to relaxation did not bring about additional improvements. The findings of studies such as this are of tremendous clinical value as they provide tools for patients who are suffering from severe pain, such as in those with cancer-related pain. A classic study by Grzesiak (1977) employed relaxation training in assisting patients who were suffering from persistent pain due to spinal cord lesions. In addition to relaxation training, the patients were taught to use peaceful imagery to enhance pain management. All the patients reported a reduction in pain and an improvement in their overall mood.

Relaxation techniques that have been supported empirically include: autogenic training, breathing exercises, imagery techniques, transcendental meditation, progressive relaxation, and yoga training. Because of their importance and their relevance to pain management, these techniques will be briefly discussed in this section.

Autogenic Training

A clinically well-recognized technique for improving stress and pain management is autogenic training (Schultz & Luthe, 1959). The term autogenic is derived from the Latin, autos (from within), and genos (generated and developed) (Jencks, 1979). That is to say, autogenic training helps to bring about changes that are generated from within. The main task of this training is to allow the body's self-regulating, homeostatic mechanism to become activated in order to initiate any needed repair (Schultz & Luthe, 1969). This training is designed to enhance self-regulatory mechanisms for counteracting the effects of stress. It consists of exercises that primarily focus on heaviness and warmth in the extremities. This highly advanced relaxation strategy is based on a strong psychophysiological theory of tension reduction and self-regulation. Schultz and Luthe (1969) stated that the purpose of autogenic training is to bring about a shift from an anxiety state to the autogenic state, which facilitates and mobilizes the recuperative and self-normalizing brain mechanisms. Luthe (1983) reported that autogenic training can be highly effective in the treatment of several stress-related disorders such as rheumatoid arthritis, chronic pain, bronchial asthma, hypertension, and gastric ulcers.

Autogenic training consists of six standard exercises. These exercises primarily emphasize warmth and heaviness in the extremities, regulation of cardiac activity, respiration, abdominal warmth, and finally cooling of the forehead (Schultz, 1932). Pelletier (1979) stated that autogenic training is the most comprehensive method of relaxation and can serve as a model for all others that address themselves to clinical treatment of pain and stress-related disorders. Labbe and Williamson (1984) found autogenic training to be highly effective in the treatment of common and classical migraine headaches. The subjects in this study maintained their improvements in a six-month follow-up study.

Breathing Exercises

Almost all relaxation techniques incorporate breathing exercises. Benson (2000) observed that all traditional forms of meditation begin with breathing. It is believed that breathing techniques directly influence the functioning of the autonomic and the central nervous systems and can play an important role in inducing a state of relaxation. On the other hand, improper and shallow breathing can increase muscle tension and may result in an agitated state. Most panic or anxiety attacks have been related to improper breathing habits. Smith (1989) stated that breathing plays a central function in relaxation training because it is a "natural barometer" which can provide the person with information about his or her state of tension and relaxation. Also, breathing exercises by themselves can promote a meditative state that can be highly peaceful and rejuvenating.

A simple but highly effective form of breathing-relaxation technique is counting one's exhalations. The purpose of this technique is to bring full attention to breathing and to quiet mental activity. All that matters is the counting of the exhalations. As soon as a thought is perceived or recognized, the attention is guided back to the breath and the counting. If one persists in the practice of this technique, he or she is likely to notice a significant degree of tension reduction both mentally and physically. One application of this technique is to combat insomnia, especially when difficulty with falling asleep seems to be the issue.

Imagery Techniques

Imagery techniques are commonly used forms of relaxation that are often combined with other stress-reduction strategies (Lavey & Taylor, 1985). Achterberg (1985) defined imagery as mental processes that summon and utilize the five senses, vision, audition, smell, taste, and touch. Because imagery primarily focuses on cognitive/mental phenomena, Davidson and Schwartz (1976) stated that it may have some limitations when reducing somatic or bodily tension. To rectify this, one may wish to combine imagery with other forms of relaxation such as breathing or progressive relaxation.

Lazarus (1985) suggested that imagery exercises not only result in a deeper state of relaxation, but they have also been shown to enhance alertness to ongoing feedback from autonomic and muscular systems. Pelletier (1979) reviewed several studies in which imagery techniques were shown to have successfully affected cancer growth. He concluded that imagery may be a powerful method in treating various stress-related illnesses. Imagery is often combined with other forms of stress management to enhance one's ability to avoid negative or self-damaging thoughts. As described previously, visualization and imagery can be highly helpful in stress-inoculation training and the process of cognitive restructuring. Imagery exercises are particularly used by sports psychologists who have found them highly effective in reducing stress and anxiety related to performance (Neiss, 1988).

Progressive Relaxation

Progressive relaxation is one of the most popular and widely used forms of relaxation. The technique was originally developed by Edmund Jacobson (1938) who studied the importance of rest and relaxation in the treatment of stress-related disorders.

Jacobson (1938) theorized that a reduction of muscle tension would lead to a reduction of autonomic nervous system activity, especially sympathetic activity. Progressive relaxation is comprised of two major steps: (1) learning to identify excessive tension in certain muscles; and (2) learning to reduce and, if possible, eliminate that tension. First, the muscle is contracted and held tense for a moment so as to help the individual learn to identify the sensation of tension. The individual is then told to relax the muscle to experience the sensation of relaxation. This procedure is repeated with various muscle groups of the body (Olton & Noonberg, 1980). Wolpe (1958) drew upon Jacobson's model of progressive relaxation and theorized that a condition of muscle relaxation would be incompatible with an anxiety response. Based on this assumption, Wolpe initiated the use of progressive relaxation in systematic desensitization for treatment of phobias and some psychosomatic disorders (Lehrer, Wolfolk, & Sime, 2008).

Transcendental Meditation

Meditation is a method of relaxation that has been practiced in the East for thousands of years. In the West, the most widely practiced and extensively studied form of meditation is transcendental meditation (TM), which was adopted from Indian Yogic traditions (Benson, 2000). The TM method is deceptively simple to perform and is easily learned. It consists of assuming a comfortable position with eyes closed and silently repeating a special sound or word which is referred to as a "mantra." A mantra is a Sanskrit word derived from the Hindu scriptures and has a special significance to the mediator. In the traditional practice of this approach, one is required to meet with an adept, a highly qualified teacher to receive a personalized mantra to use during the practice of the technique. Also, additional instructions are needed for the appropriate practice of this form of meditation that can be provided only by the teacher.

As a result of extensive psychophysiological research with TM, Benson (2000) found this technique highly effective in treating hypertension as well as a variety of cardiovascular complications. The two modern forms of meditation that are based on TM, and whose effectiveness have been supported empirically, are the relaxation response (Benson, 2000) and clinically standardized meditation (Carrington, 1977). Benson's technique has in a sense demystified transcendental meditation by suggesting that instead of repeating a "secret mantra" one can achieve the same physiological results by repeating a simple, one-syllable word such as "one" or "peace." In addition to repeating a simple word, Benson suggests three other ingredients for effective meditation: a relaxed posture, a quiet place, and a passive attitude. An additional item that needs to be added to this list is regular practice, without which the effects of this or other techniques are likely to be unnoticed.

YOGA TRAINING

The word Yoga is derived from the ancient language of Sanskrit, Yuj, which means to join or bind (Vahia & Doongaji, 1977). Similar to several other relaxation procedures, this approach focuses on mind-body integration. According to sacred Hindu texts, the practice of yoga brings about a state of total tranquility and allows one to transcend the limitations of the material universe. According to the *Bhagavad Gita*, "When his mind, intellect and self are under control, freed from restless desire, so that they rest in spirit within, a man becomes one in communion with God. He who has achieved this shall not be moved by the greatest sorrow. This is the real meaning of Yoga, a deliverance from contact with pain and sorrow" (Iyengar, 1972, p. 20).

There are a number of different yoga techniques, also called paths, which attempt to bring about a uniting of the body and the mind. These include Kundalini Yoga, which attends to the body's energy centers; Bhakti Yoga, which emphasizes primarily prayer and heartfelt devotional practices; Raja Yoga in which mastery over the self is achieved through total stillness and silence; Karma Yoga, which achieves unity through work, good deeds and serving others; Jnana Yoga, which underscores reading and meditating on the Hindu scriptures and gaining knowledge through such means; and finally Hatha Yoga, which is the most well-known form of yoga in the Western world, and which focuses on assuming certain positions, conducive to profound relaxation (Rama, 1985). The various paths of yoga are often combined to achieve self-mastery and transcendence.

Patel (1984) considered Hatha Yoga to be a way of improving health and self-control, and decreasing the harmful impact of environmental influences. The key activity underlying yoga exercises is the focused stretch. Various muscle groups are gently stretched and un-stretched while rhythmic breathing is maintained. Focused breathing is an important aspect of this form of training (Seaward, 2011). Patel (1984) found Hatha Yoga training to be especially effective in treating essential hypertension, heart disease, and bronchial asthma. Vahia and Doongaji (1977) found yoga training to be highly effective in treating various stress-related disorders, such as gastrointestinal disorders, headaches, arthritis, and others. Finally, Schultz (1950) stated that Hatha Yoga enhances muscle relaxation, improves circulation, sharpens concentration and brings about an overall state of rest and relaxation.

Models of Relaxation

Several important questions need to be asked at this point. Are all relaxation techniques the same? Do they all produce the same effects? And finally, which one is the best technique for me? Although many books on relaxation techniques do not simply address the theoretical models of relaxation procedures, I strongly feel that it is important for the reader to have an understanding of some of these models and to have a greater knowledge as to why certain techniques are best for different people at different times.

The underlying formulations by which relaxation techniques produce their results fall into one of two categories or models. The first model is based on a unitary model of stress and relaxation. This model, presented by Benson, Beary, and Carol (1974), stated that all relaxation techniques produce a common integrated relaxation response, which is the opposite of an aroused or activated state. According to Benson (2000), the relaxation response results in a reduced metabolic state which is consistent with decreased autonomic system activity. As discussed earlier, this means that there tends to be a marked decrease in oxygen consumption and carbon dioxide elimination, a reduction in the concentration of blood lactate, and a lowering of cardiac and respiratory rates (Benson & Friedman, 1985). Benson (2000) argued that since all relaxation/meditation procedures can bring on the same general effects, the best procedure would be the least difficult one to learn and to teach. A simple technique espoused by this camp is repeating a simple word with each exhalation as a way of inducing this relaxation response.

English and Baker (1983) investigated the efficacy of progressive relaxation, transcendental meditation, and a control condition in reducing blood pressure and heart rate, before, during, and after immersion of a hand in cold water, which was defined as the stressor. Both relaxation groups showed significant reductions in blood pressure, but not heart rate across the treatment intervals. This and similar studies have suggested that techniques such as progressive relaxation and transcendental meditation mobilize similar psychophysiological mechanisms and result in one generalized "relaxation response."

An alternative model of relaxation that has been conceived by Davidson and Schwartz (1976) is the multi-process model. According to this model, relaxation procedures are divided into two general categories of somatic (focusing on the physical activity) and cognitive (focusing on the mental activity) relaxation. This categorization is based on the premise that somatic and cognitive elements of arousal would respond differently to various relaxation techniques. It is believed that those relaxation procedures which influence physical or somatic processes will be effective in the reduction and the treatment of somatic tension. On the other hand, techniques that affect cognitive events are likely to reduce cognitive over-activity or anxiety (Davidson & Schwartz, 1984).

To illustrate the distinction between somatic and cognitive anxiety, Davidson and Schwartz (1976) provided the example of a person who is physically relaxed but cannot fall asleep because his or her mind is overactive. As defined by this model, this person is said to be experiencing cognitive symptoms of anxiety. Alternatively, somatic anxiety may be viewed as the characteristic of the person who experiences physical tension and discomfort without the cognitive symptoms (e.g., negative thoughts, worries). Schwartz, Davidson, and Goleman (1978) labeled progressive relaxation as a somatically oriented technique because it requires paying attention to physical sensations and muscle tension. Conversely, they conceived of mantra meditation (repeating or focusing on a word), such as transcendental meditation, as a cognitively oriented technique since repeating the mantra is likely to result in reducing constant cognitive activity.

Oringel (1983) compared somatic versus cognitive processes in relaxation training. Subjects received three sessions of either somatic (progressive) relaxation, cognitive relaxation (guided imagery), or a placebo procedure. The results supported the belief of somatic versus cognitive anxiety. Cognitive anxiety subjects showed more tension as measured by electromyography (a method of measuring muscle tension) than did the somatic subjects. The somatic subjects reduced muscle activity levels more than cognitive subjects did. No significant changes were observed in the placebo group. Elsewhere, Lehrer, Wolfolk, and Sime (2008), in their extensive review of the literature on different relaxation modalities, concluded that meditation and progressive relaxation appear to have significant differences in their effects.

From a clinical standpoint, especially when it comes to the treatment of chronic pain, I prefer the multiprocess approach to relaxation. The multiprocess approach can be quite helpful to patients who cannot figure out why a technique works at certain times and may actually cause tension at another time. For example, a few years ago, a colleague of mine who extensively uses biofeedback in his practice consulted with me about a difficult case in which his extremely successful and pleasing imagery technique was actually making one of his patients tenser and even agitated. After discussing the patient's history, it became obvious that the patient was experiencing such high levels of physical pain and tension that focusing on mental imagery was almost useless, because as the patient later remarked, "No matter how hard I try I can't seem to visualize the beach because my pain says that I am stuck right here." This patient needed a more somatic technique focused on reducing his physical tension. As this was accomplished, the patient was more inclined to consider pleasant visual images or thoughts.

Many patients throughout the years have related that they had difficulty using techniques such as transcendental meditation to reduce their pain because their physical symptoms were so distracting. After a while they became so frustrated that they had to simply drop out of therapy. I am by no means suggesting that such techniques should not be attempted by chronic pain sufferers. However, if they do not work for one person, it does not mean that he or she should give up on relaxation training altogether or conclude, "I just can't do it." The problem is very likely with the technique — or possibly because the individual has not given it enough time to work.

Summary

Considerable evidence supports the effectiveness and strength of relaxation techniques in combating pain and stress-linked complications. Also, it may be concluded that psychological and physiological changes that are brought about as a result of the practice of these techniques are long lasting, and stand the test of time. During the last several decades there has been a debate over whether different forms of relaxation procedures have unique effects or whether they all produce a single, generalized relaxation response. The unitary and the multiprocess models attempt to answer such questions and explain the nature of relaxation therapy. Although there is some support for each of these models in the treatment of chronic pain, it may be important to choose a technique that addresses both physical and mental sources of tension and anxiety.

Based on my research and clinical experience, I have concluded that the autogenic technique addresses both somatic and cognitive sources of tension and can be effectively used as a means of coping with chronic pain. This is the only technique that has benefited from nearly a century of close scientific scrutiny and the only one that has a scientific explanation for how and why it works. As Pelletier (1979) has stated, autogenic training "is the most comprehensive [technique] and can serve as a model for all others that address themselves to the clinical treatment of mind-body disorders" (p. 121).

In following chapters the reader will have an opportunity to learn about the intricacies of this technique, and will be provided with detailed instructions on how to use the technique to effectively reduce and manage pain, and to enhance sleep. Almost everything a practitioner needs to know about this technique is included in this book. I only ask that the reader closely follows the instructions for each step of the training.

4
History and Basic Principles

Autogenic training is the oldest Western approach for facilitating self-regulation and promoting recovery from psychophysiological symptoms and disorders. This technique was originally developed by the German neuropsychiatrist, Johannes Heinrich Schultz (Schultz, 1932; Schultz & Luthe, 1959), and was introduced to the medical community in the early 1920s. Although this training has gained much popularity and recognition, especially in Europe and Japan, it suffers from a lack of recognition by researchers and clinicians in the United States. This may be partially because much of the literature on the subject remains in German. Although attempts are continually being made to translate some of the original manuscripts and the research findings, a wealth of knowledge remains untapped. Another reason for the lack of proliferation of the training is the recent emphasis on quick techniques that can be easily taught and learned. Autogenic training is not such a technique. It is a series of potent therapeutic exercises that can make a significant contribution to promoting health and well-being — it is not merely another relaxation exercise. In fact, one must note that Schultz and later his protégé, Luthe, defined autogenic training as a psychophysiological form of therapy, a therapeutic approach that addresses itself to the mind-body interconnections and intercommunications (Schultz & Luthe, 1959).

The Birth of Autogenic Training

The birth of autogenic training can be traced to the latter part of the 1800s and the pioneering work of the prominent neuropsychiatrist, Oskar Vogt. Vogt devoted his life to research and exploration in the area of body-mind (somato-psychic) medicine (Luthe, 1977; Schultz & Luthe, 1969). His research in the areas of hypnosis, hypno-analysis, and sleep provided important knowledge regarding the brain's many mysteries, particularly as applied to self-regulation and psychophysiological maintenance. Vogt's observations about mind-body interactions were so astute and advanced that even today's scientists would find some of his findings accurately supportive of the latest discoveries in medicine. His research clearly suggested that what is referred to as "mind-body dichotomy" is indeed a unified entity that cannot be fully researched in a linear, reductionistic fashion. Indeed, the person as a whole is greater and different than the sum of his or her parts.

Among other areas of exploration into the self-regulatory activities of the nervous system, Vogt and his collaborator, another brilliant psychiatrist and neuropathologist, Korbinian Brodmann, became interested in the many functions of sleep, especially in terms of its psychophysiological, recuperative properties (Luthe, 1973). Hypnosis, they conjectured, was a logical method of exploring the body's self-healing properties. Hence, they began researching a variety of hypnotic, autohypnotic, and hypnoanalytic techniques and procedures. Brodmann was particularly responsible for developing a form of hypnosis, called fractioned hypnosis, which further explored the various psychophysiological changes during the hypnotic state. This line of research later enabled them to develop some of the earliest conceptualizations with regard to the various stages of sleep (Schultz, 1950).

At the same time, Vogt, his wife Cecil, and some of their collaborators continued to delve into the many mysteries of the brain from both structural and functional standpoints. In time, it became more and more obvious that by activating certain natural processes within the nervous system, a state of balance and recovery could be achieved, particularly after exposure to stress and trauma. Specific exercises called prophylactic rest-autohypnosis were developed to promote such healing processes. After practicing these techniques, patients began to spontaneously recover from a variety of physical and emotional disorders (Luthe, 1973).

Meanwhile the young physician Johannes Heinrich Schultz, who had training in internal medicine (Richard Stern and Paul Ehrlich Institutes), dermatology, and neurology, became interested in Vogt's work with mind-body regeneration techniques. Shortly after his association with his brilliant mentor, Schultz began his exploration of hypnosis and its applications in the treatment of psychosomatic disorders. He was, however, aware of and sensitive to some of the undesirable aspects of hypnotic and hypnotherapeutic techniques such as dependence on the therapist, the need for passivity, and hypnotizability (Lindemann, 1973). By the early 1900s, Schultz became convinced that through the use of some basic training, he could teach his patients to benefit from a brain-directed, self-regulatory process to improve their psychological and physical health. This process of activating the body's natural repair and regulation mechanism came to be known as autogenic therapy, or a self-generated process of repair and healing.

Early observations regarding this process of repair and regeneration suggested the experience of heaviness and warmth in the extremities while the patient was experiencing a pre-sleeplike state of profound relaxation. Schultz attempted to induce a similar state in his patients by having them repeat simple formulas (phrases) that focused on the experience of heaviness and warmth in the arms and the legs. The patients learned to quickly induce these sensations merely by repeating the formulas and concentrating on a sensation of heaviness and warmth, with the passive, or non-volitional, concentration on the formulas playing a key role in achieving the autogenic state (see Chapter 6 for a detailed explanation of passive concentration). Soon it was discovered that by focusing on additional formulas, which suggested a calm heartbeat, regular breathing, abdominal warmth, and finally, a cool forehead, the depth of the relaxation process and replenishment of the physiological resources could be profoundly enhanced. In time, these came to be known as the Standard Autogenic Training Exercises. As a result of practicing these exercises, a neurophysiological "key," or an activating mechanism was discovered which brought on a shift from an active and/or stressed state to a profound state of repair — a state of recovery which reestablished the body's homeostasis. One other especially important discovery was that after a short time, the subject could learn to benefit from the training with little or even no dependence on the therapist. This independence from the therapist came to be known as one of the hallmarks of autogenic training.

Both Vogt and Schultz made a most significant discovery: the brain had the ability to effectively correct and eliminate a variety of psychophysiological disorders brought about by imbalances within the nervous system. Hence, the term autogenic embodies two indivisible principles. First, autogenic training encompasses all the inborn capabilities of the nervous system that make it possible to bring about the optimum state of balance and health. Second, since such changes are self-generated the reliance on the therapist is minimized. Basically, and at least initially, the task of the therapist is to train the patient to activate such internal, self-regulatory mechanisms so as to effectively combat disease and internal disharmony.

Indeed, it is a most persuasive discovery that nature has provided our bodies with the necessary ingredients for promoting health that require little intervention from the outside to accomplish this task (Luthe & Blumberger, 1977). However, due to ongoing exposure to daily stress, various physical and psychological traumas, over-medication, and ineffective or even damaging interventions (e.g., unnecessary invasive procedures), we continue to weaken the body's self-healing mechanisms. Fortunately, with approaches such as autogenic training, the body's own self-recuperative capabilities can be further enhanced, and the state of inner balance reestablished.

A psychophysiologically based, corrective phenomenon often experienced during the practice of autogenic exercises is an autogenic discharge. This phenomenon may assume a variety of forms and may include experiences such as muscle twitches, sudden appearance of headaches, and physical discomfort. It has been postulated that the main purpose of autogenic discharges is to release disturbing neuronal buildup as a way of restoring normal brain functions (Schultz & Luthe, 1959). In other words, such phenomena are attempts at unloading unpleasant and traumatic experiences that may be interfering with appropriate neurophysiological activity, resulting in a variety of symptoms. If autogenic discharges persist in their occurrences, it is necessary to address them by temporarily discontinuing training and exploring the nature of such experiences.

Some of the more advanced autogenic techniques address such phenomena from a psychotherapeutic standpoint. Autogenic abreaction, for example, is a method of autogenic neutralization whereby the trainee is asked to passively disclose his or her negative experiences from a spectator's point of view without any active involvement in the experience at all, which will in time promote a discharge of disturbing neuronal load (tension) (Luthe, 1979). This approach often addresses and may promote the resolution of deeper issues that may be causing the unpleasant, psychophysiologically-based episodes (see Chapter 17 in this volume).

Elements of the Autogenic Process

In his early research, Schultz discovered two principal elements in the activation of the autogenic process. These were: (1) mental repetition of specific formulas (phrases) which focused on sensations of heaviness and warmth in the extremities (consistent with sensations experienced during hypnosis and shortly before falling asleep); and (2) the need for the patient to achieve and maintain an attitude of detachment and indifference toward any outcome that may be brought on by the repetition of the aforementioned formulas. This state of "passive concentration" is crucial in allowing the brain-directed, self-regulatory mechanisms to function optimally (Schultz & Luthe, 1959). If the concept of passive concentration is not adequately and effectively implemented by the patient, the repetition of the various formulas may actually bring about opposite results. That is to say, if the person forces himself or herself to experience heaviness or warmth, he or she may actually become more tense and stressed. We shall return to this important concept later in Chapter 6.

Although autogenic training was initially conceived in terms of psychophysiological phenomena occurring during hypnosis and self-hypnosis, it is important to note that extensive electroencephalographic studies have demonstrated, time after time, that the autogenic state is unique and different from the hypnotic state. Luthe (1970a) emphasized this point by making the following statement:

> The steady stream of research provided has provided increasing evidence that autogenic training is associated with a specific combination of multidimensional changes which are not identical with those observed during hypnosis or sleep. A variety of more recent findings even indicate that a number of physiological changes take functional directions which are diametrically opposed to those seen during hypnosis. This development cannot be overlooked, and in the view of the knowledge resulting from advancing research, *it must be pointed out that autogenic training can no longer be regarded as a form of hypnosis which is practiced without the hypnotist.* Likewise, on the basis of relevant findings, it is not justified and it would be confusing to continue to use the term "autohypnosis" in connection with autogenic training [p. 104; emphasis added].

It must be noted also that while the autogenic state shares some similarities with the recuperative changes that occur during certain stages of sleep, it is not a sleep state.

Autogenic training may be best described as a pre-sleep state with unique psychotherapeutic and psychophysiological properties that are brought on by observing certain training requirements, such as passive concentration, and through the daily practice of the standard training formulas (Luthe, Jus, & Geissmann, 1965).

Nearly a century has passed since the field of autogenic training began its experimental and clinical sojourn as a method of enhancing health and well-being as well as combating the ever-deleterious exposure to long-term stress. For example, a recent study by Goto, Nakai, and Ogawa (2011) found autogenic training to be an effective treatment for patients with Ménière's disease. Ménière's disease is a disorder of the inner ear with severe symptoms of vertigo, tinnitus, and even hearing loss, all of which can significantly impair functioning in the sufferer. Although no single theory for the exact cause of this disorder exists, stress seems to bring on the symptoms or exacerbate them. In this study the effectiveness of autogenic training persisted even after two years following the initial treatment. In Goto et al.'s study, when compared to the control group, those receiving autogenic training showed significant improvements in symptoms and demonstrated a better ability to cope with stress related to their diagnosis.

In another study, Schinozaki and colleagues (2010) compared autogenic training against an educational control group, in the treatment of patients who suffered from severe irritable bowel syndrome (IBS). Those receiving autogenic training showed significant improvements as far as IBS symptoms were concerned in comparison to the control group. Additionally, the autogenic groups saw improvements in social functioning. This is a very promising discovery as most IBS patients tend to reduce social activity due to the distressing nature of this condition and its impact on interpersonal relationships.

In addition to the above example, there are literally thousands of published studies attesting to the effectiveness of autogenic training and the following areas and studies may be considered:

- treatment of pain (Blacker, 1980)
- treatment of experimental pain (Milling et al., 2002)
- treatment of insomnia (Coursey et al., 1980)
- treatment of night terrors (Sadigh & Mierzwa, 1995)
- treatment of post-traumatic nightmares (Sadigh, 1999)
- Raynaud's disease (Freedman, Ianni, & Weing, 1983)
- treatment of myofascial trigger points (Banks et al., 1998)
- headaches (Janssen & Neutgens, 1986)
- infertility (O'Moore et al., 1983)
- anxiety disorders (Banner & Meadows, 1983; Sakai, 1997)

Many authors in the United States have lamented that autogenic training has not received the attention it deserves (Lichstein, 1989; Pelletier, 1977). Pelletier (1979) suggested that AT can serve as a model for all relaxation and meditative techniques that attempt to treat stress-related disorders.

Autogenic training has been taught in medical schools in most European countries such as Germany, Switzerland, France, Belgium, Spain, Italy, Poland, and also extensively in Japan (Luthe, 1965). Many authors have suggested that only a fraction (10 to 20 percent) of the clinical publications on this technique have been translated into the English language. Another possible explanation for the lack of recognition of this psychophysiological approach may be the emphasis that is placed on pharmacological treatments in the United States. Also, much like all behaviorally based techniques, it takes some time for the effects of autogenics to be noticed and appreciated by the trainee. However, once the technique has been mastered, its recuperative properties can be easily summoned in minutes of concentrated practice. Jencks (1977) suggested that some of the almost immediate (in roughly two weeks) benefits of this technique that can be experienced by the patient include a reduction in anxiety, improved sleep, enhanced memory, and an improvement in the ability to cope with daily stress. Gradually and with focused practice, improvements in coping with pain, cardiovascular and gastrointestinal disorders, and chronic conditions are acquired.

Conclusions

The main purpose of this chapter has been to provide the reader with some of the basic principles of the technique of autogenic training and its clinical applications. Again, it is important to note that this nearly century-old psychophysiological approach is far more than a simple technique of relaxation. Indeed, autogenic training may be viewed as a formidable method of psychotherapy, cognitive restructuring, and behavior modification. Those who have had first-hand experience with the training and have practiced it for some time will attest to the experience of spontaneous physical and psychological phenomena that are of significant healing potential. Many of these phenomena are discussed in several texts under the topics of autogenic meditation, autogenic discharges, and autogenic neutralization (see Schultz & Luthe, 1969). The study and exploration of techniques similar to autogenic training should convince us of the self-recuperative potentials of the mind-body connection and the intricate mechanisms involved in such a process. It must be emphasized that a powerful technique such as autogenic training is, nevertheless, only a technique and needs to be methodically combined with other medical and psychological approaches to address patients' needs. The treatment of chronic conditions, such as chronic pain syndrome and other stress-related disorders, requires a systematic, multidisciplinary approach. Without a doubt, autogenic training can be a worthy and reliable component of such an approach.

5

Medical and Psychological Screening

Medical Screening

Meditative or relaxation training in any form should be preceded by appropriate medical screening. This statement may come as a surprise to some of the readers, who might have been especially exposed to numerous books and articles on relaxation training with no mention of any precautions whatsoever. This is unfortunate since similar to medications, relaxation exercises can potentially have some uncomfortable side effects. Lazarus and Mayne (1990) suggested that the rapid alterations in autonomic activity, especially a decrease in sympathetic tone brought on by relaxation exercises may result in parasympathetic rebound. This rebound is likely to cause a variety of unpleasant sensations and symptoms. These may include dizziness, disorientation, headaches, anxiety, and panic attacks, and in some cases, hallucinations. However, with appropriate screening, education, and adherence to certain principles, these side effects can be avoided.

In the forthcoming pages, as we discuss autogenic training in a step-by-step fashion, the reader will be provided with detailed information about how to perform each exercise. These instructions need to be followed to the letter. When people have a negative experience during the practice of meditation or relaxation training, almost without an exception, they tend to stop practicing and are likely to drop out. Again, this can be avoided and patients can go on benefiting from these techniques by simply following certain instructions. It is best to take the necessary time and learn one step at a time rather than rush the process and end up avoiding the training altogether. I have observed a similar phenomenon with those who suddenly decided to lose weight or get in shape by doing hundreds of push-ups or go for a five-mile walk the first day.

Usually these people are in such pain and discomfort by the next day that even the thought of exercising is painful to them. While the initial intentions were healthy and noble, the outcome proved to be disastrous. But such outcomes can be avoided and patients need to be encouraged to take their time while learning the basics of autogenic training — and for that matter any other exercise — to maximize the extraordinary, health-enhancing benefits it has to offer.

Due to the potent nature of autogenic training, it is especially imperative that the patient is evaluated by a physician prior to starting the exercise. People with disorders related to the endocrine system (e.g., diabetes, hypo- or hyperthyroidism) must remain under close monitoring of a physician while undergoing this training since significant biochemical changes may occur. Although these changes are positive and beneficial, the patients' physicians need to be aware of the need to possibly change some of their medications. For example, people with hyperglycemia who are insulin dependent may, in time, need a lower dose of insulin because autogenic training can improve their condition thus necessitating an adjustment in the medication dosage. For a number of years I have worked with many diabetics who successfully practiced with autogenic training and benefited from it considerably because they followed their physicians' instructions and received regular checkups. The family physician, especially, needs to be aware of any steps the patient is taking to enhance his or her health and well-being.

The following medical conditions require physician supervision while the patient is participating in any form of meditative or relaxation training (Luthe, 1979). Even though most people with these conditions never experience any uncomfortable side effects, and such side effects are rarely observed in clinical studies, close medical supervision is required to avoid impeding the therapeutic progress.

1. Seizure disorders of any kind (petit or grand mal, etc.)
2. Labile blood pressure
3. Diabetes mellitus
4. Thyroid disorder of any kind (hyper or hypo)
5. Severe asthma
6. Glaucoma
7. An actively bleeding stomach ulcer

The autogenic technique should also be used with caution after a heart attack or the experience of a profound trauma. In such cases, it may take a few weeks before the patient can optimally benefit from relaxation training. Even then, I highly recommend a gradual, "small dose" approach, with sessions lasting somewhere between five to ten minutes, to be followed by a few minutes of discussing physical and emotional experiences and sensations.

While a variety of gastrointestinal disorders respond well to autogenic training, it is imperative that patients who are suffering from gastric ulcers do not attempt to practice the fifth standard exercise, which induces abdominal warmth. Schultz and Luthe (1969) also warned about the use of the sixth standard exercise (forehead cooling) in those who were diagnosed with glaucoma, or other degenerative ophthalmic disorders.

It is imprudent to employ an active relaxation intervention when a person is experiencing an asthma attack. In such a situation, the activation of the sympathetic nervous system is needed and not parasympathetic activation. However, there is ample empirical data that suggest that relaxation and meditative techniques may be used quite effectively to prevent asthma attacks. Those teaching and practicing such techniques need to be familiar with the medical precautions that were listed above.

Psychological Screening

There are also a few psychological conditions that need to be kept in mind prior to relaxation training. Although common sense dictates that a person who is extremely anxious or emotionally overwhelmed needs to relax, practicing relaxation techniques may actually cause greater anxiety and the experience of a phenomenon known as relaxation-induced anxiety may result (Heide & Borkovec, 1984). This is a real phenomenon that may be experienced by those who force themselves or try too hard to relax when they are extremely agitated or distressed. It is also possible that a patient may experience profound levels of relaxation-induced anxiety because of the fear of losing control. In addition, a weakened ego-defense mechanism as a result of a traumatic experience or exposure to prolonged, unremitting stress may predispose a person to the experience of such relaxation-related, disturbing phenomena. In such cases, psychotherapy or pharmacological interventions may be more helpful until the severity of the symptoms have at least somewhat subsided. Relaxation exercises should not be attempted during panic attacks. However, prior to an attack or afterward, relaxation exercises may be most beneficial.

Those who may present with symptoms suggesting a loosening of the ego boundaries need to be further examined and may be considered for other forms of treatment before training in the autogenic technique. Following is a list of psychological symptoms and diagnoses that should be kept in mind prior to the training (Luthe, 1979).

Once again, if a patient is currently experiencing any of these symptoms, make sure that his or her condition is being monitored by a physician and/or mental health professionals.

1. Severe anxiety
2. Major depressive illness
3. Active psychosis
4. Severe manic episode
5. Dissociative identity disorder (during the active phase)
6. Severe distress shortly after a trauma
7. Thought disorder due to psychological or organic causes

A patient who is suffering from major depression is unlikely to respond well to various forms of meditative-relaxation. Autogenic training is not an exception, especially because it demands a relatively high level of motivation from the patient. Additionally, depressed patients may have a difficult time maintaining passive concentration. This will render the practice of the standard exercises almost useless. If a patient has a level of mastery with this approach and does become depressed due to personal or interpersonal reasons, it is possible to use his or her knowledge of the technique during brief periods of practice to address the underlying causes of depression. Also, in such cases, the more advanced forms of autogenic therapy may be used to help ameliorate some of the symptoms of depression. But again, the patient must have mastered the intricacies of the technique in the past for this to work. The best approach would be to bring the patient's depression under control so as to make the practice of this or other techniques more effective.

In conclusion, I need to emphasize that if patients are experiencing any of the previously mentioned medical or psychological symptoms, this does not mean that they cannot practice autogenic training or other relaxation techniques. However, they need to be under physician supervision to avoid any negative experiences. As a general rule, these techniques should not be implemented during severe crises of a medical, psychological, or interpersonal nature.

When people have been exposed to prolonged levels of physical and psychological stress, it may be helpful to gradually expose them to various relaxation techniques to avoid phenomena such as parasympathetic rebound. The training sessions, for example, can be made very brief with focus on physical relaxation, simple phrases, or breathing techniques. Once the patient begins to feel more comfortable and the process of "letting go" is not as anxiety provoking, the sessions can be made longer in duration. With regard to specific standard autogenic formulas, attenuated formulas can be used initially to reduce their potency and to avoid any unpleasant experiences. For example, in the sixth autogenic exercise, instead of repeating the standard formula,

"My forehead is cool," an attenuated version ("My forehead is slightly cool") may be repeated to avoid dizziness, or other uncomfortable reactions by anxious or highly stressed patients. Additional helpful instructions are provided throughout the following training based chapters, which address the proper use of specific standard autogenic exercises.

6
Requirements for Achieving the Autogenic State

Through many years of meticulous research and clinical work, the pioneers of autogenic training developed a set of criteria for promoting the brain-generated state of normalization. These criteria have since been incorporated into a variety of relaxation techniques, although they use slightly different terminologies. There are five major requirements for achieving and facilitating the autogenic state (Figure 6.1). These are: (1) reducing environmental (afferent) stimulation; (2) passive concentration; (3) making mental contact with a specific body part or function (for example, breathing); (4) repetition of specific phrases (called formulas) for a period of time; and (5) practice of these exercises on a daily basis. In this chapter these requirements will be explored in great depth. Prior to starting the training, it is imperative that the practitioner reads this chapter at least once, and reviews it from time to time to make sure that he or she is adhering to these principles that are so central to this training.

Figure 6.1. Steps in promoting the autogenic state.

To fully experience the effects of the standard autogenic exercises and to enhance the process of mind-body rejuvenation and repair, all environmental stimuli (sound, light, etc.) need to be reduced to a minimum. This is especially critical during the initial phases of training. In time, it is possible to achieve some of the benefits of autogenic training even in those situations when attenuation of environmental stimuli is not possible, such as at a train station or the airport. Also, specific positional postures recommended by Schultz and Luthe (1969) can facilitate the achievement of the autogenic state and will be discussed in this section. I have introduced an additional posture for the fifth exercise, which has shown to enhance the achievement of warmth in the abdominal region.

From time to time, I hear people make such statements as "I relax best when I am watching television." Although they may experience a quieting of their "busy" thinking and television may be an effective form of distraction, in reality it may actually cause more tension because of the constant audio-visual stimulation. Research clearly shows that the most effective way of facilitating a shift from a stress state into a recuperative-relaxation state is to reduce environmental and physical sources of stimulation. To fully appreciate the importance of this critical step, we need to learn some of the basic concepts that were discovered in investigations dealing with sensory deprivation and the restricted environmental stimulation therapies (REST).

Lessons from Restricted Environmental Stimulation Therapy

In the late 1950s, a group of researchers at McGill University conducted the first systematic research project using sensory deprivation with human subjects. During the research, subjects were either placed in a dark, soundproof chamber, or they were immersed in dark tanks filled with water. Psychophysiological measures of subjects in these early studies showed profound decreases in arousal levels and sympathetic activity, suggesting a relaxation effect. That is to say, without practicing any particular relaxation or meditative techniques, these subjects were able to achieve deep levels of rest and relaxation by merely being placed in an environment that was free of any form of stimulation.

However, the initial reactions to such experiments were mixed. Some viewed sensory deprivation studies as unethical, horrifying, and dangerous, while others considered them a breakthrough in better understanding the human nervous system. Several decades ago, many authors argued that sensory deprivation was an inaccurate description of these experiments (Lilly, 1977; Weiss, 1973). Whether the person is resting in a dark, quiet chamber or buoyant in a water tank, he or she has a variety of sensory sensations. Auditory stimuli are also received from inside the body. Hence, the term sensory deprivation was replaced with "stimulus reduction" or what is now known as restricted environmental stimulation therapy, or REST for short. Simply put, REST entails placing a person in an environment with as little sensory stimulation as possible.

Although there is still a need for further systematic research with REST, it has been convincingly demonstrated that this approach is a powerful way of eliciting positive change in a variety of psychological, physiological, and behavioral processes (Suedfeld, 1980). Currently, there are two approaches for achieving restricted environmental stimulation. The first approach requires placing the subject in a dark and soundproof room for approximately one hour. The second approach is flotation. The subject is placed in a dark and soundproof flotation tank filled with buoyant liquid (a liquid with extremely high salt concentration). The temperature of the liquid is kept at approximately 95.0°F. Because of the high salt concentration, the subject can float in a buoyant state during the treatment period which lasts ten to sixty minutes (Lilly, 1977). The buoyant state significantly reduces stimulation from the muscular system to the brain, which will consequently promote a deeper state of relaxation.

Restricted Environmental Stimulation and Stress Management

A person who has been bombarded with stressful stimuli throughout the day will naturally seek a place of rest and solitude to reduce the physical and psychological tension that he or she has been experiencing. To accomplish this, the individual may retreat to a quiet room, dim the lights, and close his or her eyes for a short time. Even if such retreats are brief and temporary, they are likely to bring about some degree of relaxation and revitalization.

The need for seeking solitude and a quiet place to replenish one's depleted resources is by no means a new idea. The Bible, for example, is full of examples of how periods of retreat to a "desert" place can be restorative and highly beneficial. Even in today's world many religious and cultural practices require people to spend a brief period in isolation at some point during the day. Such periods of isolation have been viewed as necessary for one to maintain and improve one's health, and also to experience a state of higher consciousness.

Although the Western world has been somewhat reluctant to subscribe to such practices and rituals, there is now strong empirical evidence that forms of meditative-relaxation which require some degree of physical isolation can be highly effective in treating pain and stress-linked disorders. The effortless passive relaxation of REST may provide an advantage over methods requiring a trial-and-error approach toward achieving a deep state of relaxation.

One explanation for the effectiveness of REST is that restricted stimulation has a direct effect on the hypothalamic-pituitary-adrenal cortex axis activity (HPAC) which was described in Chapter 2. The HPAC is considered to be an important mechanism that is mainly involved in the stress response. It has been shown that the hypothalamus directs the pituitary gland to release several hormones in stress situations (Selye, 1976). The most critical hormone released by the pituitary gland in stress situations is the adrenocorticotropic hormone (ACTH).

The primary function of ACTH is to stimulate the outer layer of the adrenal glands and the adrenal cortex. The adrenal cortex then produces and releases cortisol and aldosterone. These hormones are generally responsible for providing the body with needed energy and fluid retention in stressful situations. In addition to generating energy through the process of gluconeogenesis, cortisol can effectively reduce inflammation.

As previously discussed, continuous and prolonged secretion of these hormones, results in structural damage, especially affecting lean and connective tissue. Another important role of stress hormones is their influence on the immune system. Too much cortisol significantly suppresses immune activity and if its excessive production is prolonged, a dysfunction of the immune system may ensue.

A study by Turner and Fine (1983) found REST resulted in a significant reduction of both ACTH and cortisol levels. These authors concluded that REST-assisted relaxation produces a state of relaxation that is associated with significant decreases in the pituitary-adrenal cortex activity. Also, Lilly (1977) reported improved cognitive functioning in subjects who received REST for several sessions. REST has also been used successfully in the treatment of hypertension, eating disorders, and a variety of psychosomatic disorders.

The First Requirement: Reducing Environmental Stimulation

By following specific requirements established by the pioneers in autogenic training, patients can achieve a state of reduced environmental stimulation without needing a flotation tank or an isolation chamber. First, at least during the initial phases of training, patients need to find themselves a quiet room (as noise free as possible) where they will not be disturbed for at least twenty to thirty minutes, the length of a standard exercise. They may use a sign on the door, if necessary, to inform others that they do no wish to be disturbed. It is also important to close the drapes and dim the lights to the lowest possible levels and turn off phones and pagers.

Positions for Relaxation

The next step is to reduce physical stimulation by finding a position that places the least amount of tension on muscles and joints. First, patients need to be instructed to loosen all tight clothing, loosen belts, and remove shoes if necessary. Second, they need to discover a postural position that is most agreeable to them. Most people find it helpful to lie on their back on a couch or a comfortable bed. This position may result in tension in the muscles of the lower back which will undoubtedly interfere with the ability to achieve the autogenic state. To remedy this, patients should be encouraged to experiment by placing pillows under their knees until their lower back muscles are in a neutral or stress-free position. The arms should be placed slightly away from the trunk in a comfortable, "unlocked" position.

Next, attention must be paid to the position of the neck. A soft pillow may be used to place the muscles of the neck in a relaxed position. To avoid overextending or flexing the neck, experiment with pillows of varying sizes. Photograph 6.1 depicts a comfortable horizontal position. One of the drawbacks of this position, usually during the earlier stages of training, is that some people tend to fall asleep while practicing the exercise. To avoid this, the individual may choose one of the sitting positions.

The first sitting position (Photograph 6.2) requires the use of a reclining chair with a high back and comfortable armrests that are neither too high nor too low. If the armrests of the recliner are uncomfortably positioned, a possible remedy may be to use pillows or towels to discover a position that is least stressful to the arms and the shoulders. Another problem with recliners is that they may place undue stress under the lower calves. Again, a soft pillow may be the solution.

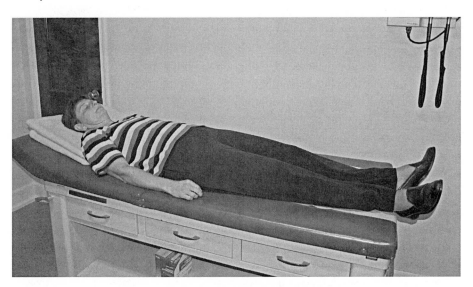

Photograph 6.1. The horizontal position.

Photograph 6.2. The reclined position.

Finally, the muscles of the lower back may be quite vulnerable in a reclined position because of the lower back extension that such chairs tend to promote. Pillows or rolled up towels may be used to reduce the stress on the lower back muscles. In my office I have several pillows that I use to make sure that the recliner fits the needs of all patients. With each patient, the recliner is transformed into a custom-made chair that promises the most comfortable position. Take your time and experiment. The outcome of each training session may be significantly improved by finding out which positions work best for the patient.

Another sitting position which is of pragmatic utility is presented in Photograph 6.3. To best benefit from this position, patients need to make sure that their feet are firmly placed on the floor. Next, they need to comfortably place their arms in their laps, with the palm of the hands facing down. Next, the head and the trunk may be dropped forward until a stress-free, relaxed position is achieved. Patients need to be cautioned not to place their upper body weight on their arms. If done correctly, the torso should comfortably balance the upper body's weight. This postural position may be used at work or when neither a bed nor a recliner is available. The position is also excellent for the abbreviated exercises which will be discussed later on.

A specific position is highly recommended for the third standard autogenic exercise, which focuses on cardiac activity. To best achieve the objectives of this exercise, the patient is asked to assume the horizontal position (see

Photograph 6.4). The next step is to comfortably place the right hand on the chest region, slightly to the left. To achieve this position with the least amount of tension, it is best to place a pillow under the right arm and elevate it slightly so that the arm is raised to the level of the chest. This position should be used for as long as necessary until the patient can comfortably make contact with the cardiac activity.

Finally, the horizontal position can be used effectively in the fifth standard exercise which focuses on generating warmth in the abdominal region. For this particular exercise, patients are

Photograph 6.3. The sitting position.

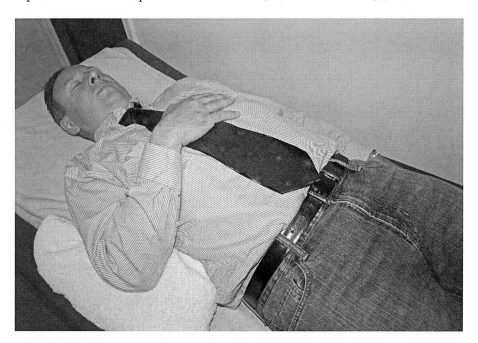

Photograph 6.4. The horizontal position for exercise three (heart) (note the comfortable position of the right hand on the chest).

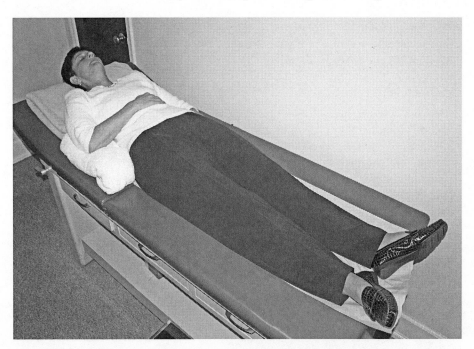

Photograph 6.5. Specially designed horizontal position for the fifth exercise (solar plexus) (note the light placement of the right hand on the upper region of the abdominal cavity).

asked to comfortably, but very lightly, place their right hand on the upper abdominal region, right below the tip of the sternum (see Photograph 6.5). Again it may be helpful to place a pillow under the arm in order to minimize any undue stress on the arm. This posture can significantly expedite the objectives of the fifth exercise as will be discussed in Chapter 12.

The Second Requirement: Passive Concentration

As mentioned earlier, passive concentration is a key principle in autogenic training. This may initially appear to be an obviously contradictory message and one may understandably ask, "How can I concentrate and be passive at the same time? Doesn't concentration require at least some level of active volition?" As we explore the intent of the original developers of this concept, it will become clear as to what they had in mind by these words and why they made it such a central concept in this form of psychophysiological training. Meanwhile, it may help to think of passive concentration as an effortless state of passive focusing or passive attention to a specific task — as if one is observing a task but is not actively participating in it. Many people have some difficulty with this concept mainly because they feel that to make something of value take place they need to be trying hard. For example, if one wants to develop stronger muscles or to flatten the abdominal muscles, he or she must exercise hard, work at it, and sweat a lot. A patient recently remarked, "My whole life I was told that if I wanted to accomplish anything, I had to work hard at it. Now I am learning that sometimes I can accomplish things without trying at all." While trying hard may make sense with regard to developing strong muscles, the process of psychophysiological repair and regeneration actually requires the opposite.

If one were to try to force falling asleep, it is quite likely that the result would be quite disappointing — remaining wide awake hour after hour. Falling asleep is an effortless process; it cannot be accomplished forcefully, which is why it is called "falling" asleep. In other words, no active participation is required as long as certain conditions are met; *it will happen by itself.* The key here is identifying certain conditions and how one can make sure that they are met efficaciously. In pages to come, detailed instructions will be provided on how to promote a state of regeneration and recuperation in its most natural way. Emphasis will be placed on discovering how people tend to interfere with this natural state of recovery and how autogenic training can reestablish this process. Meanwhile, we need to spend some more time exploring the concept of passive concentration or as it was suggested, passive attention.

Figures 6.2 and 6.3 depict the relative position of the autogenic state within the wake-sleep continuum. Initially it was conceived that the autogenic state lay somewhere between wakefulness and sleep, specifically, in the drowsy state, shortly before falling asleep (see Figure 6.1) (Jus & Jus, 1965). This was a general conceptualization that was helpful in emphasizing the importance of maintaining passive concentration, as without it one was either likely to fall asleep or become easily distracted due to attention to a variety of external or internal sources of stimulation, such as environmental noises or cognitive over-activity.

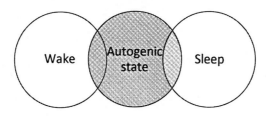

Figure 6.2. The general location of the autogenic state within the wake-sleep continuum.

However, the growing number of electroencephalographic studies of the autogenic state provided further, and more detailed, information about its occurrence within the wake-sleep continuum as seen in Figure 6.2 (Luthe, Jus, & Geissman, 1965, p. 8). This more expanded formulation of the "location" of the autogenic state placed even greater emphasis on maintaining passive concentration. Hence, greater emphasis was placed on the proper use of the standard formulas, as well as other postural suggestions to make sure that the autogenic state is achieved and maintained, with the latter being the key to bringing about psychophysiological corrections. The use of this continuum may be instructive in helping patients understand the importance of following the requirements of this intervention. For example, if instead of passive concentration the trainee tries to actively attend to the formulas (for example, to try to make the arms heavier), he or she is likely to become more alert and experience somatic and cognitive arousal. If the proper positions for the exercises are not followed, one is likely to experience undue physical tension or become overly drowsy and fall asleep. Finally, as mentioned before, if the trainee fails to maintain adequate focus on the formulas, he or she is likely to drift toward the drowsy state, which leads to falling sleep. After a few sessions of autogenic training, trainees learn how to recognize that they have indeed entered the autogenic state, which is a pleasant state of attending passively, as an observer to the effects of the various formulas.

Schultz and Luthe (1969) defined passive concentration in the following manner: "[It] implies a casual attitude and functional passivity toward the intended outcome of [the person's] concentrative activity, whereas 'active concentration' is characterized by the person's concern, interest, attention and goal-directed active efforts during the performance of a task and in respect to the final functional result" (p. 14). This brief statement is filled with some very critical concepts that require our attention. First, it implies that a casual attitude needs to be maintained during each exercise — observing or watching without active participation. Second, "functional passivity" further emphasizes

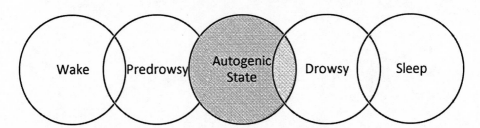

Figure 6.3. A more precise location of the autogenic state within the wake-sleep continuum (based on Luthe, Jus, & Geissman, 1965, p. 8).

that patients should be instructed to avoid any attempt at directly affecting or interfering with the body's natural functioning. Finally—and the most difficult concept for most people—"goal-directedness" needs to be dropped from one's vocabulary during the practice of autogenic exercises. Emphasize to patients that they should refrain from setting a specific agenda at the beginning of each exercise with regard to their accomplishments such as "I am going to raise my hand temperature by ten degrees by the end of the exercise." Such an attitude is most likely to have paradoxical effects and may indeed result in an increase in levels of tension and stress. Consequently, the hand temperature is likely to decrease by the end of the exercise. Many instances of relaxation-induced anxiety can be effectively avoided by adhering to these instructions.

At the same time, as patients learn to detach from the results of the exercise during the repetitions of the formulas, they need to learn to remain focused on the task at hand. This is the concentration or the attention part. If they stop paying attention to specific body parts or stop repeating a particular formula, it is likely that either they will fall asleep or become very alert, at which time they start thinking about subjects that have nothing to do with the exercise. Hence, a perfect balance between passivity and attention to each formula needs to be maintained throughout each session. Now that we have a better understanding of passive concentration, let us examine the focal points of one's attention.

The Third Requirement: Making Mental Contact with a Specific Body Part or Function

During the standard autogenic exercises, patients are instructed to pay attention principally to their arms and legs, cardiac activity, breathing, abdomen, and finally, the forehead. The process of attending to these body parts is termed *making mental contact.* That is to say, mental activity needs to be directed at a particular body part, such as the right arm, or left leg. This is another critical principle that must be met for effective training. I often ask my patients to imagine that they were looking at a body part with their eyes closed. Although this may appear to be a simple task at first, many, especially chronic pain patients, have some initial difficulty in accomplishing this. When people are in pain, they tend to gradually distance or disconnect themselves from those body parts that are in pain or distress. This form of distraction will eventually result in exhaustion of their resources because so much of their energy is consumed by trying to remain detached. To remedy this, prior to the practice of autogenic exercises I have introduced certain preparatory exercises that should significantly improve the ability to pay attention to specific body parts or to "make mental contact" with them. These exercises are described in detail in Chapter 7.

The Fourth Requirement: Repetition of Specific Phrases (Formulas)

The silent repetition of specific phrases, which are referred to as formulas, constitutes the core emphasis of autogenic training. Schultz and Luthe (1969) referred to these as "technical keys which, when applied correctly, unlock or facilitate a psychophysiologic complexity of brain-directed (autogenic) processes aiming at multidimensional readjustment and gradual normalization" (p. 14). Each standard autogenic formula is meant to promote a gradual process of repair, regeneration, replenishment, and balance. Formulas are positively stated and are repeated in the present tense such as "My right arm is heavy." As a particular formula is repeated, patients are asked to passively focus on specific sensations of heaviness and warmth in a particular body part. Other formulas focus on calm and regular breathing or a calm and steady heartbeat.

Some patients may focus on these formulas visually (seeing the actual phrase before their eyes), acoustically (focusing on the sound of the phrase) or merely focus on the feelings and the sensations that are embodied in the formula such as heaviness and warmth. It is also important to pause briefly between each repetition to better focus on specific sensations and to further enhance mental contact with a particular body part. For example, one may think of the following visual representation while repeating each formula: "My right arm is heavy ... (pause) ... my right arm is heavy ... (pause) ... my right arm is heavy ... (pause) ... my right arm is heavy ... (pause)..."

Patients are instructed to silently and slowly repeat each formula five to seven times. Also, a "background" formula that suggests a relaxing state may be used in between each standard formula. For example, as one moves from the right to the left hand, it may be helpful to repeat a transitional or a background formula to further enhance relaxation. These transitional or background formulas can also be used to pace the training process and avoid any sudden autonomic shifts that can result in unfavorable reactions.

The original literature on autogenic training uses the word "tranquility" (*ruhe* in German) as such a background. The English translations, however, suggest the formula "I am at peace." I highly recommend using one of these two while moving from one formula to the next. These can be instrumental in significantly enhancing the ability to enter a deeper state of rest and relaxation. Again, it is important to point out that any active volition (goal orientedness) needs to be avoided during the repetition of the formulas. Instruct the patient not to try to "make" anything happen.

Shortly before repeating each formula, the patient must make mental contact with a specific body part (as implied in the formula). The repetition of the formula may then commence. Finally, these formulas can serve as an effective anchor during those times when the mind begins to wander. As soon as distracting thoughts are recognized, one needs to return to making mental contact with the body part and repeat the formula.

In addition to the standard formulas, I have also introduced several others which are consistent with the autogenic principles and can be extremely helpful, especially to those suffering from fibromyalgia, chronic fatigue, and chronic pain. These will be discussed during specific chapters which deal with the various exercises.

The Fifth Requirement: Daily Practice

As powerful as autogenic training is, without daily practice it is unlikely, if not impossible, to benefit from its psychophysiological and therapeutic effects. During the early phases of training, patients are asked to practice for approximately ten to twenty minutes, twice a day. To achieve the best possible results, they need to continue practicing for three to six months. In time, most people will be able to enter the autogenic state after repeating one or two formulas for under two minutes. To "get there," they need to practice, practice, and then practice a little more. The benefits of learning to achieve the various levels of autogenic training are so tremendous that the initial, intensive practice of these exercises will be a small investment of time when one considers the lasting therapeutic effects that will ensue. That is to say, the benefits of regular practice will by far outweigh any inconveniences.

A Quick Summary

To enhance and facilitate the achievement of the autogenic (self-generated repair) state, the following conditions need to be met.

1. *Reducing environmental or afferent stimulation.* Patients need to practice in a dark or dimly lit room with as little noise or sources of distraction as possible. Second, it is critical to assume a body position that is comfortable and as stress free as possible. This is referred to as finding the right training positions (postures). There are five training positions or postures that should help achieve this objective.

2. *Passive concentration.* Here the patient is asked to focus on a particular formula without trying to make or force anything to happen. This may be viewed as a state of passive attention — that is, one's focus is maintained on the task at hand but he or she is detached from achieving a certain goal. Use an example such as "Think of wanting to fall asleep without forcing yourself to fall asleep."

3. *Making mental contact.* Throughout the autogenic exercises, patients are asked to pay close attention to a body part or a function such as breathing or cardiac activity. For instance, when they are asked to repeat a formula that involves the right arm, they need to become as aware of that right arm as possible. They may be asked to imagine looking at their right arm with their eyes closed. For most people who are suffering from chronic pain, this may be, at least initially, a difficult task to accomplish, especially if they are asked to focus on an area that tends to be painful. To help overcome such impediments, I highly recommend that patients familiarize themselves with the two preliminary exercises (see Chapter 7) that will considerably improve the ability to make mental contact with specific body parts and bodily functions.

4. *Repetition of specific phrases.* This constitutes the very core of autogenic training. During each exercise, patients are asked to repeat specific phrases or formulas that focus on the experience of certain sensations. Think of these as "keys" to activating the recuperation and self-repair process. Each formula is repeated five to seven times with brief pauses between each phrase.

5. *Daily Practice.* The need for daily practice cannot be over emphasized. Patients need to practice autogenic exercises twice a day, for approximately ten to twenty minutes. As they begin to master the exercise, it is possible to enter the autogenic state by repeating one or two phrases, often under several minutes. This usually occurs after three to six months of consistent, daily practice.

7
The Preliminary Exercises

As mentioned in Chapter 6, an important step in promoting the autogenic state is to make mental contact with specific body parts. One of Schultz's techniques for achieving this was to have his patients shake their hands (one at a time) as vigorously as possible. This was then followed by quietly observing the relaxing sensation that ensued after the shaking. Shortly after this the repetition of the autogenic formulas would commence. After years of using this technique in clinical practice, I have discovered that the patient can gain the necessary momentum for effective and successful practice by learning two preliminary techniques. The first exercise, which incorporates aspects of progressive muscle relaxation, increases awareness of specific muscle groups through the experience of gentle levels of muscle tension. This is followed by a close observation of ensuing sensations. The other involves gaining awareness of tension in various muscle groups through observation and passive attention. These techniques need to be practiced for at least two or three sessions and, in my experience, can significantly improve the ease with which the patient begins the standard autogenic exercises. (The following instructions may be read to the patient.)

General Instructions

Before beginning any relaxation exercise, you need to make certain preparations. First, spend a few minutes and complete the Autogenic Pain or Tension Checklists (see the end of chapter and also Appendix A), Form A. Form B is completed at the end of each session. This will help you to accomplish two goals: (1) to gain greater awareness about the intensity of pain in different body parts; and (2) to assess your improvements. These simple forms will also assist you in developing a better understanding about changes in your pain and discomfort from day to day. In time, you can share this information with your physicians and therapists, which should prove to be of help in further evaluating and treating your condition.

Second, it is imperative that you are not disturbed during these and the autogenic exercises. Please turn off your phone and if necessary put a sign on your door to make sure that no one interrupts your practice time. Sudden interruptions should be avoided at all costs. Third, make sure that you loosen up any tight clothing — take off your shoes if you like. Finally, finding the right position is an extremely important step that requires some experimentation. (Review the postural photos in Chapter 6.) Remember, the point of assuming the postures is to make sure that you are not inadvertently holding your body in a tense position. Make the necessary adjustments so that your body is in its most effortlessly relaxed position. If you choose to sit in an upright position, make sure that your feet are flat on the floor to ensure that if you fall asleep during the exercise, you are safely protected against an accidental fall. Especially during the first few weeks of training, I recommend that you either use the supine position or the reclined position. Spend enough time to discover what position works best for you.

Preliminary Exercise I

Now we are ready to begin the first preliminary exercise. While resting in a comfortable position, take a few deep breaths and as you exhale, allow your body to sink into the bed or the chair. In a few moments you may find yourself focusing on different thoughts. This is a very common experience and although you may initially try to block your thoughts, you will notice that the more you try to stop your thoughts, the less successful you become at this task. Therefore, do not try to fight your thoughts, but as soon as you notice that you are focusing on anything other than the instructions for the exercise, gently shift your attention from stray thoughts and bring your attention back to the task at hand. As you practice this method of passively refocusing your thoughts, you will notice that, in time, your mind becomes quieter. Meanwhile, remember that you do not need a totally still mind to perform these exercises.

Now focus your attention on your right hand and your right arm. Gently press your arm against the surface of the bed or the arm of the chair. Hold this position for a few seconds and then allow your arm to go totally limp. Observe any sensations that you might be experiencing in your right hand and arm (it helps to label these sensations, such as smooth, tired, tense, cold, warm). Shift your attention to your left hand and arm. Gently press your arm against the surface of the bed or the arm of the chair. After holding this position for a few seconds, allow your arm to go totally limp. Observe any sensations that you might be experiencing.

We now move to the shoulders and the muscles of the neck. Simply, and very gently, push your shoulders and neck back — push them against the back of the chair or the surface of the bed. Hold this position for a few seconds and then allow your shoulders to become limp and relaxed. Observe the sensations in the muscles of your shoulders and the muscles of your neck. *Do not* force yourself to relax your shoulder or your arms. Merely observe your sensations, which may be subtle or pronounced. Repeat this portion of the exercise twice.

While keeping your arms and shoulders in a comfortable position, pay attention to the muscles of your jaw. In a very gentle manner, clench your teeth and hold the tension for five to eight seconds. Then allow your jaw to sag. Observe any sensations in the muscles of your jaw and the back of your neck. As we will explore in the next exercise, your upper and lower teeth should never touch except when you eat. However, most chronic pain patients discover a tendency to clench their teeth. This can result in pain and discomfort not only in the muscles of the jaw, but the neck and the upper back as well. With the help of these exercises you will soon catch yourself when clenching your teeth. Gradually, and without much thought, you will be able to avoid a great deal of pain and discomfort.

Now let us move to the lower extremities, the legs and the feet. Gently press your right leg against the seat of the chair or the surface of the bed. Hold this position for a few seconds and then allow your leg to become limp. Observe your sensations. You may then gradually point your right toes toward your trunk. Please do this very slowly and hold the tension for a brief time (three to five seconds). Then allow your foot and toes to become limp. Focus on your sensations.

Shift your attention to your left leg. Gently press your leg against the seat of the chair or the surface of the bed. Hold the tension and then allow your leg to go limp. Observe your sensations. Now gently point your left toes toward your trunk. Hold this position for a few seconds and then allow your foot and toes to go limp. Pay attention to your sensations and allow your body to be calm and quiet. Give yourself about two minutes before you proceed to the next segment of the exercise.

Now let us return to the upper extremities. Once again pay attention to the muscles of your right hand and arm. Without moving your arm, simply make a fist (not too tightly) with your hand and hold the tension for a few seconds and then allow your fist to relax and let your arm become limp. Observe your sensations. Notice if you have difficulty allowing your hand to relax fully. Give yourself about a minute and then move to your left hand and arm. Make a fist with your left hand and hold the tension for a few seconds. Then allow your fist to relax; let your arm go limp. Pay close attention to any sensation that you might be experiencing in your hand and arm.

While keeping your arms as relaxed as possible, gently shrug and lift up your shoulders. Hold the tension for a few seconds and then allow your shoulders to comfortably relax. Observe your sensations. See whether your shoulders tend to lift themselves up and become tense again. Repeat this procedure twice so that you can gain greater awareness about the levels of tension in these muscles. Again, resist the temptation to force your shoulders to relax. Simply observe them as closely as you can.

Let us now move to the muscles of the jaw. If you are suffering from symptoms of temporomandibular joint disorder (TMJD), it is critical that you pay close attention to these instructions. Gently open your mouth as wide as you can *without* causing any pain. If you notice pain or discomfort, you have gone too far. Close your mouth and gently start again. The purpose of this exercise is not to see how wide you can open your mouth but to gain awareness about tension in the muscles of the jaw. The experience of a slight sensation of tension is sufficient for this task. After holding your mouth open for five to eight seconds, allow your mouth to gently close. Again notice that your upper and your lower teeth should not touch. Observe your sensations; especially note any sensations on your temples and the back of your neck.

The fifth autogenic exercise focuses on generating a soothing sensation of warmth in the abdominal region. Hence, we need to learn to pay closer attention to this region. Gently pull in your abdominal muscles and hold the tension. Do not take a deep breath — simply hold your breath for a few seconds and as you breathe out allow your abdominal muscles to relax. Pay special attention to your upper abdominal region. Observe your sensations. Allow your breathing to be calm and regular.

Now with great care, gently push your abdomen out and arch your lower back. Please do this very gently and go to the point where you notice tension but no pain. Hold this position for a few seconds and then relax. Pay close attention to the muscles of your lower back. For example, notice the curvature in the small of your back. As you perform this exercise, you may notice that the muscles of the lower back begin to gradually relax and in time the relaxation of the muscles becomes very pronounced.

We will now turn to the muscles of the legs and the feet. Gently stretch out your right leg and then point your toes toward your trunk. (Just a slight move in the direction of the trunk is sufficient. Do not force this.) Hold this position briefly and then allow your legs, foot, and toes to relax and go limp.

Pay attention to your sensations. You may suddenly discover your tired and tense calves through this exercise. Simply observe these sensations.

Then shift your attention to your left leg and foot. Stretch out your left leg and then point your toes toward your trunk (remember to do this gently). Hold this position and then allow your leg, foot, and toes to relax. Observe your sensations.

You have now completed the first preliminary exercise. Give yourself a few minutes to enjoy some peace and calm. At this point most people notice that their mind is not as "busy" or "noisy." If this is not your experience, give it time and you will have a quieter mind in a little while. When you are ready to get up, please take a few deep breaths, flex your arms and stretch out your legs, open your eyes, and gently stand up. Remember, you need to repeat this exercise for several days before proceeding to the next preliminary exercise. Take a few moments and complete the Pain or Tension Checklists (Form B).

Preliminary Exercise II

During the first preliminary exercise, you gained greater awareness of certain muscle groups by actively tensing and relaxing these muscles. In this second exercise, you will further enhance your awareness of these areas by passively making mental contact with them through a process of focused attention. After a few days of practicing this technique, you should be ready to more easily and comfortably begin the standard autogenic exercises. Remember that it is best to take these preparatory steps to avoid any frustration during the advanced part of the training.

As with the first preliminary exercise, find yourself a comfortable position. Make sure that you are left undisturbed for approximately fifteen to twenty minutes. Also, make sure that you complete the Pain Checklist (Form A) prior to beginning your session. Because this exercise uses a more passive method of making mental contact with specific body parts, you may notice that initially your mind tends to wander a little more than during the first exercise. Again, I need to remind you that you should not force yourself to remain focused on the task at hand. Any forceful attempt to accomplish the goals of these exercises will actually result in the experience of greater levels of tension. Merely refocus your attention as soon as you notice that you have become distracted.

To begin the exercise, simply close your eyes and take a few deep breaths. Do not hold your breath. After a deep inhalation, breathe out and allow your body to sink effortlessly into the bed or the chair. Give yourself about two to three minutes to settle down and to quiet your thoughts. Now begin focusing on the muscles of your right hand and arm (up to your right shoulder). Imagine that you are looking at your arm with your eyes closed. Breathe naturally and comfortably. With each exhalation, silently say to your right hand and arm: "Relaxed and calm." Repeat this for three to five breaths. While keeping your right arm totally still, shift your attention to your left hand and arm. Again imagine that you are looking at your arm with your eyes closed. With each exhalation silently repeat to yourself "Relaxed and calm." Repeat this for three to five breaths.

An excellent method of paying attention to the muscles of your shoulders is to notice how your breathing affects (no matter how subtly) the movement in your shoulders. If you are a shallow breather, you will notice a greater rate of movement in this area. Do not try to control your breathing; your awareness of these muscles is all that is required of you. Breathe naturally and with each exhalation say: "Relaxed and calm." You may notice subtle movements in the muscles of your neck and a gradual release of tension. Make sure that you do not interfere with this process. Repeat this for three to five breaths.

We now move to the muscles of the jaw. Begin by paying attention to whether your upper and lower teeth are touching. Allow your jaw to sag slightly. Imagine that the force of gravity is naturally pulling your jaw down, quite effortlessly. Breathe comfortably and naturally. Exhale through slightly parted lips. With each exhalation silently say: "Relaxed and calm." Repeat this for three to five breaths.

Because the third autogenic exercise requires paying attention to cardiac activity, it is important that you can comfortably become more aware of the muscles of your chest and then more aware of the activity of your heart. During this exercise you need to simply pay attention to the muscles of your chest. Again, you may find it helpful to focus on your breathing and the movement of your chest, or just imagine that you are looking at the muscles of your chest with your eyes closed. Most people who are chest breathers will notice more activity in these muscles. This will in time change as you begin the fourth autogenic exercise on breathing. Meanwhile, breathe naturally and comfortably and with each exhalation silently say to yourself: "Relaxed and calm." Repeat this for three to five breaths.

Gaining greater awareness of the abdominal region, especially internally, is the focus of the fifth autogenic exercise. During the preliminary exercises, we simply pay attention to the abdominal muscles. Again, simply pay attention to any movements in the abdominal region as you inhale and exhale. Abdominal breathers will notice much more movement in this area than in the chest. Breathe naturally and without trying to interfere with your breathing process. With each exhalation, silently say: "Relaxed and calm." Repeat this for three to five breaths. The muscles of the lower back are perhaps the most neglected muscles in the human body. We pay attention to them only when we suffer from back pain. Although the standard autogenic exercises do not offer any special phrases or formulas for the muscles of the lower back, I have introduced several phrases that focus on heaviness and warmth which patients have found quite helpful in relaxing these muscles of the lower back. Hence, it is important to gain a greater awareness of this area.

Allow your attention to shift to the muscles of your lower back. Try to focus on the small of your back. Abdominal breathers may find it much easier to pay attention to this area because the activity of the abdomen during breathing directly affects the muscles of the back. You may also wish to imagine how your lower back touches the back of the chair or the surface of your mattress. (If the patient finds this to be a difficult task to accomplish, I highly recommend that he or she returns to the first preliminary exercise and repeat the section which focuses on tensing and relaxing the muscles of the back.) As you remain focused on the muscles of your lower back, simply repeat with each exhalation: "Relaxed and calm." Repeat this for a slightly longer period, such as five to eight breaths.

The final segment of this exercise concerns making mental contact with the lower extremities. It is best to perform this in several small steps. Begin by focusing on the muscles of your right thigh, from your hip to the knee. If it helps, imagine that you are looking at the muscles of your right thigh with your eyes closed. With each exhalation, silently repeat: "Relaxed and calm." After three to five exhalations, move to the muscles of the lower leg, from your knee to your ankle, and then pay attention to the muscles of your right foot. With each exhalation silently repeat to yourself, "Relaxed and calm." Now concentrate on your entire leg and repeat: "Relaxed and calm."

Now shift your attention to your left leg, from your hip to your knee. With each exhalation silently repeat to yourself, "Relaxed and calm." After three to five breaths, move to the muscles of your lower leg, from your knee to your ankle and then all the way down to your foot. Silently repeat, "Relaxed and calm" for three to five breaths. Then focus on your entire leg and repeat, "Relaxed and calm."

Upon completing this segment, allow your body and mind to be calm and peaceful. When you are ready to end the exercise, take a few deep breaths, stretch out your arms and your legs, and get up very gently. You need to repeat this exercise for several days before beginning the standard autogenic exercises. If you find yourself having difficulties with this second exercise, especially after practicing for two or three times, return to the first exercise for a day or two and then repeat this exercise once again. There is no reason to rush the process. Take your time and you will reap the benefits of your patience and perseverance.

Make sure to complete the Pain or Tension Checklist (Form B) at the end of the exercise. After practicing the preliminary exercises for several days, I highly recommend that you review the data that you have been collecting before and after each relaxation session. In time, you will have a reliable and useful record of your progress. Also, I urge you to use these every time you practice the standard autogenic exercises.

Remarks

At times people with chronic pain and stress-related disorders wonder with great frustration why suddenly they have a bad day after several exceptionally good days. By asking my patients to develop a process of active data collection regarding their pain, sleep, and other activities, I have been able to help them solve some of the mysteries regarding the fluctuations in their symptoms. Remember, the more they learn about their condition, the easier it is to predict certain (but not all) changes in symptoms, which should help them develop better strategies for coping. This approach should considerably help mitigate the sense of helplessness that is often a concomitant of any chronic condition. As it was pointed out, the checklists (see the end of the next chapter or Appendix A) can be most helpful in assisting patients gain a better understanding of their pain levels, especially before and after each training session. They can also be used effectively for gathering outcome data at the end of the treatment period. Another useful instrument, the Autogenic Progress Index, appears in Appendix B. This form is especially helpful for clinicians to determine when the patient is ready to move to the subsequent standard exercise.

8

The First Standard
Exercise: Heaviness

Autogenic training and all of its adjunctive modalities begin with the standard exercises, the first of which lays the foundation for the rest of the exercises. Hence, promoting the sensation of heaviness in the extremities becomes the required step for promoting warmth, rhythmic cardiac activity, relaxed breathing, etc. One way of conceiving of the relationship between these exercises is to think of them as a series of six interconnected rings that form a chain. In time, after much practice, it becomes possible to bring about the sensations of the more advanced exercises, let us say, abdominal warmth, by simply repeating the heaviness formula. The first standard autogenic exercise, and for that matter all subsequent exercises, needs to begin by reducing environmental stimulation to the lowest possible level. Lights may be dimmed, sources of noise should be effectively eliminated, and finally the patient needs to position him or herself in a fashion that is restful and as free from discomfort as possible.

Review the specific autogenic postures as described in Chapter 6 and help the patient choose a position that is most agreeable. Also, inform the patient that the best time for practicing these exercises is usually twenty minutes after lunch or dinner and before retiring for the evening. An important point to remember is that autogenic exercises should *never* be abruptly ended (indeed, it is inadvisable to conclude any form of relaxation or meditative exercises in a sudden fashion). The body requires a period of adjustment to the physiological changes that have occurred as a result of the practice of autogenic exercises. Patients may experience dizziness, disorientation, and light-headedness if they attempt to stand up quickly at the end of the exercise. Although such sensations usually do not last very long, they can be most disturbing. These experiences can be avoided by concluding each exercise slowly and by allowing the body enough time to make the appropriate adjustments.

A brief set of guidelines for each training session is provided in Table 8.1. These guidelines need to be reviewed by the therapist at the beginning of each session.

Introducing the First Exercise

Heaviness

The first standard exercise focuses on inducing a pleasant sensation of heaviness in the extremities, which is similar to that experienced shortly before falling asleep. Patients are instructed to repeat specific formulas over and over while maintaining a casual or a non-goal-oriented attitude. That is to say, they should refrain from forcing themselves to make anything happen. Remember, forcing oneself to experience a particular sensation is most likely to result in the experience of greater levels of tension and stress, the exact opposite of what we are trying to achieve. The next step is to help patients passively imagine or visualize what it would feel like if their arms and legs were becoming heavier. Green and Green (1977) describe this process by stating, "One just tells the body what to do, usually by visualizing the desired state, then detaches from the situation — steps aside, gets out of the way, so to speak — and allows the body to do it" (p. 54). Although one may find it tempting to think of carrying a heavy object to induce the sensation of heaviness, or imagining that one's arms are "lead-like," this is against Schultz's advice. He emphasizes that the sensation of heaviness should be a normal, agreeable, and comfortable one — very similar to what is experienced before falling asleep — which is akin to a profound experience of muscle relaxation. For example, patients may be asked to ponder, "My right arm is comfortably, or pleasantly, heavy." After a period of consistent daily practice, thinking or repeating the formula several times is sufficient to bring about the experience of muscle relaxation in the arms and the legs.

Table 8.1. A review of guidelines for autogenic training sessions.

1. Prior to each training session, the therapist needs to describe, in depth, the rationale and the goals for that session. It is imperative that the patient feels comfortable with his or her understanding of this rationale.

2. The therapist needs to emphasize the importance of "no volition" or "passive concentration" to the fullest at the beginning of each and every session. The therapist may suggest appropriate images for each exercise such as, "Imagine a cool breeze brushing against your forehead as you repeat the forehead cooling formula." Although the patient is not required to use the same visual suggestions, such images may serve as a tentative guideline. They will also help the patient differentiate between effective versus ineffective or harmful images (e.g., holding a warm cup of coffee while repeating, "My right arm is warm" instead of immersing one's hand in boiling water).

3. Each session needs to be intentionally terminated by having the patient flex the arms, take a deep breath, and open the eyes.

4. The patient needs to feel quite comfortable with each exercise before moving on to a more advanced exercise. That is to say, if the patient does not experience the sensation of heaviness in the arms, do not introduce the warmth formula. The use of the Autogenic Progress Index (Appendix B) is highly recommended. The index needs to be completed at the end of each training session. The clinical data generated by this form can be most helpful in determining when the patient is ready to transition to the next standard exercise. Emphasize at the onset of the training that it is the patient's responsibility to practice the assigned exercise at least twice a day for approximately fifteen minutes. Little progress can be made without commitment to daily practice. Encourage the patient to express his or her feelings, thoughts, and sensations at the end of each training session. The therapist's openness and nonjudgmental attitude toward exploring such experiences, whether mental or physical, serves as a crucial facet of the training.

As discussed earlier, patients should be instructed that they can substantially facilitate the experience of this sensation by ensuring that their arms, shoulders, legs, and lower back are well supported. They need to be sure that no undue stress is placed upon these areas during the exercise. If they attempt to perform these exercises while holding their muscles in a rigid manner, it is quite likely that they will not be able to achieve the desired effects. That is why the therapeutic, autogenic postures described in Chapter 6 are so crucial in achieving the desired effects.

Prior to the start of the first exercise, I highly recommend reviewing the pre-exercise checklist (see Table 8.2) to ensure that the appropriate physical or environmental preparations have been made. Next, attention needs to be paid to "the appropriate mind-set" before repeating the specific formulas for this exercise.

Table 8.2. The pre-exercise checklist.

1. Complete the Autogenic Pain (or Tension) Checklist (Form A)
2. Reduce environmental stimulation and assume a training posture
3. Passive concentration on the formulas and physical sensations
4. Make mental contact with specific body parts
5. Repeat the autogenic formulas
6. Daily practice (Reminder)

One of the most concise statements that captures the process of autogenic exercises is eloquently stated by Norris, Fahrion, and Oikawa (2007, p. 189). You may wish to place a bookmark here and return to this paragraph at the beginning of each training session.

At this point you will be given some autogenic training phrases, and I want you to [silently] say each phrase over and over to yourself. First, your attitude as you do this is quite important. This is the kind of thing where the more you try to relax, the less it will happen. So the best approach is to have the intention to relax, but to remain detached about your actual results. Since everyone can learn voluntary control of these processes, it is only a matter of time until you do, therefore you can afford to be detached about the results. Second, saying the phrases is good because it keeps them in mind, but it is not enough. The part of the brain that controls these processes, the limbic system, doesn't understand language well, so it is important to translate the content of the phrase into some kind of image. One of the phrases is "My hands are heavy and warm." If you can imagine what it would feel like if your hands did feel heavy or if they did feel warm, that helps to bring about the changes that we are looking for. Or use a visual image: Imagine that you are lying at the beach in the sun, or that you are holding your hands over a campfire. Whatever works for you as a relaxing image or a warmth-inducing image is the thing to use, but the imaging itself is important. Finally, if you simply trust your body to do what you are visualizing it as doing, then you will discover that it will.

In some of the original literature on autogenic training, Schultz (1932) suggested that as a way of promoting a deeper state of rest and relaxation special background formulas may be used. In some of the earlier manuals, he had his patients repeat the word "tranquility" (*ruhe* in German) between each formula. In later English publications, the formula "I am at peace" was introduced. I encourage my patients to use this formula or the word tranquility throughout each exercise, as suggested in the following training sequence.

Again, it is highly recommended that prior to starting the autogenic exercises, patients familiarize themselves with the preliminary exercises that were described in Chapter 7. These exercises will help them gain much greater momentum while practicing the standard exercises. As mentioned before, the preliminary exercises need not be practiced for long. Perhaps four or five times should be sufficient to master the desired effects of achieving mental contact with specific body parts.

Each formula used during the first training session is to be repeated for approximately two minutes. The choice of beginning the training with the right or the left arm solely depends on the patient's handedness. That is, if he or she is right-handed it is best to make mental contact initially with the right arm and hand. Throughout the years of using autogenic training with chronic pain patients, especially those suffering from fibromyalgia, I have come to realize that certain additional formulas can be most helpful in reducing pain and discomfort. These additional formulas (marked with an asterisk) are consistent with those developed by Schultz and actually seem to enhance the training process significantly. For example, I have observed that during the pre-sleep state (similar to the autogenic state), the muscles of the jaw tend to relax. By repeating a formula that suggests a heavy and relaxed jaw, this process of entering a deeper state of relaxation is accelerated. Also, since many chronic pain patients tend to suffer from temporomandibular joint disorder (TMJD), the focus on a relaxed jaw can be most helpful in reducing pain and discomfort as well as making them aware of the tendency to possibly grit or grind their teeth due to extremely tense muscles. I have also included additional formulas for reducing muscle tension in the shoulders and the lower back.

The Brief Exercise

Remind patients to complete either the Tension Checklist or the Pain Checklist, Form A, prior to beginning each session. The following instructions may be read to the patient:

You are now ready to begin the first exercise. For the first two or three sessions, I recommend a shorter form of the exercise to be followed by the extended exercise. (Please make sure that you have reviewed with the patients the requirements for the effective practice of autogenic training as described in Chapter 7.) Remember that it is quite likely that from time to time you will be distracted by a passing thought. As soon as you become aware of this, gently guide yourself back to the formula and the specific body part that is the focus of your attention. Now assume a comfortable position. Close your eyes and take a few deep breaths. If you find it difficult to take deep and comfortable breaths, you may want to shrug your shoulders as you inhale and slowly drop your shoulders. Let go of the tension as you exhale. Then, gently and silently begin repeating to yourself the following formulas. Each formula needs to be repeated five to seven times.

- I am at peace.
- My right arm is heavy.
- My left arm is heavy.
- I am at peace.
- My right leg is heavy.
- My left leg is heavy.
- I am at peace.

- My entire body is heavy and relaxed.
- I am at peace.

To conclude the exercise, take a deep breath and as you exhale gently flex your arms and open your eyes. Give yourself a few minutes before standing up. Repeat this exercise for three consecutive days. (Make sure that the patient completes the Tension Checklist or the Pain Checklist, Form B, upon finishing the exercise.)

The Extended Exercise

Approximately four days after practicing the brief exercise, patients may begin the extended exercise. Again, make sure to remind patients to complete either the Tension Checklist or the Pain Checklist, Form A, prior to beginning each session. The following instructions may be read to the patient:

After assuming your desired, comfortable posture, take a few deep breaths and begin repeating the following formulas, each for five to seven times.

- I am quiet and relaxed.
- I am at peace.

Now begin making mental contact with various body parts as you repeat the following formulas.

- My right (left) arm is heavy.
- I am at peace.
- My left (right) arm is heavy.
- I am at peace.
- Both arms are heavy.
- I am at peace.
- My shoulders are heavy.
- I am at peace.
- My jaw is heavy.
- I am at peace.
- My right (left) leg is heavy.
- I am at peace.
- My left (right) leg is heavy.
- I am at peace.
- Both legs are heavy.
- I am at peace.
- My lower back is heavy.
- My entire body is comfortably relaxed.
- I am at peace.

Now take a deep breath, and as you exhale, stretch out your arms and your legs several times, and then open your eyes. (Make sure that the patient completes the Pain or Tension Checklist, Form B, upon finishing the exercise.)

Green and Green (1977) suggest saying the following affirmation as a way of concluding the exercise: "I feel life and energy flowing through my arms, my legs, and my whole body. The energy makes me feel light and alive" (p. 338). A statement such as this may be used to more smoothly make the transition from the autogenic state to an alert state.

It is of significant therapeutic value that patients express their experiences and observations at the end of each exercise. A record of such experiences can, in time, provide valuable insight into ways of improving the benefits of the training. Each exercise needs to be practiced twice a day for approximately ten to fifteen minutes. It is not uncommon for certain stress-related symptoms such as headaches and gastrointestinal distress to spontaneously disappear during the practice of the heaviness exercise. However, it may take some time for the corrective properties of autogenic training, in terms of reestablishing a systemic state of balance and healing, to occur.

Before proceeding to the next standard formula, it is imperative that patients have been able to comfortably experience a "volition-free" sensation of heaviness in their extremities. For optimum results, it is best to practice each standard exercise twice a day for at least a week. Also, it is not prudent to move to a more advanced exercise without achieving the particular sensations suggested in each and every phase of the training. Before moving to the second standard exercise, which focuses on the sensation of warmth, patients need to be able to comfortably experience the sensation of heaviness in their arms and legs. Once this has been achieved after several practice sessions, they are ready to proceed to the next exercise.

Common Difficulties with the First Standard Exercise

The most common difficulty with the first exercise (experienced by roughly 20 percent of patients) concerns the inability to stay focused. Distractions are quite common during the practice of any relaxation or meditative exercise. Patients need to be reassured that as long as they adhere to the requirements for the correct practice of the autogenic exercises, it is only a matter of time before they can effectively overcome intrusive thoughts. However, there are several clinical guidelines that practitioners should keep in mind when patients report persistent, intrusive, and distressing thoughts. In my opinion, the most effective method of stopping distressing thoughts is to talk about them. The training process may need to be put on hold, often briefly, so that the patient may openly discuss the nature of the thoughts.

Another method of reducing distress from the experience of mental distractions is to initially shorten the length of the exercises, such as reducing the number of the repetitions to three to five times, so as to help the patient maintain better concentration. As the ability to maintain focus increases, the exercises are gradually made longer with additional repetitions.

For those patients who have difficulty experiencing the heaviness sensation, my recommendation is to reassure them that with passive concentration and repetition of the formulas, this will occur in a short while. In rare cases, when patients continue to show difficulty with the experience of heaviness in the extremities, it may be helpful to have them hold a small weight in each hand prior to starting the exercise. They should merely focus on what it feels like to experience the sensation of heaviness as they hold the weights.

An ingenious idea proposed by Thomas (1967) is to have the patient perform the exercise in a bathtub and briefly and gently lift up his or her arm while repeating the heaviness formula. I have found this method to be of great value even in the most difficult and resistant cases. This approach needs to be attempted only once for the patient to make the appropriate connections between the formulas and the desired sensation of heaviness.

In rare cases, when patients are not adhering to the principle of passive concentration, they may report a tense, aching sensation in their arms while practicing the first standard exercise. They should be instructed "not to try to make anything happen" and pay close attention to the requirements for the exercises.

Finally, if the patient reports difficulty with making mental contact with a specific body part during the repetition a formula, I highly recommend spending more time with the preliminary exercises which were discussed in Chapter 7. Also, prior to a training (exercise) session some patients find it helpful to lightly touch the body part with which they cannot make mental contact.

Case Example 1

MJ is a 42-year-old woman who was diagnosed with fibromyalgia pain syndrome approximately two years ago. In addition to some of the common symptoms of fibromyalgia, MJ was particularly distressed because of pain and constant discomfort in her forearms. At times the discomfort was so severe that she could not even slightly raise her hands and arms to pick up the lightest of objects. On those "bad" days she was completely dependent on her children for basic grooming, such as brushing her hair.

She described her arms as being "in constant spasm." Prior to the treatment, her forearm surface electromyographic activity (EMG) showed to be well above average. After familiarizing herself with the preliminary exercises (Chapter 7), MJ was trained in the first autogenie exercise for approximately three weeks. She initially found it difficult to make mental contact with her arms because she wanted to avoid her painful arms at all costs. This tendency to avoid focusing on her arms was apparently contributing to the worsening of her symptoms. By practicing the heaviness exercise she began experiencing a comfortable sensation of heaviness in her arms. Later in the treatment when additional exercises were introduced, MJ gained greater strength in both arms and the constant, aching sensation began to disappear. Even on the bad days she was able to use the exercises effectively to manage her pain and discomfort.

Case Example 2

Restless leg syndrome is a condition that can profoundly influence a person's quality of sleep, which will in turn compromise his or her daily activities. Although newer medications are being introduced to the market for the treatment of this condition, autogenic training may be an effective intervention, especially for those who prefer a psychophysiological approach.

AG was a 64-year-old woman who suffered from frequent bouts of restless leg syndrome. She had been taking anxiolytic agents for several years before her family physician warned her that she was developing resistance to her medication and she seemed to need higher doses in order to control her symptoms. This made her very concerned as she was afraid of becoming totally dependent on medications for a good night's rest. She was highly motivated and willing to practice the autogenic technique on a regular basis. Curiously, during her first treatment session, when she was repeating the formula "My right leg is heavy," she felt the need to move her leg so forcefully that she opened her eyes and reported the sensation. She was asked to maintain the principle of passive concentration and merely observe specific body parts without interfering with any of her observations and sensations. Once again we began with the first formula and slowly moved to the lower extremities. Patient had a few mild autogenic discharges during the exercise, which she found rather amusing to observe. About a week of practicing the exercise in bed, she noticed several "massive" autogenic discharges in her legs followed by total relaxation. She had learned not to interfere with such discharges as their corrective nature was explained to her in much depth. After two weeks of practice, before proceeding to the second exercise, patient reported that she was beginning to fall asleep with no medication and that her symptoms were not as unsettling. We decided to stay with the first exercise and observe her symptoms. During the second week she reported that she was falling asleep with the use of the autogenic exercises without any noticeable restlessness in her legs. She was able to maintain such improvements during a six-week follow-up. This identical protocol has been helpful to several patients who presented with similar symptoms. Although it is a good idea to proceed with the training in its entirety, it appears that sustained symptom relief can be achieved through the practice of the first standard exercise.

The Autogenic Pain Checklist

Form A

EXERCISE: I (Heaviness)

INSTRUCTIONS: Complete this form before your autogenic training session. Simply rate your pain levels by circling the number on a scale of 0 to 10. A score of 0 indicates the absence of pain, whereas a score of 10 indicates severe pain in that body part.

1. My right arm is

0	1	2	3	4	5	6	7	8	9	10

2. My left arm is

0	1	2	3	4	5	6	7	8	9	10

3. My shoulders are

0	1	2	3	4	5	6	7	8	9	10

4. My neck is

0	1	2	3	4	5	6	7	8	9	10

5. My forehead is

0	1	2	3	4	5	6	7	8	9	10

6. My jaw is

0	1	2	3	4	5	6	7	8	9	10

7. My chest is

0	1	2	3	4	5	6	7	8	9	10

8. My abdomen is

0	1	2	3	4	5	6	7	8	9	10

9. My lower back is

0	1	2	3	4	5	6	7	8	9	10

10. My right leg is

0	1	2	3	4	5	6	7	8	9	10

11. My left leg is

0	1	2	3	4	5	6	7	8	9	10

12. Overall my body is

0	1	2	3	4	5	6	7	8	9	10

The Autogenic Pain Checklist

Form B

EXERCISE: I (Heaviness)

INSTRUCTIONS: Complete this form after your autogenic training session. Simply rate your pain levels by circling the number on a scale of 0 to 10. A score of 0 indicates the absence of pain, whereas a score of 10 indicates severe pain in that body part.

1. My right arm is

0	1	2	3	4	5	6	7	8	9	10

2. My left arm is

0	1	2	3	4	5	6	7	8	9	10

3. My shoulders are

0	1	2	3	4	5	6	7	8	9	10

4. My neck is

0	1	2	3	4	5	6	7	8	9	10

5. My forehead is

0	1	2	3	4	5	6	7	8	9	10

6. My jaw is

0	1	2	3	4	5	6	7	8	9	10

7. My chest is

0	1	2	3	4	5	6	7	8	9	10

8. My abdomen is

0	1	2	3	4	5	6	7	8	9	10

9. My lower back is

0	1	2	3	4	5	6	7	8	9	10

10. My right leg is

0	1	2	3	4	5	6	7	8	9	10

11. My left leg is

0	1	2	3	4	5	6	7	8	9	10

12. Overall my body is

0	1	2	3	4	5	6	7	8	9	10

The Autogenic Tension Checklist

Form A

EXERCISE: I (Heaviness)

INSTRUCTIONS: Complete this form before your autogenic training session. Simply rate your tension levels by circling the number on a scale of 0 to 10. A score of 0 indicates the absence of tension, whereas a score of 10 indicates extreme tension in that body part.

1. My right arm is

0	1	2	3	4	5	6	7	8	9	10

2. My left arm is

0	1	2	3	4	5	6	7	8	9	10

3. My shoulders are

0	1	2	3	4	5	6	7	8	9	10

4. My neck is

0	1	2	3	4	5	6	7	8	9	10

5. My forehead is

0	1	2	3	4	5	6	7	8	9	10

6. My jaw is

0	1	2	3	4	5	6	7	8	9	10

7. My chest is

0	1	2	3	4	5	6	7	8	9	10

8. My abdomen is

0	1	2	3	4	5	6	7	8	9	10

9. My lower back is

0	1	2	3	4	5	6	7	8	9	10

10. My right leg is

0	1	2	3	4	5	6	7	8	9	10

11. My left leg is

0	1	2	3	4	5	6	7	8	9	10

12. Overall my body is

0	1	2	3	4	5	6	7	8	9	10

The Autogenic Tension Checklist

Form B

EXERCISE: I (Heaviness)

Instructions: Complete this form after your autogenic training session. Simply rate your tension levels by circling the number on a scale of 0 to 10. A score of 0 indicates the absence of tension, whereas a score of 10 indicates extreme tension in that body part.

1. My right arm is

0	1	2	3	4	5	6	7	8	9	10

2. My left arm is

0	1	2	3	4	5	6	7	8	9	10

3. My shoulders are

0	1	2	3	4	5	6	7	8	9	10

4. My neck is

0	1	2	3	4	5	6	7	8	9	10

5. My forehead is

0	1	2	3	4	5	6	7	8	9	10

6. My jaw is

0	1	2	3	4	5	6	7	8	9	10

7. My chest is

0	1	2	3	4	5	6	7	8	9	10

8. My abdomen is

0	1	2	3	4	5	6	7	8	9	10

9. My lower back is

0	1	2	3	4	5	6	7	8	9	10

10. My right leg is

0	1	2	3	4	5	6	7	8	9	10

11. My left leg is

0	1	2	3	4	5	6	7	8	9	10

12. Overall my body is

0	1	2	3	4	5	6	7	8	9	10

9
The Second Standard
Exercise: Warmth

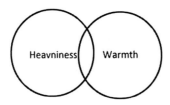

Almost invariably, many chronic pain patients, or those who are suffering from certain stress related disorders, complain of cold hands and feet. Some wear heavy socks to bed to avoid giving their spouse an unpleasant experience should the spouse rub against the patient's "icy feet." The experience of cold extremities is a common occurrence when a source of threat is perceived. One of the body's methods of protecting itself against loss of blood in case of injury or laceration is to constrict the blood vessels in the periphery. The human body is equipped to cope effectively with such blood volume changes in the short term. However, this form of vasoconstriction can, in time, place unnecessary demands on the various organs of the body, especially the heart. In some people, the experience of prolonged pain can result in a state of peripheral chronic vasoconstriction, which may bring about additional complications.

Most people who learn how to properly induce a pleasant sensation of heaviness in their extremities report that at the end of the exercise they began to feel a mild sensation of warmth in their hands. They are on their way to the next phase of the training. The second standard autogenic exercise focuses on generating a soothing warmth in the extremities. This constitutes a critical stage in the process of training because it paves the way for some of the more advanced exercises (especially the fifth exercise and the additional formulas for pain control and sleep enhancement). The resultant peripheral vasodilation from the practice of this exercise may be viewed as a shift from a "stress" to a "relaxation" state influenced by changes in the hypothalamic-adrenal cortex axis, a major mechanism involved in the stress response brought on by pain and other sources of demand. As the body moves from an activity state (catabolic) into a regeneration mode (anabolic), the blood vessels tend to dilate and a pleasantly agreeable sensation of warmth in the arms and the legs is experienced. Initially, such a sensation may be limited to the hands and the arms, but in time the shoulders, legs, and feet will be affected. During the fifth standard exercise, emphasis will be placed upon generating warmth in the abdominal region that will significantly deepen the relaxation state. Please note that it is imperative that prior to moving to the second exercise, patients must be able to almost effortlessly experience a sensation of heaviness in their arms and legs after repeating the formulas from the first exercise. It is inadvisable to initiate the second exercise as long as this objective has not been achieved.

Long before the advent of anti-anxiety medications such as Valium, Xanex, and Ativan, hot baths were used to reduce anxiety and tension. The second autogenic exercise accomplishes this reduction of anxiety and tension through the activation of the appropriate centers in the brain which promote a normalizing effect in the vascular system. Indeed, during the practice of this exercise most anxious patients report the experience of a pleasantly drowsy, tranquil state which is similar to the feeling experienced after taking a tranquilizer, but without the common side effects. As it will be discussed in the chapter on sleep (Chapter 16), the sensation of warmth can be used quite effectively as a method of initiating and enhancing sleep. At the same time, keep in mind that upon concluding the second exercise, patients need to give themselves some extra time before they stand up and return to their daily routines. This will help to avoid any unpleasant sensations such as disorientation or dizziness.

During this second phase, patients are asked to passively repeat formulas that suggest a sensation of heaviness and warmth in their extremities. Again it is helpful to consider imagining what it would be like if they were experiencing a soothing and pleasant sensation of warmth in the arms and the legs. For example, you may suggest that patients consider the image of lying on warm sand at the beach on a sunny day. Ask them to think of their body as a sponge that is slowly absorbing the heat from the sand. Or you may suggest imagining what it would be like if they were soaking in a warm bath and were beginning to gradually experience a soothing sensation of heaviness and warmth in the arms and legs.

Here it is important that certain precautions are observed with regard to the content of imagery. First, ask the patients to refrain from forcing themselves to think of the beach or the warm bath. They need to be instructed not to limit themselves to these specific images and should feel free to use whatever comes naturally. For instance, one may think of holding a warm cup of tea between the hands and then allow the warmth to travel from the hands into the arms and shoulders. Second, and this is a most critical requirement, these images *should never include touching something that is hot.* Such images can result in a rapid instead of a gradual increase in peripheral vasodilation and may cause uncomfortable sensations. On the other hand, an image that focuses on something hot may actually result in the activation of a stress response and bring about a paradoxical effect. Always suggest sensations that promote a pleasant sensation of warmth, preferably a sensation that is experienced gradually.

Once in a while, and in extremely rare cases, some people may find it difficult to experience the sensation of warmth in their arms. I recommend two methods for making progress in such cases. First, I highly recommend using temperature biofeedback in conjunction with the warmth formula for brief periods of time and with eyes open. This is to reinforce the slightest change in hand temperature. However, if a temperature unit or even a hand thermometer is not available, or the person finds it difficult to benefit from this suggestion, another option based on observations of Schultz and Luthe may be used. They recommended that it may be helpful to have the individual immerse his or her arms in a basin of warm *(not hot)* water prior to the practice of the warmth formulas (Schultz & Luthe, 1959). I have found this to be of particular benefit for achieving the main objective of the second exercise. In my experience, even in the most refractory cases, this technique seems to work.

The actual training sequence in the second standard exercise is similar to the first exercise.

The Warmth Exercise

Remind patients to complete either the Tension Checklist or the Pain Checklist, Form A, prior to beginning each session. The following instructions may be read to the patient:

After quieting yourself for a few minutes, gently close your eyes and silently begin repeating the following formulas:

- I am quiet and relaxed.
- I am at peace.
- My right arm is heavy and warm.

- I am at peace.
- My left arm is heavy and warm.
- I am at peace.
- My shoulders are heavy and warm.
- I am at peace.
- My jaw is heavy and warm.
- I am at peace.
- My right leg is heavy and warm.
- I am at peace.
- My left leg is heavy and warm.
- I am at peace.
- My right foot is heavy and warm.
- I am at peace.
- My left foot is heavy and warm.
- I am at peace.
- My lower back is heavy and warm.
- My entire body is comfortably relaxed.
- I am at peace.

To conclude the exercise, take a deep breath and as you exhale gently flex your arms and gently open your eyes. Give yourself a few minutes before standing up. (Make sure that the patient completes Form B of the Tension Checklist or the Pain Checklist upon finishing the exercise.)

The induction of a sensation of warmth in the extremities may bring about a profound sensation of relaxation and even sleepiness. Therefore, it is of clinical importance that patients are fully awakened upon the completion of the exercise. Often, stretching the arms and the legs and opening the eyes is sufficient for this purpose. Taking several deep breaths may actually expedite the process.

Before concluding this section, it may be helpful to consider an interesting case report that appeared in the second volume of *Autogenic Therapy* (Luthe & Schultz, 1969a), which deals with the many medical applications of this approach. This case effectively portrays how the warmth exercise can be a life-saving tool.

> A well-known sportsman who had learned autogenic training for the purpose of improving his performance was caught by an avalanche. He and his companions were buried under the snow in below 30 degrees Centigrade temperatures and had to stay motionless for several hours until they were rescued. The advanced trainee applied the autogenic approach and focused on warmth in nose, fingers, toes and ears in rotation. He was the only person who escaped without frostbite or any other injury from the cold [Luthe & Schultz, 1969a, p. 80].

While I hope that those suffering from chronic pain or stress related disorders will not find themselves in the predicament of these sportsmen, the inspiration from this report should help those who avoid the frozen food section in a grocery store because of severe sensitivity to cold. I have instructed many of my patients with extremely cold hands to practice portions of the warmth exercise before entering the grocery store or prior to leaving home on a cold day. These patients report rewarding applications of this and other standard exercises.

Common Difficulties with the Second Standard Exercise

If the first standard exercise, heaviness, is performed adequately, the experience of warmth should come almost naturally during the practice of the second standard exercise. Since the second exercise requires closer attention to the principle of passive concentration, patients need to be reminded to resist any tendency to make their hands warmer. Any such attempts will inevitably result in paradoxical experiences, such as cooling of the hands and the arms or a sudden experience of pain and tension with or without stiffness. Although such experiences are rare and occur on those occasions when the patient is trying to warm the extremities, it is prudent to end the exercise if distressing sensations are experienced for more than a few minutes. The most effective method of intervention is to have the patient flex the arms, take a deep breath, and open the eyes during exhalation. This is as effective as the "cancellation method" used during hypnosis. As mentioned earlier, it is important to process the sessions by having the patient discuss his or her experiences and sensations, especially on those occasions when persistent, distressing sensations begin to emerge. There is no need for exploring the cause of such sensations. A simple verbal expression of the various sensations is often sufficient.

To assist patients who have difficulty experiencing the sensation of warmth, I highly recommend Schultz's warm water immersion which was discussed earlier. This technique is especially of great help to patients with very cold extremities. Simply have them immerse one arm in warm water for a few minutes and pay attention to the soothing sensation of warmth. I have used this technique effectively with patients who had very cold feet and found it difficult to focus on a sensation of warmth in their feet. The period of immersion needs to be brief and very much focused. To maintain the necessary focus, the practitioner should instruct the patient to pay close attention to his or her arm as it is being slowly immersed in warm water, especially as the sensation of warmth begins to spread (this is best done with the eyes closed for greater focus). The practitioner may ask questions such as "where in your hand or arm are you experiencing the sensation of warmth?" "Is the sensation of warmth traveling up your arm?" "Are you experiencing a change in the volume of your hands?"

Finally, a brief and sudden decrease in the temperature of the extremities may suggest an autogenic discharge. This should not be interfered with as long as the sensations are brief and not distressing. Patients need to be instructed to simply observe such passing sensations and allow the nervous system to make the appropriate adjustments. As a rule, I always have the patient's non-dominant hand monitored via a thermistor during each training session, even when the patient is not provided with direct feedback. Such information can be very helpful in assessing the process of training and to make the necessary adjustments when needed.

Case Example 1

One of the first patients whom I treated with autogenic training was a very distressed bartender who was about to lose his job because of a gradual loss of sensation in his hands several hours after touching ice-filled glasses and cold drinks. On several occasions, he had actually cut his hands without being aware of it. Medical tests had ruled out any neurological causes for this, although it had been suggested that he was suffering from a mild to moderate form of Raynaud's syndrome. (Some fibromyalgia patients may also experience this condition.) After four weeks of autogenic training with emphasis on the second exercise, the patient was able to gradually raise the temperature of his hands. The immersion technique was used on two occasions to help him more easily move to the second standard exercise. He was also provided with a bulb thermometer which he used to monitor his improvement before and after each exercise session at home. His steady improvements were highly motivating, and in time he was able to generate a soothing sensation of warmth in his hands with his eyes open. He reported to me that he often repeated some of the warmth formulas to himself while at work and was able to effectively combat his condition with confidence.

Case Example 2

GW was a 22-year-old athlete who had suffered an injury in her groin area. Detailed medical examination did not show any pathological causes of the pain a year after her initial injury. However, the pain persisted. After an intensive course of physical therapy, she continued to be in a great deal of physical distress. Her greatest concern was that she was becoming addicted to her pain medications. She was realizing that she could not function without them, while at the same time they made her feel tired, groggy, and unable to get motivated to attend college. She was becoming more and more depressed because of the refractory nature of her pain, especially due to the fact that no matter what she did she could not "make the pain go away." During our initial consultation session, she was asked if there was anything that helped alleviate her pain even slightly. She responded that applying a warm compress at night to the injured region seemed to "calm the pain," especially while she rested in her bed.

GW was provided with detailed instructions about the process of autogenic training and was asked to make a commitment to the treatment protocols, including the required daily practice of assigned exercises. After she was able to achieve the sensation of heaviness in her extremities, GW was introduced to the second standard exercise. She learned how to induce a pleasant sensation of warmth in her arms within days. She reported that she started to sleep better as the sensation of warmth made her feel drowsy. Her overall attitude began to improve but the groin pain remained. She was then instructed to take a warm bath and practice the second exercise while in the tub. Additionally, after completing the exercise, she was asked to focus on the injured area and use two Organ-Specific formulas (see Chapter 14), which were, "Warmth dissolves the tension" followed by "Warmth dissolves the pain." After the second time she practiced the procedure, GW reported that she felt a strong pulsation in her groin followed by total relaxation. The next phase of the treatment required her to go through the same process while sitting in a chair, in the absence of a warm compress, and while attempting to generate the same sensation of warmth on her own. The intensity of the groin pain began to drop rapidly to the point that throughout the day she was almost unaware of any discomfort. When she felt any pain or tension in the injured area, she would simply focus on the heaviness and warmth sensations in her extremities, followed by the two organ specific formulas. Within six months after the start of treatment, the patient was free of pain and was able to discontinue all of her medications.

The Autogenic Pain Checklist

Form A

EXERCISE: II (Warmth)

INSTRUCTIONS: Complete this form before your autogenic training session. Simply rate your pain levels by circling the number on a scale of 0 to 10. A score of 0 indicates the absence of pain, whereas a score of 10 indicates severe pain in that body part.

1. My right arm is

0	1	2	3	4	5	6	7	8	9	10

2. My left arm is

0	1	2	3	4	5	6	7	8	9	10

3. My shoulders are

0	1	2	3	4	5	6	7	8	9	10

4. My neck is

0	1	2	3	4	5	6	7	8	9	10

5. My forehead is

0	1	2	3	4	5	6	7	8	9	10

6. My jaw is

0	1	2	3	4	5	6	7	8	9	10

7. My chest is

0	1	2	3	4	5	6	7	8	9	10

8. My abdomen is

0	1	2	3	4	5	6	7	8	9	10

9. My lower back is

0	1	2	3	4	5	6	7	8	9	10

10. My right leg is

0	1	2	3	4	5	6	7	8	9	10

11. My left leg is

0	1	2	3	4	5	6	7	8	9	10

12. Overall my body is

0	1	2	3	4	5	6	7	8	9	10

The Autogenic Pain Checklist

Form B

EXERCISE: II (Warmth)

INSTRUCTIONS: Complete this form after your autogenic training session. Simply rate your pain levels by circling the number on a scale of 0 to 10. A score of 0 indicates the absence of pain, whereas a score of 10 indicates severe pain in that body part.

1. My right arm is

0	1	2	3	4	5	6	7	8	9	10

2. My left arm is

0	1	2	3	4	5	6	7	8	9	10

3. My shoulders are

0	1	2	3	4	5	6	7	8	9	10

4. My neck is

0	1	2	3	4	5	6	7	8	9	10

5. My forehead is

0	1	2	3	4	5	6	7	8	9	10

6. My jaw is

0	1	2	3	4	5	6	7	8	9	10

7. My chest is

0	1	2	3	4	5	6	7	8	9	10

8. My abdomen is

0	1	2	3	4	5	6	7	8	9	10

9. My lower back is

0	1	2	3	4	5	6	7	8	9	10

10. My right leg is

0	1	2	3	4	5	6	7	8	9	10

11. My left leg is

0	1	2	3	4	5	6	7	8	9	10

12. Overall my body is

0	1	2	3	4	5	6	7	8	9	10

The Autogenic Tension Checklist

Form A

EXERCISE: II (Warmth)

INSTRUCTIONS: Complete this form before your autogenic training session. Simply rate your tension levels by circling the number on a scale of 0 to 10. A score of 0 indicates the absence of tension, whereas a score of 10 indicates extreme tension in that body part.

1. My right arm is

0	1	2	3	4	5	6	7	8	9	10

2. My left arm is

0	1	2	3	4	5	6	7	8	9	10

3. My shoulders are

0	1	2	3	4	5	6	7	8	9	10

4. My neck is

0	1	2	3	4	5	6	7	8	9	10

5. My forehead is

0	1	2	3	4	5	6	7	8	9	10

6. My jaw is

0	1	2	3	4	5	6	7	8	9	10

7. My chest is

0	1	2	3	4	5	6	7	8	9	10

8. My abdomen is

0	1	2	3	4	5	6	7	8	9	10

9. My lower back is

0	1	2	3	4	5	6	7	8	9	10

10. My right leg is

0	1	2	3	4	5	6	7	8	9	10

11. My left leg is

0	1	2	3	4	5	6	7	8	9	10

12. Overall my body is

0	1	2	3	4	5	6	7	8	9	10

The Autogenic Tension Checklist

Form B

EXERCISE: II (Warmth)

INSTRUCTIONS: Complete this form after your autogenic training session. Simply rate your tension levels by circling the number on a scale of 0 to 10. A score of 0 indicates the absence of tension, whereas a score of 10 indicates extreme tension in that body part.

1. My right arm is

0	1	2	3	4	5	6	7	8	9	10

2. My left arm is

0	1	2	3	4	5	6	7	8	9	10

3. My shoulders are

0	1	2	3	4	5	6	7	8	9	10

4. My neck is

0	1	2	3	4	5	6	7	8	9	10

5. My forehead is

0	1	2	3	4	5	6	7	8	9	10

6. My jaw is

0	1	2	3	4	5	6	7	8	9	10

7. My chest is

0	1	2	3	4	5	6	7	8	9	10

8. My abdomen is

0	1	2	3	4	5	6	7	8	9	10

9. My lower back is

0	1	2	3	4	5	6	7	8	9	10

10. My right leg is

0	1	2	3	4	5	6	7	8	9	10

11. My left leg is

0	1	2	3	4	5	6	7	8	9	10

12. Overall my body is

0	1	2	3	4	5	6	7	8	9	10

10
The Third Standard Exercise: Heart

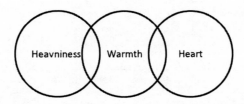

The third "ring" in the autogenic process is the heart exercise. Again, one may not proceed to this level of the training process without mastery of the two previous stages. After the first two standard exercises have been effectively mastered to the point that the sensations of heaviness and warmth can be induced comfortably and relatively rapidly, patients will be ready to begin the third standard exercise, which focuses on the activity of the heart. The relaxation and self-regulatory effects that are often observed in the first two exercises are further enhanced at this level. Many stress related symptoms may either disappear or are significantly reduced in intensity during the practice of the heart exercise.

This exercise requires further preparation and it is important that some additional time is spent to familiarize patients with some of its intricacies. For example, to gain a better sense of cardiac activity, a specific resting posture plays a crucial role. As shown in Photograph 6.4 (Chapter 6), this may be achieved by assuming the supine position with the right hand comfortably placed on the chest region, directly above the heart. Schultz and Luthe (1959) suggested that most of us need to "discover" our heart. It is noteworthy that most people initially state that they have little or no awareness of their cardiac activity. However, this type of awareness can easily be achieved by observing certain conditions. Again, special attention is placed on assuming a particular training posture. As seen in Photograph 6.4, note that the right arm is slightly elevated to make the positioning of the hand on the chest as comfortable as possible. The head and the shoulders are elevated by the use of a soft pillow. As it was mentioned earlier, patients must refrain from trying to force anything to happen. Passive concentration plays a more crucial role in this exercise than in the previous sessions. In time, such therapeutic awareness will be achieved quite effortlessly, naturally, and very quickly. Before instructing patients to make mental contact with their heart during the exercise, it is best to allow them a few minutes to explore and experience the heart rate prior to repeating the new formula. The next step is to begin repeating the formulas from the first two standard exercises and then introduce the new formulas:

• My heartbeat is calm.
• My heartbeat is calm and regular.
• My heartbeat is calm and strong.

Note that these formulas are not about consciously changing the heartbeat or making the heartbeat faster or slower. Instead, the focus is on a calm and regular heartbeat, which is a hallmark of a relaxed and tranquil state. This sets the stage for the natural self-regulatory mechanisms to take over and bring about the necessary changes that are health enhancing. What is most important in this exercise is the patient's ability to be patient and allow the gradual experience of the sensations of relaxation.

Throughout the years, I have noticed that soon after engaging in the third exercise many patients begin to enter a profound state of tranquility and psychophysical calmness which results in falling asleep. A large majority of my patients have stated that they begin to truly appreciate the experience of a deepening in their ability to relax after they complete the third exercise. This is a natural juncture in the training where a tendency for anxiety and panic attacks can be significantly and effectively corrected. Such improvements may occur spontaneously and without a need to specifically treat such symptoms.

Although usually we may not be aware of the activity of the heart, we constantly maintain a subconscious, yet profound, contact with this organ as its activity can either arouse us or gently put us to sleep. Schwartz (1989) reported that "self-attention" to cardiac activity in a relaxed fashion can, by itself, initiate a self-regulatory process with potential "localized healing." That is to say, passive attention to the activity of the heart may bring about a state of greater order and balance within the body. Also, *symptomatic* relief from mild forms of mitral valve prolapse (MVP), which are often quite distressing, can be effectively achieved within a matter of weeks with the use of the cardiac formulas. However, if a patient is suffering from any form of cardiac condition, it is imperative that he or she consults a physician prior to engaging in this exercise. Although in a clinical setting I have never observed any complications with this exercise, certain necessary precautions should be observed so that the progress in this training is not hindered. Jencks (1979) further supports these observations and experiences by stating, "Occasionally one meets with the opinion that the observation of the rhythm of the heart leads to undue concern with the heart. The author has never observed this, nor noticed any reference to it in the autogenic training literature. In fact, the contrary seems to occur" (p. 28).

To begin this exercise, please observe the requirements that were described previously. Assist patients in finding a comfortable position while lying on their back. Next, have them place their right hand on the chest and allow a few minutes to comfortably make mental contact with the heart. This requires patience! There is no reason to rush the process.

The Heart Exercise

Remind patients to complete Form A of either the Tension Checklist or the Pain Checklist, prior to beginning each session. The following instructions may be read to the patient:

When you feel ready, gently close your eyes and silently begin repeating the following formulas:

- I am quiet and relaxed.
- I am at peace.
- My right arm is heavy and warm.
- I am at peace.
- My left arm is heavy and warm.
- I am at peace.
- My shoulders are heavy and warm.
- I am at peace.
- My jaw is heavy and warm.
- I am at peace.
- My right leg is heavy and warm.
- I am at peace.
- My left leg is heavy and warm
- I am at peace.
- My right foot is heavy and warm.
- I am at peace.
- My left foot is heavy and warm.

- I am at peace.
- My lower back is heavy and warm.
- I am at peace.

Now begin paying attention to your heart in a passive and relaxed way. After a few moments, repeat to yourself:

- My heartbeat is calm.
- I am at peace.
- My heartbeat is calm and regular.
- I am at peace.
- My heartbeat is calm and strong.
- I am at peace.
- My heartbeat is calm and steady.*
- I am at peace.
- My entire body is comfortably relaxed.
- I am at peace.

Now allow yourself to be calm and quiet and enjoy the feeling of total relaxation and tranquility. When you feel ready, take a deep breath, flex and then stretch out your arms and open your eyes. You may also wish to gently stretch out your legs. Give yourself a few moments before you sit up from the supine position. (Make sure that the patient completes the Tension Checklist or the Pain Checklist, Form B, upon finishing the exercise.)

Common Difficulties with the Third Standard Exercise

The third standard exercise may initially appear as difficult to teach and to learn. Although the main focus of the first two phases of training was on inducing heaviness and warmth in the extremities, the third exercise focuses on an internal organ which may present difficulties as far as the requirement of "making mental contact" is concerned. The specific training posture developed for the third exercise should make the task of "discovering" the activity of the heart much easier. Most patients require assuming the training position with the right hand placed on the chest cavity only for a few sessions before they can perform the exercise in a horizontal or a reclined position without the hand placement.

The practitioner needs to instruct the patient to take his or her time and develop a sense for the cardiac rhythm prior to initiating this phase of treatment. As it was stated, it is critical in this exercise to emphasize to the patient

---

*This is an additional formula that was added to support the other standard formulas. It enhances the overall effectiveness of the exercise.

that the objective is not to reduce or to increase the activity of the heart. The need for emphasizing passive concentration on the activity of the heart becomes even more crucial during the third exercise. Jencks (1979) reported that by having patients focus on the rhythm of the heart, such passive concentration may be maintained more effectively. Some patients may initially report an increase in their cardiac activity immediately after repeating the heart formulas. They should be instructed not to interfere with this phenomenon and should continue to passively repeat the formula. When necessary, patients may repeat the background formula, "I am at peace," more frequently before repeating, "My heartbeat is calm and steady." Again, if distressing sensations persist, the exercise may be concluded by flexing the arm, taking a deep breath, and opening the eyes. Luthe reported that in those rare cases when patients present with difficulties regarding heart formulas, it is probable that they have certain fears about their cardiac health, possibly due to their medical history (in Lindemann, 1973). In addition to appropriate screening prior to commencing the training, it may be helpful to explore patients' fears and concerns.

As stated earlier in this chapter, when performed correctly, the relaxing, tranquilizing, and rejuvenating effects of this exercise can be so profound that many patients report a spontaneous improvement in their sleep. Also, home practice of the exercises begins to improve health, especially in terms of a deepening of relaxation and a reduction in the overall experience of pain and tension. This phase of training is so important because of its therapeutic benefits that Luthe (1977) advises against moving to the next exercise until the objectives of the third exercise have been achieved.

Case Example 1

JA was a healthy, active woman prior to a motor vehicle accident which resulted in the development of symptoms of wide-spread pain to the point that her entire body was "constantly aching." As she was beginning to learn ways of coping with her pain and discomfort, she began experiencing dizziness and panic-like experiences. The symptoms became so disturbing that eventually she was referred to a cardiologist for further evaluation. JA was diagnosed with mitral valve prolapse and was asked to learn stress management strategies to cope with her symptoms. Also, she was instructed to follow a diet free of stimulants.

I began working with JA for over a month before she was ready to begin the third standard autogenic exercise. An entire session was devoted to helping her discover her cardiac activity. This was done in brief five-minute segments with time for reporting subjective experiences and encouraging passive concentration. Although initially she was apprehensive about paying attention to her heartbeat, her anxiety began to subside and disappear after she began following the instructions and practicing the exercise on a regular basis. Her cardiologist, who referred her to me, was also pleased with her improvements and gradually began reducing her medications. JA often remarked that "the heart tape" was her favorite — her "audio tranquilizer." Similar sentiments are often expressed by patients after mastering the third standard exercise.

Case Example 2

BD was a 14-year-old who had a difficult time falling asleep. She stayed up until 3 A.M. before she could "lose consciousness." She was a good student whose grades had started to suffer mainly because of lack of sleep. She did not watch television late at night, nor did she work on her computer, cell phone, etc. She simply could not fall asleep. Thoughts about the day before and plans for the next day would enter her mind, but she reported that she did not obsess about them, nor was she preoccupied by such thoughts. They would simply run through her mind almost incessantly. After working with a cognitive therapist, she had learned how to isolate and later reframe some of her negative ideations, and to confront them effectively. However, her idiopathic insomnia persisted. BD often described her insomnia as persistent tension all over her body and the inability to completely "turn off" her mind even when it was "as close to a blank" as possible.

After a comprehensive evaluation, she was found to be a good candidate for autogenic training. At the end of each of the treatment sessions, she was provided with an instructional MP3 file that she listened to as she tried to fall asleep. After successful completion of the first two exercises, she reported that her body would become "incredibly relaxed," however, she still could not fall asleep until the early hours of morning. Despite this, she felt more refreshed when she awoke in the morning. When we began the training in the third exercise, for the first time, I noticed that she fell asleep during the session. She was pleasantly surprised when I woke her at the end of the exercise. After practicing the third exercise for a week, with the use of the audio instructions, she woke up in the morning with her headphones resting on her head, in disbelief that she had fallen asleep while listening to the exercise (normally she would remove her headphones after the exercise, even when she was lying in bed). During the second and the third night of practicing the heart exercise, she became very sleepy but it took her an additional 15 minutes to fall asleep after she listened to the exercise. She was discharged from my care after 12 sessions of treatment. Even though we covered all the standard exercises, the exercise that she used most frequently to fall asleep was the third exercise.

The Autogenic Pain Checklist

Form A

EXERCISE: III (Heart)

INSTRUCTIONS: Complete this form before your autogenic training session. Simply rate your pain levels by circling the number on a scale of 0 to 10. A score of 0 indicates the absence of pain, whereas a score of 10 indicates severe pain in that body part.

1. My right arm is

0	1	2	3	4	5	6	7	8	9	10

2. My left arm is

0	1	2	3	4	5	6	7	8	9	10

3. My shoulders are

0	1	2	3	4	5	6	7	8	9	10

4. My neck is

0	1	2	3	4	5	6	7	8	9	10

5. My forehead is

0	1	2	3	4	5	6	7	8	9	10

6. My jaw is

0	1	2	3	4	5	6	7	8	9	10

7. My chest is

0	1	2	3	4	5	6	7	8	9	10

8. My abdomen is

0	1	2	3	4	5	6	7	8	9	10

9. My lower back is

0	1	2	3	4	5	6	7	8	9	10

10. My right leg is

0	1	2	3	4	5	6	7	8	9	10

11. My left leg is

0	1	2	3	4	5	6	7	8	9	10

12. Overall my body is

0	1	2	3	4	5	6	7	8	9	10

The Autogenic Pain Checklist

Form B

EXERCISE: III (Heart)

INSTRUCTIONS: Complete this form after your autogenic training session. Simply rate your pain levels by circling the number on a scale of 0 to 10. A score of 0 indicates the absence of pain, whereas a score of 10 indicates severe pain in that body part.

1. My right arm is

0	1	2	3	4	5	6	7	8	9	10

2. My left arm is

0	1	2	3	4	5	6	7	8	9	10

3. My shoulders are

0	1	2	3	4	5	6	7	8	9	10

4. My neck is

0	1	2	3	4	5	6	7	8	9	10

5. My forehead is

0	1	2	3	4	5	6	7	8	9	10

6. My jaw is

0	1	2	3	4	5	6	7	8	9	10

7. My chest is

0	1	2	3	4	5	6	7	8	9	10

8. My abdomen is

0	1	2	3	4	5	6	7	8	9	10

9. My lower back is

0	1	2	3	4	5	6	7	8	9	10

10. My right leg is

0	1	2	3	4	5	6	7	8	9	10

11. My left leg is

0	1	2	3	4	5	6	7	8	9	10

12. Overall my body is

0	1	2	3	4	5	6	7	8	9	10

The Autogenic Tension Checklist

Form A

EXERCISE: III (Heart)

INSTRUCTIONS: Complete this form before your autogenic training session. Simply rate your tension levels by circling the number on a scale of 0 to 10. A score of 0 indicates the absence of tension, whereas a score of 10 indicates extreme tension in that body part.

1. My right arm is

0	1	2	3	4	5	6	7	8	9	10

2. My left arm is

0	1	2	3	4	5	6	7	8	9	10

3. My shoulders are

0	1	2	3	4	5	6	7	8	9	10

4. My neck is

0	1	2	3	4	5	6	7	8	9	10

5. My forehead is

0	1	2	3	4	5	6	7	8	9	10

6. My jaw is

0	1	2	3	4	5	6	7	8	9	10

7. My chest is

0	1	2	3	4	5	6	7	8	9	10

8. My abdomen is

0	1	2	3	4	5	6	7	8	9	10

9. My lower back is

0	1	2	3	4	5	6	7	8	9	10

10. My right leg is

0	1	2	3	4	5	6	7	8	9	10

11. My left leg is

0	1	2	3	4	5	6	7	8	9	10

12. Overall my body is

0	1	2	3	4	5	6	7	8	9	10

The Autogenic Tension Checklist

Form B

EXERCISE: III (Heart)

INSTRUCTIONS: Complete this form after your autogenic training session. Simply rate your tension levels by circling the number on a scale of 0 to 10. A score of 0 indicates the absence of tension, whereas a score of 10 indicates extreme tension in that body part.

1. My right arm is

0	1	2	3	4	5	6	7	8	9	10

2. My left arm is

0	1	2	3	4	5	6	7	8	9	10

3. My shoulders are

0	1	2	3	4	5	6	7	8	9	10

4. My neck is

0	1	2	3	4	5	6	7	8	9	10

5. My forehead is

0	1	2	3	4	5	6	7	8	9	10

6. My jaw is

0	1	2	3	4	5	6	7	8	9	10

7. My chest is

0	1	2	3	4	5	6	7	8	9	10

8. My abdomen is

0	1	2	3	4	5	6	7	8	9	10

9. My lower back is

0	1	2	3	4	5	6	7	8	9	10

10. My right leg is

0	1	2	3	4	5	6	7	8	9	10

11. My left leg is

0	1	2	3	4	5	6	7	8	9	10

12. Overall my body is

0	1	2	3	4	5	6	7	8	9	10

11

The Fourth Standard Exercise: Respiration

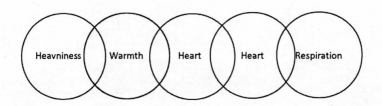

Stressed people interfere with their breathing and will inadvertently add greater tension to their body. Improper breathing will also influence mental states, even though most people are unaware of such a connection. Efficient and effective breathing is perhaps one of the most central elements in enhancing self-regulation. The old adage that "breath is life" is indeed an accurate one and may be expanded to "ineffective breathing can interfere with healthy living." That is, although respiration is an automatic process, we can, at will, affect the rate and the depth of our breathing. Jencks (1977) observed that most children use their diaphragm quite well to allow their respiration to maintain an optimum level of inhalation and exhalation. Most adults on the other hand, and especially those suffering from chronic pain, tend to breathe in a shallow, controlled fashion. Many authors have suggested that conditions such as panic and anxiety attacks, chest and upper back pain, and muscle tension may be attributed to improper breathing. Smith (1989) convincingly reminds us that "breathing is the only basic physiological process that is both voluntary and involuntary" (p. 113).

Without a doubt, breathing exercises are the most commonly taught techniques in stress management courses. One of the most well-known, popular methods of relaxation, Hatha Yoga, combines deep breathing with stretching of specific muscle groups. Diaphragmatic breathing is another prevalent relaxation procedure through which people are taught to enhance their process of respiration by focusing on abdominal instead of chest breathing. If used ineffectively and too forcefully, this technique can actually have paradoxical effects, which may cause greater tension, stress, and possible symptoms such as dizziness, numbness in the hands, and other disturbing sensations.

The autogenic approach for improving proper respiration is quite different from other, more popular techniques. Without active intervention or volition, patients report improved respiration through the use of specific autogenic formulas. However, I am by no means against the use of various breathing techniques and strongly feel that they can be used quite effectively in clinical settings and at home. If patients are familiar with such techniques, they may wish to use them during the preliminary exercises but I advise against using them during an autogenic session. This concern was also shared by Schultz and Luthe (1969) who made the following remark: "In trainees with healthy respiratory systems, training difficulties are relatively rare and are reported chiefly by trainees who have learned and practiced some sort of respiratory exercises before starting autogenic therapy. These trainees find it exceptionally difficult to remain passive and to let 'it' (the respiratory system) work without interference" (p. 100).

It is quite likely that by the time patients are ready to begin the fourth standard autogenic exercise, they have already become aware of a deepening in their breathing and the concomitant experience of more profound calmness. As with the previous exercises, patients need to be reminded that any conscious attempt to change their breathing should be avoided at all cost. Any active form of intervention may result in a greater level of arousal, which is likely to make respiration more irregular. Impress upon them the importance of following the instructions for the previous exercises and allowing the inborn physiological mechanisms to make the appropriate transition into a more pronounced state of recuperation and regeneration. This state is further reinforced and enhanced during the respiration exercise. Similar to the heart exercise, patients are asked to bring a greater level of passive concentration or passive attention to an inward focus on the internal rhythms of the body, which in this case is breathing rhythm. Jencks (1977) suggested spending a few minutes prior to the exercise observing the respiratory activity in terms of inhalations, exhalations, and changes in movements in chest and abdominal areas. The formulas for this session, which are to be repeated after the heaviness, warmth, and heart formulas, are described below.

- My breathing is calm.
- My breathing is calm and regular.

- I breathe comfortably and naturally.*
- It breathes me.

Schultz's original formula for this exercise was "It breathes me." Although it is difficult to do justice to the profound philosophical and psychophysiological wisdom of such a phrase in a few paragraphs, it is also true that most people have difficulty comprehending or relating to this formula. The word "it" embodies a critical concept in understanding the process of self-regulation. At any moment, there are innumerable bodily events taking place that are not even remotely perceived by our conscious awareness. The body's physiological mechanisms are self-supporting and do not require active participation to maintain their function. In reality we can interfere with these mechanisms by trying to force changes in their activities, a process that is antithetical to the autogenic philosophy. "It" denotes those unconscious physiological mechanisms that allow the body to maintain its state of balance. In other words, "it knows" how to breathe, how to maintain proper temperature, how to promote effective digestion. Awake or asleep, "it" brings the necessary changes that are needed for survival. Unfortunately, due to exposure to traumatic events and long-term stressors such as pain, this innate mechanism of self-regulation (it) can lose its effectiveness in generating an internal state of balance and harmony.

Prior to using the key formula, "It breathes me," at least initially, an appropriate substitution may be a formula that suggests calm and regular breathing. Ultimately, the most salient point of this exercise is that we often interfere with natural breathing, which by itself can induce undue stress. The brain's own self-regulatory mechanisms are capable of maintaining optimal breathing without any assistance from the conscious mind: "it" knows how to breathe and how to do so effectively and efficiently, as while we sleep. By entering the autogenic state through the repetition of such formulas, the body's innate abilities are summoned to make the appropriate and necessary psychophysiological adjustments.

Because the respiration formulas are preceded by the heart exercise, a supine position is highly recommended, at least initially, to achieve the optimum level of relaxation from this exercise.

The Respiration Exercise

Remind patients to complete Form A of either the Tension Checklist or the Pain Checklist, prior to beginning each session. The following instructions may be read to the patient:

---

*This is not one of the original, standard formulas. However, after many clinical and empirical observations, it was added to further enhance the effectiveness of the breathing formulas.

When you are ready, gently close your eyes and silently begin repeating the following formulas.

- I am quiet and relaxed.
- I am at peace.
- My right arm is heavy and warm.
- I am at peace.
- My left arm is heavy and warm.
- I am at peace.
- My shoulders are heavy and warm.
- I am at peace.
- My jaw is heavy and warm.
- I am at peace.
- My right leg is heavy and warm.
- I am at peace.
- My left leg is heavy and warm.
- I am at peace.
- My right foot is heavy and warm.
- I am at peace.
- My left foot is heavy and warm.
- I am at peace.
- My lower back is heavy and warm.
- I am at peace.

Now pay attention to your cardiac activity in a passive and relaxed fashion:

- My heartbeat is calm.
- I am at peace.
- My heartbeat is calm and regular.
- I am at peace.
- My heartbeat is calm and strong.
- I am at peace.

Now passively begin paying attention to your breathing. After a brief pause begin repeating to yourself:

- My breathing is calm.
- I am at peace.
- My breathing is calm and regular.
- I am at peace.
- I breathe comfortably and naturally.
- I am at peace.
- It breathes me.

- I am at peace.
- My entire body is comfortably relaxed.
- I am at peace.

After repeating the last formula, allow yourself to be calm and quiet for a few minutes. Then after taking a deep breath, flex your arms and slowly open your eyes. Again, please keep in mind that you should not get up too quickly in order to avoid any uncomfortable sensations. (Make sure that the patient completes the Tension Checklist or the Pain Checklist, Form B, upon finishing the exercise.)

A generalized sensation of warmth, warmth all over the body, is often experienced during the practice of this exercise. Muscle tension tends to dissolve considerably, hence, it is only prudent to make sure that the patient is comfortable and ready to assume a sitting and/or a standing position. If necessary, have the patient gently stretch out his or her arms and legs several times before standing up.

Common Difficulties with the Fourth Standard Exercise

The most challenging difficulty with the breathing exercise is presented by those who attempt to breathe in a particular fashion, such as "doing" diaphragmatic breathing. These tendencies should be resisted and the patient should be instructed not to use previous training in other forms of breathing while performing the fourth standard exercise. As soon as some patients begin repeating the formula, "My breathing is calm and regular," they tend to consciously slow their breathing, or use their abdomen "to do the breathing." Helping them to become aware of these tendencies is very critical at this stage of training.

Unless the patient fully understands the objective of this exercise, it is best to use examples, emphasize passive concentration, and perform brief experiments with the new formulas, until he or she can perform the exercise in a volition free state. In difficult cases, to "undo" contradictory instructions and habits, it is important to proceed slowly by shortening the training sessions and emphasizing the need for passive concentration. The importance of fully emphasizing the meaning and the implications of the formula "It breathes me" cannot possibly be overemphasized, especially when persistent difficulties and/or resistance are encountered.

By the time they reach the fourth standard exercise, the majority of patients have already become aware of a pleasant deepening in their breathing. Once they learn not to force this process, they will soon become aware of the profoundly quieting effect of this exercise. A common observation that is often made by chronic pain patients after training in the fourth exercise is that their shoulders feel much more relaxed. An almost total disappearance of cognitive and somatic anxiety is another typical observation during and after each practice session.

Case Example 1

One of the most difficult cases of post-traumatic nightmare disorder I treated involved a young woman who had developed a phobia of not being able to breathe while asleep. The patient, KS, was in a severe motor vehicle accident, which in addition to physical injury resulted in her experiencing frequent and very disturbing nightmares. To help her sleep better, one of her physicians had prescribed an anti-anxiety medication. Although such medications can be quite helpful for a brief period of time, KS began experiencing even more distress and anxiety because she could not wake from the nightmares. Shortly after that, she became preoccupied with the thought that she was not going to be able to breathe while asleep. This further complicated her recovery because she avoided falling asleep until the early hours of the morning when she would pass out. During the fourth autogenic training session, I spent some time describing to her the importance of the formula "It breathes me." I indicated to her that her body was capable of breathing quite effectively without her assistance. Soon "It breathes me" became one of her favorite formulas and she learned to use it to gradually control some of her symptoms of anxiety. In time, with the use of autogenic exercises and an advanced autogenic technique known as autogenic abreaction, the disturbing dreams ceased altogether (see Sadigh, 1999).

Case Example 2

Panic attacks are inherently very distressing as they affect a person's mind and body, and often relationships, in profound ways. One of the most disturbing forms of panic attacks is when they occur during sleep, a phenomenon which often occurs in NREM sleep approximately during the first two cycles of sleep. Such attacks may result in a challenging form of phobic anxiety that is extremely difficult to treat. People who suffer from panic attacks during sleep find ways of avoiding sleep so as to avoid the horrifying experience of not being able to breathe while in the deeper stages of sleep. This maladaptive behavior of avoiding sleep will in time result in further complications, one of which may be an increase in the frequency of these panic attacks. The fourth standard autogenic exercise is an excellent intervention for coping with and even avoiding panic attacks. The key to the success of this exercise has to do with a thorough explanation of the formula "It breathes me." The meaning of this formula was explained in much detail earlier in this chapter.

RM was a 35-year-old driven member of a successful company who suddenly began experiencing panic attacks during sleep. Initially, he was thought to be suffering from sleep apnea. Extensive sleep studies did not support this hypothesis. After a while, RM would read at night and try to keep himself busy when he would just "pass out." He no longer slept in his bed, a choice that was having a damaging effect on his marriage. He preferred reading in a recliner late at night, although this offered no guarantees that he could avoid the nocturnal panic attacks. When I first met him, he looked exhausted and very worried that his lack of sleep was affecting his job performance. He did not want to be demoted, as he had climbed the "ladder of success" in his organization very quickly and confidently. He had addressed many of his concerns with his "talk therapists." This had given him greater insight into his driven nature and the need to be successful; however, he was haunted by the attacks at night. As an athletic person, he was not interested in taking medications. He expressed an interest in learning a form of relaxation exercise. He was provided with detailed information about autogenic training and it was emphasized to him that it was not simply a form of relaxation but a form of psychophysiological psychotherapy.

After the first few weeks of treatment, he was able to fall asleep much more quickly while seated in a recliner. During the practice of the fourth standard exercise, he reported that he was gaining some confidence that his brain was doing the breathing and that it did not need his help or vigilance. He gradually started to sleep in his bed while practicing the exercises. He began to fall asleep to two final formulas: "It breathes me ... and ... I am at peace."

He completed the autogenic training approximately 6 months after our first meeting. During a follow up meeting he reported that he had not had any attacks for a while. He was urged to continue with the autogenic formulas each night, while in bed, and to make time during the week to practice the exercises in their entirety.

The Autogenic Pain Checklist

Form A

EXERCISE: IV (Respiration)

INSTRUCTIONS: Complete this form before your autogenic training session. Simply rate your pain levels by circling the number on a scale of 0 to 10. A score of 0 indicates the absence of pain, whereas a score of 10 indicates severe pain in that body part.

1. My right arm is

0	1	2	3	4	5	6	7	8	9	10

2. My left arm is

0	1	2	3	4	5	6	7	8	9	10

3. My shoulders are

0	1	2	3	4	5	6	7	8	9	10

4. My neck is

0	1	2	3	4	5	6	7	8	9	10

5. My forehead is

0	1	2	3	4	5	6	7	8	9	10

6. My jaw is

0	1	2	3	4	5	6	7	8	9	10

7. My chest is

0	1	2	3	4	5	6	7	8	9	10

8. My abdomen is

0	1	2	3	4	5	6	7	8	9	10

9. My lower back is

0	1	2	3	4	5	6	7	8	9	10

10. My right leg is

0	1	2	3	4	5	6	7	8	9	10

11. My left leg is

0	1	2	3	4	5	6	7	8	9	10

12. Overall my body is

0	1	2	3	4	5	6	7	8	9	10

The Autogenic Pain Checklist

Form B

EXERCISE: IV (Respiration)

INSTRUCTIONS: Complete this form after your autogenic training session. Simply rate your pain levels by circling the number on a scale of 0 to 10. A score of 0 indicates the absence of pain, whereas a score of 10 indicates severe pain in that body part.

1. My right arm is

0	1	2	3	4	5	6	7	8	9	10

2. My left arm is

0	1	2	3	4	5	6	7	8	9	10

3. My shoulders are

0	1	2	3	4	5	6	7	8	9	10

4. My neck is

0	1	2	3	4	5	6	7	8	9	10

5. My forehead is

0	1	2	3	4	5	6	7	8	9	10

6. My jaw is

0	1	2	3	4	5	6	7	8	9	10

7. My chest is

0	1	2	3	4	5	6	7	8	9	10

8. My abdomen is

0	1	2	3	4	5	6	7	8	9	10

9. My lower back is

0	1	2	3	4	5	6	7	8	9	10

10. My right leg is

0	1	2	3	4	5	6	7	8	9	10

11. My left leg is

0	1	2	3	4	5	6	7	8	9	10

12. Overall my body is

0	1	2	3	4	5	6	7	8	9	10

The Autogenic Tension Checklist

Form A

EXERCISE: IV (Respiration)

INSTRUCTIONS: Complete this form before your autogenic training session. Simply rate your tension levels by circling the number on a scale of 0 to 10. A score of 0 indicates the absence of tension, whereas a score of 10 indicates extreme tension in that body part.

1. My right arm is

0	1	2	3	4	5	6	7	8	9	10

2. My left arm is

0	1	2	3	4	5	6	7	8	9	10

3. My shoulders are

0	1	2	3	4	5	6	7	8	9	10

4. My neck is

0	1	2	3	4	5	6	7	8	9	10

5. My forehead is

0	1	2	3	4	5	6	7	8	9	10

6. My jaw is

0	1	2	3	4	5	6	7	8	9	10

7. My chest is

0	1	2	3	4	5	6	7	8	9	10

8. My abdomen is

0	1	2	3	4	5	6	7	8	9	10

9. My lower back is

0	1	2	3	4	5	6	7	8	9	10

10. My right leg is

0	1	2	3	4	5	6	7	8	9	10

11. My left leg is

0	1	2	3	4	5	6	7	8	9	10

12. Overall my body is

0	1	2	3	4	5	6	7	8	9	10

The Autogenic Tension Checklist

Form B

EXERCISE: IV (Respiration)

INSTRUCTIONS: Complete this form after your autogenic training session. Simply rate your tension levels by circling the number on a scale of 0 to 10. A score of 0 indicates the absence of tension, whereas a score of 10 indicates extreme tension in that body part.

1. My right arm is

| 0 | 1 | 2 | 3 | 4 | 5 | 6 | 7 | 8 | 9 | 10 |

2. My left arm is

| 0 | 1 | 2 | 3 | 4 | 5 | 6 | 7 | 8 | 9 | 10 |

3. My shoulders are

| 0 | 1 | 2 | 3 | 4 | 5 | 6 | 7 | 8 | 9 | 10 |

4. My neck is

| 0 | 1 | 2 | 3 | 4 | 5 | 6 | 7 | 8 | 9 | 10 |

5. My forehead is

| 0 | 1 | 2 | 3 | 4 | 5 | 6 | 7 | 8 | 9 | 10 |

6. My jaw is

| 0 | 1 | 2 | 3 | 4 | 5 | 6 | 7 | 8 | 9 | 10 |

7. My chest is

| 0 | 1 | 2 | 3 | 4 | 5 | 6 | 7 | 8 | 9 | 10 |

8. My abdomen is

| 0 | 1 | 2 | 3 | 4 | 5 | 6 | 7 | 8 | 9 | 10 |

9. My lower back is

| 0 | 1 | 2 | 3 | 4 | 5 | 6 | 7 | 8 | 9 | 10 |

10. My right leg is

| 0 | 1 | 2 | 3 | 4 | 5 | 6 | 7 | 8 | 9 | 10 |

11. My left leg is

| 0 | 1 | 2 | 3 | 4 | 5 | 6 | 7 | 8 | 9 | 10 |

12. Overall my body is

| 0 | 1 | 2 | 3 | 4 | 5 | 6 | 7 | 8 | 9 | 10 |

12

The Fifth Standard
Exercise: Abdominal Warmth

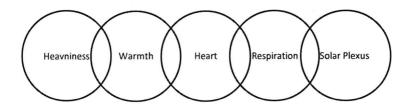

Long before the birth of autogenic training, it was common practice in hospitals to apply a hot compress to the abdominal region to bring about a calming and tranquilizing effect, especially to promote sleep and to reduce anxiety. In the same fashion, passive concentration on generating warmth in the abdominal region further enhances the body's self-regulatory mechanisms already initiated through the first four standard exercises. Such effects are even further enhanced as abdominal warmth is induced. That is, as the formulas for the fifth exercise are repeated, one may actually experience more profound sensations of heaviness and warmth in the extremities, followed by more regular cardiac activity and deeper, more relaxed breathing.

There is one critical point that needs to be considered prior to training in the fifth formula. Those who suffer from severe gastrointestinal symptoms, especially bleeding ulcers, may not be appropriate candidates for this phase of training. An increase in the circulation of the abdominal region may inadvertently worsen such conditions. In such cases, the fifth exercise may be postponed until the condition is brought under control (through medication, changes in diet, etc.), or the condition is no longer in an acute state. In severe cases of gastrointestinal (GI) disorders, the exercise may be abandoned altogether and the patient may proceed to the sixth standard exercise, which focuses on cooling the forehead. There have been reports of minor abdominal pain that completely disappeared after the use of the fifth exercise because of its profoundly relaxing properties, but it should not be attempted by those who are suffering from a bleeding ulcer or ulcerative colitis.

Diabetes is another condition that needs to be kept in mind prior to training in the fifth standard exercise. It has been postulated that the induction of warmth in the abdominal cavity may affect carbohydrate metabolism, which will consequently cause changes in insulin levels. Under the close supervision of an endocrinologist, and with the use of the fifth exercise, I have been able to help a number of diabetics lower their doses of injected insulin. Although the benefits of the effective use of this exercise can be quite rewarding for the patient, I recommend caution and a slower pace for this particular level of training. Above all, make sure that the patient is under close medical supervision (as discussed in Chapter 5, patients with endocrinological symptoms and disorders need to be treated only in collaboration with a treating physician). Schultz and Luthe (1959) reported the following case, which, although rare, may serve as an important example of the potency of these exercises.

> A young diabetic who required relatively high quantities of insulin and who mastered the standard exercises was asked to continue autogenic training by emphasizing the development of warmth in the upper regions of the abdomen. After effective exercises had been practiced frequently, the patient began to suffer from hypoglycemic shocks because he continued injecting the same amount of insulin as he took before. After taking 20 units less, the patient felt well even though he was not too careful about dietary indiscretions [p. 71].

As with the third standard exercise (heart), we are going to move from the periphery (the arms and the legs) toward the internal organs. The focus of the fifth exercise is not to bring about a sensation of warmth on the surface of the abdominal region or the skin. The primary objective is, however, to improve circulation and to promote a pleasant sensation of heat in a deep region of the upper abdominal cavity referred to as the solar plexus. This region of the abdomen sits behind the stomach and is immediately located in front of the spine, and contains an intricate interweaving of fibers of the autonomic nervous system. Thus, this region plays a crucial role in the regulation of the activities of many of the internal organs, especially in terms of the blood supply to the stomach, liver, kidneys, pancreas, and many other organs. Figure 12.1 shows the location of the solar plexus. It is important that the patient has some sense of the location of this region prior to practicing the appropriate formula.

Traditionally, the main formula for this exercise has been "My solar plexus is warm." However, I have found it equally effective to have patients repeat to themselves, "My abdomen is warm." Again, as long as they know that by "abdomen" we mean a deeper region of the upper abdominal cavity and not the surface area, either formula should work quite effectively in accomplishing the goal of this exercise. In the original autogenic writings, Schultz and Luthe (1959) suggested that as a method of improving circulation in the abdominal region, therapists might want to hold a hand between the tip of the sternum and the umbilicus and have the patient focus on the sensation of warmth and allow it to gradually move deeper into this region. They also suggested that, at least initially, while the patient was focusing on the heat from the therapist's hand, the following formula should be repeated: "Heat rays are warming the depth of my abdomen." This was to be followed by the formula "My solar plexus is warm."

As indicated in Chapter 7, I have developed a new postural position for this exercise which significantly enhances the effectiveness of the formula. This position is considerably similar to the one recommended for the heart exercise with two exceptions. First, the hand is placed (very lightly) on the center of the upper abdominal region, right below the breastbone. Second, one may use either hand as long as the position of the arm is as comfortable as possible. It is important that patients experiment with this position until they discover the position that places the least amount of stress and tension on the abdomen and the arm. I recommend repositioning a pillow under the arm until this objective is achieved.

Another way of facilitating the effects of this exercise is to combine the formula with the following image: "Imagine drinking a warm liquid and follow the warmth as it moves down the esophagus, enters the abdomen, and a soothing heat begins to concentrate in the solar plexus region." If it is possible for the patient to visualize the heat penetrating the abdominal region and especially concentrating behind the stomach

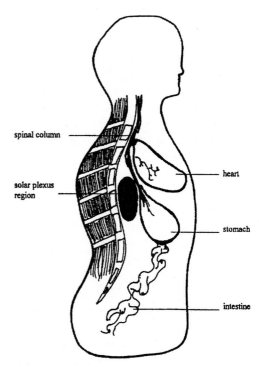

Figure 12.1. The location of the solar plexus.

and in the front of the spine, he or she will quickly notice a profound state of relaxation affecting the entire body. As stated earlier, many may actually fall asleep during the practice of this exercise because of its tranquilizing properties. To remedy this, an additional formula is suggested to be repeated at the beginning of the fifth exercise: "I remain peacefully alert during the exercise."

Given the potent properties of this exercise, and the concern that some patients might have about irritable bowel syndrome and/or occasional stomach upset, a gradual process of increasing the sensation of warmth in the abdominal region is advised. This can be accomplished by attenuating or diluting the key formula. For example, I suggest that all patients initially repeat to themselves: "My abdomen (solar plexus) is slightly warm." Then the formula is replaced with "My abdomen (solar plexus) is pleasantly warm." And finally, "My abdomen (solar plexus) is warm." This approach quite effectively safeguards the patient against any unpleasant sensations that may be brought on by a sudden increase in circulation. Again I must emphasize that if a patient is currently suffering from an actively bleeding ulcer or a severe case of colitis, this exercise should be postponed until the condition has been treated medically and has been brought under control.

At this juncture in the training, the many benefits of the fifth exercise can also make it easier to address musculoskeletal pain. This is usually the time when I introduce some additional formulas for pain management and coping. Luthe and Schultz (1969a) reported a spontaneous reduction in pain while focusing on an agreeable sensation of warmth both in the periphery and in the abdominal region. Most chronic pain patients suffer from diffuse and widespread pain that seems to be, at least partially, the result of vasoconstriction and ischemia. Once this condition is counteracted through the practice of the standard exercises, beneficial effects such as a reduction in pain and stiffness may be observed. Hence, I have found it extremely useful to include an additional formula (not a standard one) for reducing pain which emphasizes the healing qualities of an increase in blood flow in certain muscle groups. The new formula, "Warmth dissolves the pain," can be used quite effectively to bring about soothing relief in painful and cramped muscles.

The basic instruction for the use of this formula is rather simple, although attention to certain specific details is required. First, to maximize the benefits of this formula, patients should not use it until they have reached the end of the fifth exercise, which sets the stage for the perfect opportunity to work on reducing pain. Second, the formula needs to be used initially in a specific way. That is to say, patients need to use it to affect pain and discomfort in a specific muscle group, for instance, the muscles of the right leg and not both legs simultaneously. Patients need to focus on one area before moving to another. Finally, if patients are experiencing a severe inflammatory condition, such as inflammation of the knees, they should wait until the condition is brought under control before using the pain formula.

Once the patients have been provided with the above instructions and precautions, they are ready to begin the fifth autogenic exercise. Again, a supine position is advised with specific attention placed upon the position of the hand (in the upper abdominal region, see Photograph 6.5 in Chapter 6). It is best not to use the abdominal exercise shortly after eating a meal. To effectively complete the training sequence, at least twenty minutes needs to be allocated to the exercise.

The Abdominal Warmth Exercise

Remind patients to complete Form A of either the Tension Checklist or the Pain Checklist prior to beginning each session. The following instructions may be read to the patient:

When you are ready, gently close your eyes and then silently begin repeating the following formulas:

- I remain peacefully alert during the exercise (optional)
- I am quiet and relaxed.
- I am at peace.
- My right arm is heavy and warm.
- I am at peace.
- My left arm is heavy and warm.
- I am at peace.
- My shoulders are heavy and warm.
- I am at peace.
- My jaw is heavy and warm.
- I am at peace.
- My right leg is heavy and warm.
- I am at peace.
- My left leg is heavy and warm.
- I am at peace.
- My right foot is heavy and warm.
- I am at peace.
- My left foot is heavy and warm.
- I am at peace.

Now passively pay attention to your cardiac activity, and then begin repeating the following formulas:

- My heartbeat is calm.
- I am at peace.
- My heartbeat is calm and regular.
- I am at peace.
- My heartbeat is calm and strong.
- I am at peace.

Now passively pay attention to your breathing.

- My breathing is calm.
- I am at peace.
- My breathing is calm and regular.
- I am at peace.
- I breathe comfortably and naturally.
- I am at peace.
- It breathes me.
- I am at peace.

Now pay attention to your upper abdominal cavity, behind the stomach and in front of the spine. Then begin repeating:

- My abdomen is slightly warm.
- I am at peace.
- My abdomen is pleasantly warm.
- I am at peace.
- My abdomen is warm.

Now pay attention to a specific muscle group that may be painful or extremely tense and then begin repeating to yourself:

- Warmth dissolves the pain.
- I am at peace.

At this point you may also wish to shift your attention to another muscle group and begin repeating the formula "warmth dissolves the pain."

- My entire body is comfortably relaxed.
- I am at peace.

Allow yourself a few minutes before ending the session. When you are ready, take a deep breath and as you exhale, flex your arms, stretch out your legs, and open your eyes. Please sit up very slowly. (Make sure that the patient completes the Tension Checklist or the Pain Checklist, Form B, upon finishing the exercise.)

Schultz and Luthe (1969) and Luthe (1970a) reported that approximately 50 percent of their trainees became quite sleepy during the practice of the fifth exercise, and roughly 10 percent actually fell asleep at the conclusion of the session. Therefore, it is quite possible that the first few times patients use this exercise they may experience a profound state of tranquility or may actually fall asleep. Because of this, during home practice, the use of an alarm clock is not recommended as its jarring sound may counteract the beneficial effects of the training. Patients may wish to have someone gently check on them twenty minutes into the exercise, or, if possible, set their alarm clock to play soft music. The use of an additional formula recommended by Lindemann (1973) may be quite helpful to avoid falling asleep. This formula is repeated approximately five to seven times prior to starting the training sequence: After closing the eyes, the patient may repeat, "I stay free and fresh while training" or "I remain calm and alert during the exercise."

Common Difficulties with the Fifth Standard Exercise

Allow me to emphasize once again that patients need to follow certain precautions before engaging in this exercise. Patients initially are advised to use the attenuated forms of the formulas, such as "My abdomen is slightly warm" in order to avoid any unpleasant sensations. With that said, there are usually few problems reported with the practice of this exercise. The special posture developed for the fifth standard exercise is sufficient to help gradually induce a pleasant sensation of warmth in the abdominal cavity. However, patients need to be reminded of resting the right hand very lightly on the upper abdominal region, and only during the first few sessions of training. If the posture or the visualization of drinking a warm liquid do not facilitate the process of warming the abdomen, it may be helpful to have the patient actually drink some warm liquid and focus on his or her sensations as the liquid enters the abdomen.

Benign abdominal sounds usually noticed during the practice of this exercise need to be ignored. It is helpful to mention this to patients before commencing this exercise so that they do not try to suddenly tense their abdomen because of such sounds, since such action results in counterproductive consequences. In most cases, in deep states of relaxation as produced during the practice of the standard exercises, internal and external distractions are rather effortlessly pushed out of conscious awareness. Patients will discover this by themselves after a period of practice, although some instruction early on may prove to be helpful.

Patients also need to be made aware of the tranquilizing nature of this exercise and should be instructed to give themselves ample time to end the exercise appropriately, especially while practicing at home. Some patients report that their muscles become soft and rubbery. They should be cautioned not to stand up too quickly after ending the exercise. Arms may need to be flexed several times to effectively conclude the training session. As with the previous exercises, opening the eyes as one flexes the arms may bring about a greater sense of alertness.

Case Example 1

CG was a 49-year-old security guard who developed severe pain in his lower back due to an injury at work. After approximately three months of grappling with his back pain, CG began experiencing some of the distinct symptoms of fibromyalgia pain syndrome. At times his muscles were so tight that he could hardly stand or sit. His sleep deteriorated significantly and he began experiencing frequent anxiety attacks and became clinically depressed. Initially, a combination of strong pain medications and anxiolytic agents were used to help him cope. Eventually, hydrotherapy became one of his favorite ways of reducing tension in his lower back, but unfortunately the effects were short-lived. During his multidisciplinary treatments he was introduced to autogenic training. He began using the techniques after doing his stretches in the morning, every afternoon, and before going to bed at night.

CG particularly liked the fifth exercise and was able to achieve a high level of relaxation while practicing it. He also noticed that he could effectively use the fifth exercise to more quickly initiate sleep. When his sleep was disrupted due to pain, he could induce the sensations of heaviness and warmth in his extremities by simply repeating "My abdomen is pleasantly warm" and "Warmth makes me sleepy." In time, he was able to use several additional formulas to bring relief to his aching back. He described this exercise as a combination of "a tranquilizer and a pain pill without the grogginess."

Case Example 2

GJ was a 24-year-old woman who suffered from severe dysmenorrhea. Her menstrual pain and cramps were so severe that often times she would become nauseous. In her late teens, as a way of controlling her menstrual symptoms, she was placed on birth control pills that were immensely helpful. However, the pills contributed to the formation of blood clots in her legs, which were fortunately treated immediately and effectively. She wrote to me and asked me if there was anything she could do to control her symptoms as she was becoming desperate and had to stay home for at least two to four days out of every month.

GJ learned the first two standard exercises very quickly and reported they were helpful. We spent more time on the third exercise, which helped her fall asleep at night. It was, however, not until we began the fifth standard exercise when she reported that she was seeing a significant decrease in her cramps and abdominal pain during the practice of this particular exercise. In addition to the formulas for this exercise, I asked her to move her left hand to the lower left quadrant of her abdomen and use the following additional formulas: "My left hand is heavy and warm and ... My lower abdomen is warm and relaxed."

A few weeks later, she amazed herself when while at a meeting, she was able to use the above formulas to calm her symptoms. As it was mentioned earlier in the book, the autogenic formulas form an interconnected set of processes, very much like a chain, whereby activation of the first "ring" will, in time, bring about the activation of the later stages almost at will. For this to happen, patients need to stay motivated and fully master each exercise prior to moving to the next level. Although GJ continued to have some premenstrual symptoms, they became much more manageable and they stopped interfering with her daily activities.

The Autogenic Pain Checklist

Form A

EXERCISE: V (Abdominal Warmth)

INSTRUCTIONS: Complete this form before your autogenic training session. Simply rate your pain levels by circling the number on a scale of 0 to 10. A score of 0 indicates the absence of pain, whereas a score of 10 indicates severe pain in that body part.

1. My right arm is

0	1	2	3	4	5	6	7	8	9	10

2. My left arm is

0	1	2	3	4	5	6	7	8	9	10

3. My shoulders are

0	1	2	3	4	5	6	7	8	9	10

4. My neck is

0	1	2	3	4	5	6	7	8	9	10

5. My forehead is

0	1	2	3	4	5	6	7	8	9	10

6. My jaw is

0	1	2	3	4	5	6	7	8	9	10

7. My chest is

0	1	2	3	4	5	6	7	8	9	10

8. My abdomen is

0	1	2	3	4	5	6	7	8	9	10

9. My lower back is

0	1	2	3	4	5	6	7	8	9	10

10. My right leg is

0	1	2	3	4	5	6	7	8	9	10

11. My left leg is

0	1	2	3	4	5	6	7	8	9	10

12. Overall my body is

0	1	2	3	4	5	6	7	8	9	10

The Autogenic Pain Checklist

Form B

EXERCISE: V (Abdominal Warmth)

INSTRUCTIONS: Complete this form after your autogenic training session. Simply rate your pain levels by circling the number on a scale of 0 to 10. A score of 0 indicates the absence of pain, whereas a score of 10 indicates severe pain in that body part.

1. My right arm is

0	1	2	3	4	5	6	7	8	9	10

2. My left arm is

0	1	2	3	4	5	6	7	8	9	10

3. My shoulders are

0	1	2	3	4	5	6	7	8	9	10

4. My neck is

0	1	2	3	4	5	6	7	8	9	10

5. My forehead is

0	1	2	3	4	5	6	7	8	9	10

6. My jaw is

0	1	2	3	4	5	6	7	8	9	10

7. My chest is

0	1	2	3	4	5	6	7	8	9	10

8. My abdomen is

0	1	2	3	4	5	6	7	8	9	10

9. My lower back is

0	1	2	3	4	5	6	7	8	9	10

10. My right leg is

0	1	2	3	4	5	6	7	8	9	10

11. My left leg is

0	1	2	3	4	5	6	7	8	9	10

12. Overall my body is

0	1	2	3	4	5	6	7	8	9	10

The Autogenic Tension Checklist

Form A

EXERCISE: V (Abdominal Warmth)

INSTRUCTIONS: Complete this form before your autogenic training session. Simply rate your tension levels by circling the number on a scale of 0 to 10. A score of 0 indicates the absence of tension, whereas a score of 10 indicates extreme tension in that body part.

1. My right arm is

0	1	2	3	4	5	6	7	8	9	10

2. My left arm is

0	1	2	3	4	5	6	7	8	9	10

3. My shoulders are

0	1	2	3	4	5	6	7	8	9	10

4. My neck is

0	1	2	3	4	5	6	7	8	9	10

5. My forehead is

0	1	2	3	4	5	6	7	8	9	10

6. My jaw is

0	1	2	3	4	5	6	7	8	9	10

7. My chest is

0	1	2	3	4	5	6	7	8	9	10

8. My abdomen is

0	1	2	3	4	5	6	7	8	9	10

9. My lower back is

0	1	2	3	4	5	6	7	8	9	10

10. My right leg is

0	1	2	3	4	5	6	7	8	9	10

11. My left leg is

0	1	2	3	4	5	6	7	8	9	10

12. Overall my body is

0	1	2	3	4	5	6	7	8	9	10

The Autogenic Tension Checklist

Form B

EXERCISE: V (Abdominal Warmth)

INSTRUCTIONS: Complete this form after your autogenic training session. Simply rate your tension levels by circling the number on a scale of 0 to 10. A score of 0 indicates the absence of tension, whereas a score of 10 indicates extreme tension in that body part.

1. My right arm is

0	1	2	3	4	5	6	7	8	9	10

2. My left arm is

0	1	2	3	4	5	6	7	8	9	10

3. My shoulders are

0	1	2	3	4	5	6	7	8	9	10

4. My neck is

0	1	2	3	4	5	6	7	8	9	10

5. My forehead is

0	1	2	3	4	5	6	7	8	9	10

6. My jaw is

0	1	2	3	4	5	6	7	8	9	10

7. My chest is

0	1	2	3	4	5	6	7	8	9	10

8. My abdomen is

0	1	2	3	4	5	6	7	8	9	10

9. My lower back is

0	1	2	3	4	5	6	7	8	9	10

10. My right leg is

0	1	2	3	4	5	6	7	8	9	10

11. My left leg is

0	1	2	3	4	5	6	7	8	9	10

12. Overall my body is

0	1	2	3	4	5	6	7	8	9	10

13

The Sixth Standard Exercise: Forehead Cooling

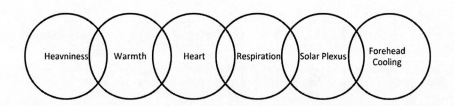

We have now reached the final ring in the chain of the autogenic process, which is forehead cooling. Generally speaking, one method of inducing a tranquilizing and drowsy state is by applying a cool compress to the forehead. A similar sensation is also perceived shortly before falling asleep. Also, people often notice that during active problem solving and intense mental activity the forehead tends to feel much warmer. Conversely, as one quiets his or her mind, a naturally pleasant, cooling sensation over the region of the forehead is experienced. Self-generated reduction in the temperature of the head is the last standard autogenic exercise — an exercise that is also extremely potent and effective. When a sensation of warmth in the trunk is combined with a cooling sensation in the forehead, a profoundly soothing state of relaxation is achieved. Each step of the autogenic training to this point has focused on achieving a psychophysiological state in which effective self-regulation and recovery from pain-induced stress can be attained. The sixth standard exercise further augments this process, although it demands the highest level of passive concentration.

Given the highly tranquilizing nature of this exercise, certain precautions need to be observed. First, to avoid any uncomfortable effects from the use of this exercise, patients need to pay close attention to the images they use to promote the cooling sensation in the forehead region. For example, they must refrain from using any images that suggest the visualization of ice or snow, a cold liquid, or a cold can of soda on the forehead (Luthe, 1979). They should be encouraged to focus on a cooling sensation and not on a cold one. Images suggesting "a cool breeze," "a cool hand placed gently on the forehead," or "a cool cloth on the forehead" can be highly effective. In other words, the cooling sensation must be pleasant and agreeable and conducive to bringing on a tranquil state. Second, this exercise is best practiced while lying down, at least initially. The possible, but brief, negative effects that one may experience are dizziness or possibly disorientation. However, this can be effectively circumvented by using the horizontal posture and by getting up very slowly at the end of the training session. By following these simple instructions, patients can benefit from the many positive effects of the forehead cooling exercise.

Up to this point, the previous exercises have extensively focused on generating a sensation of warmth in the extremities and the abdominal regions. Therefore, the initial attempt to focus on a cooling sensation over the region of the forehead may be difficult. For this reason, I suggest that prior to the first session of practicing the sixth autogenic exercise, it is helpful to perform a simple sensory enhancement technique. For example, a few minutes before starting the exercise, instruct the patients to wet one hand in cool (not cold) water and place it on the forehead. Ask them to focus on the cooling sensation and repeat this two to three times, until they know what to look for during the session. Or, on a cool and pleasant day, you may want to ask them to open the windows and allow a gentle cool breeze to blow over their face. Then have them recall this sensation during the practice of the exercise. It is important for patients to be reassured that it may take days or weeks before they actually experience the cooling of the forehead while repeating the new formula. Emphasize patience and again, at all costs, make sure they avoid thinking about something cold to accelerate the process of training.

Consistent with the other exercises reviewed thus far, after repeating the formulas from the previous exercise, patients are asked to make mental contact with the forehead and simply begin repeating the following standard formula:

• My forehead is cool.

I have found it very helpful to have patients initially use an attenuated form of this formula such as:

• My forehead is slightly cool.
• My forehead is comfortably cool.
• My forehead is pleasantly cool.
• My forehead is cool.

Perhaps the greatest challenge to achieving this final stage of autogenic training is to maintain passive concentration for long enough to reach the objectives of this exercise. This is where the demand for attending passively to the cooling sensation is so great that either people fall asleep or they try too hard to bring about the desired sensation that they become aroused. However, if the principle of passive concentration has been followed effectively to this point, it will be a matter of time before the cooling of the forehead can be achieved and maintained. I cannot emphasize the profound therapeutic benefits that are gained as a result of the practice of these advanced exercises. Often times not only the symptoms that form the focus of the treatment but also other physical and emotional symptoms tend to disappear once one reaches this level of training. Let us recall that the main function of autogenic training is to provide the brain with the optimal opportunity to activate its self-regulatory mechanisms to their fullest so as to promote normalization of the various functions.

In time, as patients begin to master these exercises to their fullest potential, they simply need to repeat one or two formulas or even think about a cooling sensation in the forehead region to activate the entire autogenic process. Until then, it is best to take time and follow a more gradual approach.

After reviewing the pre-exercise checklist and assuming a horizontal position, the training sequence may commence.

The Forehead Cooling Exercise

Remind patients to complete Form A of either the Tension Checklist or the Pain Checklist prior to beginning each session. The following instructions may be read to the patient:

When you are ready, gently close your eyes and then silently begin repeating the following formulas:

- I am quiet and relaxed.
- I am at peace.
- My right arm is heavy and warm.
- I am at peace.
- My left arm is heavy and warm.
- I am at peace.
- Both arms are heavy and warm.
- I am at peace.
- My shoulders are heavy and warm.
- I am at peace.

- My jaw is heavy and relaxed.
- I am at peace.
- My right leg is heavy and warm.
- I am at peace.
- My left leg is heavy and warm.
- I am at peace.
- Both legs are heavy and warm.
- I am at peace.
- My right foot is heavy and warm.
- I am at peace.
- My left foot is heavy and warm.
- I am at peace.
- Both feet are heavy and warm.

Now passively pay attention to your cardiac activity and then begin repeating:

- My heartbeat is calm.
- I am at peace.
- My heartbeat is calm and regular.
- I am at peace.
- My heartbeat is calm and strong.
- I am at peace.

Now passively pay attention to your breathing and then begin repeating:

- My breathing is calm.
- I am at peace.
- My breathing is calm and regular.
- I am at peace.
- I breathe comfortably and naturally.
- I am at peace.
- It breathes me.
- I am at peace.

Now begin paying attention to your upper abdominal cavity and then begin repeating:

- My abdomen is slightly warm.
- I am at peace.
- My abdomen is pleasantly warm.
- I am at peace.
- My abdomen is warm.

You may now wish to pay attention to a specific muscle group and begin repeating the following formula for pain control.

• Warmth dissolves the pain.
• I am at peace.

Give yourself a few moments prior to moving to the forehead cooling formula. You may wish to think of a pleasantly cool breeze brushing against (only) your forehead. Then begin repeating:

• My forehead is slightly cool.
• I am at peace.
• My forehead is pleasantly cool.
• I am at peace.
• My forehead is cool.
• I am at peace.
• My entire body is comfortably relaxed.
• I am at peace.

Give yourself a few minutes to enjoy the soothing sensation of relaxation. You may initially find yourself resisting the need to conclude the exercise, however, if you need to get up and go somewhere, please make sure that you end the exercises after taking a few deep breaths, flexing your arms, stretching out your legs, and opening your eyes. After opening your eyes, wait for a few moments before sitting up. Then give yourself two to three minutes before standing up. (Make sure that the patient completes the Tension Checklist or the Pain Checklist, Form B, upon finishing the exercise.)

Common Difficulties with the Sixth Standard Exercise

By the time patients are ready to begin the sixth standard exercise, they have spent weeks or even months practicing the other five preceding exercises, with the sensation of warmth playing a critical role in their structure. Hence, some difficulty may be experienced in shifting one's attention from soothing warmth to a pleasantly cooling sensation in the region of the forehead. To avoid unnecessary frustration, it is best to dampen the forehead with cool water while exploring the forehead cooling objective of the exercise. Allowing a cool breeze to blow on one's face may be another effective method of achieving the same objective. Such exploratory techniques need to be attempted only a few times prior to performing the exercise. Side effects such as dizziness and disorientation usually disappear quickly at the conclusion of the exercise.

They can be avoided by using attenuated versions of the formula for forehead cooling, such as "My forehead is slightly cool" and "My forehead is pleasantly cool."

As mentioned before, patients should initially perform the sixth standard exercise while in a horizontal position, thus assisting the nervous system to more easily make the necessary adjustments. The cooling of the forehead, when achieved slowly and cautiously, can be a very pleasant exercise with profoundly tranquilizing effects.

Case Example 1

KW is an executive secretary who works at a respected firm and enjoys her work very much. She works hard and is highly respected by her employers. Two years ago, KW was in a terrible motor vehicle accident in which the emergency crew required over an hour to rescue her from the wreckage of her car. Fortunately, her physical injuries were not that serious and she was able to recover relatively quickly. However, KW began developing some disturbing symptoms of post-traumatic stress disorder. Perhaps one of her worst symptoms manifested itself in her need to have fresh air blown on her face. Although this was a manageable problem at home, it was extremely difficult to cope with at work. She related to me that while at home, if she became anxious, she needed only to open one of the windows and spend a few minutes cooling her head. This, however, was not an easy option at work. She worked on the tenth floor of a building with sealed windows, and her only choice was to go all the way to the first floor to cope with her need for air. (In time she discovered an open window in the maintenance area on the second floor which she referred to as her "rescue window.") Another factor that complicated the situation was that at such times, she became very claustrophobic and could not ride the elevator to the first floor. Going down the steps was also problematic because of her aching back and sensitive knees (the result of the accident). She always carried tranquilizers with her which, unfortunately, had certain side effects and interfered with her work.

KW learned to quickly put some of the autogenic formulas into use to cope with her symptoms of pain and post-traumatic stress disorder. However, the sixth standard exercise became her favorite because it allowed her to experience a tranquil state of relaxation very similar to putting her head out the window. She now quite effectively practices the forehead cooling exercise while sitting up. Because of her resolve and determination, she continues to make good and steady progress.

Case Example 2

I first saw EH when he was in his late 50s, and wanted to better manage his stress and chronic headaches. He learned the standard exercises in approximately six months and was pleased with the results. Later, he was able to put the exercises to use after the traumatic loss of a family member, which caused him to have frequent disturbing dreams. We met again and I was able to teach him some additional autogenic exercises. He was adept at reaching the forehead cooling exercise in a matter of minutes. Not only did he experience symptom relief, he also regained his self-confidence.

Nearly 10-years after I last saw him, I was informed by a member of his family that EH was hospitalized in the oncology floor, perhaps living the last days of his life. When I visited him he was in a great deal of pain. At times he felt very warm and distressed by it. A gentle nurse frequently placed a cool compress on his forehead, which seemed to help him get some relief. Sadly, the other nurses did not know that this helped him rest better. He was not coherent all the time; however, the second time I visited him, he was very responsive. I gently took him through several autogenic formulas. He began to relax rather quickly. When we reached "My forehead is pleasantly cool," he smiled and his entire face began to relax. During the last few days of his life, he could achieve the cooling of the forehead rather quickly. Because he could lower the pain at least somewhat, he did not require as much pain medication. This allowed him to have a more meaningful interaction with his family in his last days. He did not require the cool compress on his forehead while he was conscious as he was able to generate the pleasant, cooling sensation almost at will.

The Autogenic Pain Checklist

Form A

EXERCISE: VI (Forehead Cooling)

Instructions: Complete this form before your autogenic training session. Simply rate your pain levels by circling the number on a scale of 0 to 10. A score of 0 indicates the absence of pain, whereas a score of 10 indicates severe pain in that body part.

1. My right arm is

0	1	2	3	4	5	6	7	8	9	10

2. My left arm is

0	1	2	3	4	5	6	7	8	9	10

3. My shoulders are

0	1	2	3	4	5	6	7	8	9	10

4. My neck is

0	1	2	3	4	5	6	7	8	9	10

5. My forehead is

0	1	2	3	4	5	6	7	8	9	10

6. My jaw is

0	1	2	3	4	5	6	7	8	9	10

7. My chest is

0	1	2	3	4	5	6	7	8	9	10

8. My abdomen is

0	1	2	3	4	5	6	7	8	9	10

9. My lower back is

0	1	2	3	4	5	6	7	8	9	10

10. My right leg is

0	1	2	3	4	5	6	7	8	9	10

11. My left leg is

0	1	2	3	4	5	6	7	8	9	10

12. Overall my body is

0	1	2	3	4	5	6	7	8	9	10

The Autogenic Pain Checklist

Form B

EXERCISE: VI (Forehead Cooling)

INSTRUCTIONS: Complete this form after your autogenic training session. Simply rate your pain levels by circling the number on a scale of 0 to 10. A score of 0 indicates the absence of pain, whereas a score of 10 indicates severe pain in that body part.

1. My right arm is

0	1	2	3	4	5	6	7	8	9	10

2. My left arm is

0	1	2	3	4	5	6	7	8	9	10

3. My shoulders are

0	1	2	3	4	5	6	7	8	9	10

4. My neck is

0	1	2	3	4	5	6	7	8	9	10

5. My forehead is

0	1	2	3	4	5	6	7	8	9	10

6. My jaw is

0	1	2	3	4	5	6	7	8	9	10

7. My chest is

0	1	2	3	4	5	6	7	8	9	10

8. My abdomen is

0	1	2	3	4	5	6	7	8	9	10

9. My lower back is

0	1	2	3	4	5	6	7	8	9	10

10. My right leg is

0	1	2	3	4	5	6	7	8	9	10

11. My left leg is

0	1	2	3	4	5	6	7	8	9	10

12. Overall my body is

0	1	2	3	4	5	6	7	8	9	10

The Autogenic Tension Checklist

Form A

EXERCISE: VI (Forehead Cooling)

INSTRUCTIONS: Complete this form before your autogenic training session. Simply rate your tension levels by circling the number on a scale of 0 to 10. A score of 0 indicates the absence of tension, whereas a score of 10 indicates extreme tension in that body part.

1. My right arm is

0	1	2	3	4	5	6	7	8	9	10

2. My left arm is

0	1	2	3	4	5	6	7	8	9	10

3. My shoulders are

0	1	2	3	4	5	6	7	8	9	10

4. My neck is

0	1	2	3	4	5	6	7	8	9	10

5. My forehead is

0	1	2	3	4	5	6	7	8	9	10

6. My jaw is

0	1	2	3	4	5	6	7	8	9	10

7. My chest is

0	1	2	3	4	5	6	7	8	9	10

8. My abdomen is

0	1	2	3	4	5	6	7	8	9	10

9. My lower back is

0	1	2	3	4	5	6	7	8	9	10

10. My right leg is

0	1	2	3	4	5	6	7	8	9	10

11. My left leg is

0	1	2	3	4	5	6	7	8	9	10

12. Overall my body is

0	1	2	3	4	5	6	7	8	9	10

The Autogenic Tension Checklist

Form B

EXERCISE: VI (Forehead Cooling)

INSTRUCTIONS: Complete this form after your autogenic training session. Simply rate your tension levels by circling the number on a scale of 0 to 10. A score of 0 indicates the absence of tension, whereas a score of 10 indicates extreme tension in that body part.

1. My right arm is

0	1	2	3	4	5	6	7	8	9	10

2. My left arm is

0	1	2	3	4	5	6	7	8	9	10

3. My shoulders are

0	1	2	3	4	5	6	7	8	9	10

4. My neck is

0	1	2	3	4	5	6	7	8	9	10

5. My forehead is

0	1	2	3	4	5	6	7	8	9	10

6. My jaw is

0	1	2	3	4	5	6	7	8	9	10

7. My chest is

0	1	2	3	4	5	6	7	8	9	10

8. My abdomen is

0	1	2	3	4	5	6	7	8	9	10

9. My lower back is

0	1	2	3	4	5	6	7	8	9	10

10. My right leg is

0	1	2	3	4	5	6	7	8	9	10

11. My left leg is

0	1	2	3	4	5	6	7	8	9	10

12. Overall my body is

0	1	2	3	4	5	6	7	8	9	10

14
Advanced Autogenic Training

Autogenic training may be viewed as a dynamic, multidimensional form of mind-body treatment whose many facets can be explored for a variety of needs and purposes. The applications of this self-regulatory approach are indeed vast as well as highly useful in a variety of clinical settings. However, the key is the mastery of standard exercises as all of its variations emerge from these basic steps. Approximately six to eight weeks after beginning the first standard autogenic exercise and after patients have achieved the basic objectives of each of the exercises (sensations of heaviness and warmth in the extremities, etc.), they may be ready for some of the more abbreviated forms of autogenic training, which will be discussed next. This chapter also includes some of the more advanced formulas that build upon the initial training that was explored previously. Therefore, before using the information explored in this chapter, patients are urged to first master the standard exercises.

After some steady practice with the autogenic exercises, most people will be able to activate the chain of responses that are generated in the standard exercises in a matter of minutes. This will be especially helpful just before or shortly after exposure to stressful situations. In a way, the advanced exercises may be viewed as methods of rapid refueling and replenishing one's psychophysiological resources. Although it is prudent to continue to use the standard exercises for a while, benefits of the training can be summoned quickly and effectively with the repetition of some key formulas. In time it is possible to initiate sleep much more quickly with the use of these advanced formulas. These formulas can also be helpful in reducing the number of sleep interruptions chronic pain patients and those grappling with extreme stress experience on a regular basis. Mothers with young children often report that they appreciate more restful sleep while using some of the advanced formulas.

Many of my patients, especially those who suffer from chronic fatigue syndrome, have noted that instead of taking ineffective naps, they have been able to replenish themselves and gain more physical and cognitive stamina by using these (advanced) autogenic formulas. Some of these patients have reported that ten to fifteen minutes of autogenic training is more "energizing" than an hour or more of napping, which often causes them to feel more tired and "groggy." I usually instruct patients to refuel as often as possible so that they can enjoy more of their daily activities. Despite these helpful techniques, the advanced formulas are not a replacement for a good night's rest and the regular practice of the standard exercises.

One of the main focuses of these advanced exercises is to more quickly generalize the sensation of heaviness and warmth. Instead of repeating six or eight formulas, one can learn to achieve the same results by repeating only three or four formulas.

The Abbreviated Sequence for Replenishment

During the practice of the abbreviated exercises, while one can use the specific postures that were described before, it is best to learn an additional sitting posture that can promote almost an instant state of relaxation, especially in the upper body portion (see Photograph 14.1). Patients are instructed to sit in a comfortable position with their feet firmly placed on the floor. Next, they are asked to close their eyes, and after taking a deep breath, exhale and allow the arms to go limp. The head is gently dropped down and is maintained in this position while comfortable breathing is encouraged. The image of this relaxing position is known as the "rag doll" posture.

For this posture, patients may be provided with the following instructions:

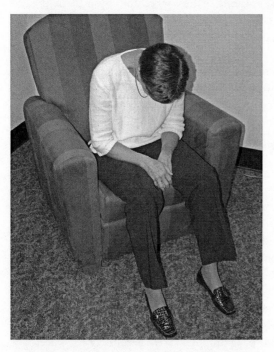

Photograph 14.1. The "rag doll" sitting position.

Imagine that a thread is attached to the top of your

head that holds your head and neck in an upright position. Your shoulders are slightly pulled back and your arms are comfortably hanging next to your trunk. Next, imagine that the thread is cut and at once your body falls into a limp and tension-free position. To further enhance the relaxing effects of this posture, slightly lift up your right arm, inhale slowly, and as you exhale let your arm become totally limp. Imagine that your arm is so limp that at this point it would be very difficult for you to move it. Now slightly lift up your left arm, inhale slowly, and as you exhale let your arm become totally limp. Now gently lift up your shoulders, inhale deeply, and as you exhale let your shoulders drop totally and allow them to assume a very limp and relaxed position. Breathe comfortably and naturally. When you are ready, begin repeating to yourself the following formulas:

- I am at peace.
- My arms (as you naturally inhale) are heavy and warm, (as you naturally exhale)
- My neck and shoulders (inhale) are heavy and warm, (exhale)
- Both legs (inhale) are heavy and warm, (exhale)
- My breathing (inhale) is effortless, (exhale)
- It breathes me.
- My entire body (inhale) is limp and relaxed, (exhale)
- My mind is quiet.
- My body is healing.
- I am at peace.

You may end the exercise by taking a deep breath, shaking your arms and repeating to yourself: "I feel refreshed and energized. My body is strong and full of vitality."

As with the previous exercises, make sure that patients get up very slowly during the abbreviated exercise as well. This abbreviated exercise can be done in less than ten minutes. Patients should make room in their schedule to practice it at least three times per day. They are also instructed not to wait until they are totally exhausted to practice these or any other techniques. It is better to have brief "refueling" sessions throughout the day than to expect full rejuvenation in the evening. As it will be discussed in Chapter 16 on sleep, total exhaustion actually prevents people from entering the deeper, recuperative stages of sleep. Therefore, it is best to include autogenic training into one's daily routine on a regular basis.

From time to time, some patients report that while using the rag doll posture, they notice a tightening of their jaw muscles. This could especially be noticed by those who suffer from Tempromandibular Joint Disorder

(TMJD). This type of tension can significantly interfere with the exercise and either weaken its effectiveness or simply render it useless altogether. This concern can be easily rectified if the following adjustments are made. Upon relaxing the neck and the head, when the face is pointing down, pay close attention to the position of the upper and the lower teeth. If the teeth are touching, this suggests a tense, anatomically unnatural, and definitely not relaxed position that is bound to add undue stress to the jaw muscles and its joints. By simply allowing a small space to form between the upper and the lower teeth, the joints begin to relax. This position needs to be maintained for the duration of the exercise. One helpful mental tool to promote proper positioning is to imagine there is a small, soft object between the teeth, preventing them from touching. A small orthodontic appliance may also be useful for this purpose if it is securely placed in the mouth, but it is not necessary when the above instructions are closely observed.

The Use of the Organ-Specific Formulas

The depth and effectiveness of autogenic training can be enhanced through the use of advanced formulas, whose very task is to bring about specific psychophysiological changes to improve symptom management and recovery from stress induced conditions. Once the standard autogenic exercises have been fully mastered, these additional formulas may be introduced to affect the functioning of specific body systems. These formulas are called "organ-specific" and their effects are consistent with those observed during the regular training. The introduction of these additional formulas has been found to be useful, especially when greater attention is needed for normalization of a specific organ, for example the lungs or the gastrointestinal tract. As with the previous formulas, patients should be cautioned not to change the wording of the formulas to achieve particular results. These formulas emerged from years of research and observation and their effects have been examined in numerous studies.

Some of the organ-specific formulas are shown in Table 14.1. They are usually introduced toward the end of a training session after the sensations of heaviness and warmth have been effectively established. Some of the following formulas were adapted from the work of Schultz and Luthe (1969, p. 177). Additional formulas are based on my own research. Patients should use these formulas with care and after they have been medically examined for the possible underlying causes of their condition. Prior to repeating each formula, it is imperative that mental contact is made with the specific organs. For example, for muscle pain in the right leg, one needs to make sure that mental con tact is made with the leg prior to repeating the formula: "Warmth dissolves the pain." One of the side effects of certain antidepressants is that of dry mouth. The organ-specific formula, "Saliva flows naturally," is highly effective in reestablishing saliva production in such cases. I also had success using this formula with a patient who had a severe dry mouth after receiving radiation for cancer of the jaw.

Table 14.1. Organ-specific formulas.

Symptoms and Conditions	*Organ-Specific Formulas*
• Constipation	My lower abdomen is warm.*
	My pelvis is warm and relaxed.*
• Mild asthma	My chest is comfortably warm.†
	Breathing is effortless.
• Heart palpitations	My heartbeat is calm and easy.*
	I am relaxed and at ease.
• Hypertension	My forehead is agreeably cool.*
	My feet are warm.
• Premenstrual cramps	My abdomen is calm and warm.
	Cramps are calm and easy.
• Raynaud's syndrome	My fingers are warm.*
	The tips of my fingers are warm and relaxed.
• Muscle pain	Warmth dissolves the pain.
	My pain is dissolving.
• Insomnia	It sleeps me.
	Warmth makes me sleepy.*
• Tingling and paresthesia	My nerves function properly.
• Restless legs	My legs are warm and smooth.
	Warmth dissolves the tension. My legs are warm and tension free.
• Hemorrhoids	My anus is heavy.*
	My anus is cool.*
	My bowels move smoothly.
• TMJ	My jaw is heavy and relaxed.
• Dry mouth	Saliva flows naturally.

*From Schultz and Luthe (1959).
†Not to be used during an asthma attack.

The Use of the Intentional Formulas

Up to this point, every formula has been based on bringing about psychophysiological changes or enhancing the functioning of a certain physiological system. Although the intentional formulas can be used in the same manner, their primary purpose is to reinforce changes in behavior and provide further support for mental and physical well-being. As one reviews these formulas, it may seem that they tend to be more like affirmations or helpful suggestions that can make day-to-day living less stressful. However, these formulas are more than simple, self-improvement affirmations, and with effective use they can bring about important changes, especially in patients who suffer from chronic pain and chronic fatigue. Think of them as behavior modification strategies that are highly focused and are consistent with the basic premise of autogenic training, which is normalization through the activation of self-regulatory mechanisms.

Schultz and Luthe (1969) provide a list of intentional formulas that are both helpful and interesting. In this section I present only a select few of their suggestions that pertain to the topic of the treatment at hand. In clinical practice, I have used only a few intentional formulas as my work has been more specifically focused on treating psychophysiological symptoms. I have also introduced several of my own formulas with a focus on recovery from chronic conditions. One intentional formula that I have used to help some anxious students with recall of information during tests is: "I recall effortlessly." Many fibromyalgia patients who often experience what is known as the "fibro-fog" have also reported that the formulas have been of great use to them. Since these individuals (students and FMS patients) were well trained in the autogenic exercises prior to the use of this formula, they were also asked to consider repeating, "I am at peace," in conjunction with the intentional formula. Hence the following sequence: "I recall effortlessly and I am at peace."

If practitioners choose to use the intentional formulas in clinical practice, it is important that they observe the same guidelines that were indicated with the organ-specific formulas. Remember that initially patients should use these formulas after promoting a sensation of heaviness and warmth in their extremities by repeating some of the preliminary, standard formulas. Patients should refrain from creating their own formulas to avoid any paradoxical phenomena that may inadvertently occur during the treatment, especially when the patient is not under clinical supervision. Table 14.2 summarizes a set of nine intentional formulas. It is important to note that only one (symptom-focused) intentional formula at a time should be introduced to promote its assimilation.

Table 14.2. Intentional formulas.

Symptoms and Conditions	Intentional Formula
• Difficulty swallowing	My throat is wide and relaxed.* Swallowing is easy.
• Compulsivity	I need not be perfect.* Details do not matter.*

- Shortness of breath   I breathe effortlessly.
                               I breathe comfortably and naturally.
- Feeling mentally blocked   Thoughts flow freely.
                               My mind is calm and clear.
- Restless legs   Restless legs do not bother me.
                               It sleeps me.*
- Recovery after surgery   My body is healing.
                               I am calm and relaxed. Recovery comes naturally.
                               Every day I am stronger.
- Tremors due to anxiety   I am calm and still.
                               My body is quiet.
- Ear noises   The ringing is fading away.
                               I need not fight the noise.
- Mental "fogginess"   I think clearly.
                               I am fresh and alert.†
- Difficulties with memory   I recall effortlessly.

*From Schultz and Luthe (1969).
†From Lindemann (1973).

The Technique of Autogenic Meditation

The term meditation often conjures up images from the Eastern world, often suggesting the repetition of secret mantras, yoga positions, and other visual connotations. The word meditation actually comes from its Latin root *Meditatio*, which suggests focused thinking. Autogenic meditation has nothing in common with ancient, religious practices and is in reality an extension of the standard exercises that requires greater, focused attention to mental phenomena such as visualization of colors, objects, images, etc. In this sense, it may be viewed as a unique method of profoundly enhancing mind-body integration, and is often introduced after the patient has reached a point where he or she can effortlessly enter into the autogenic state with the repetition of a few formulas. I have often reserved this approach for patients who, after approximately a year of practice, approach me and ask if there is more to learn. Others may stay with the standard exercises and benefit from their recuperative properties for many years without incorporating autogenic meditation into their daily practice.

Autogenic meditation relies heavily on the use of visual phenomena and the elicitation of certain feelings and concepts in a systematic fashion to promote a more advanced state of autogenic (normalization) process. This process further allows various body systems to achieve their optimum functioning through a process of "unloading" the nervous system, which occurs naturally during certain stages of sleep (Luthe, 1973). From the perspective of autogenic training, hence, dreams act as mechanisms through which excessive neuronal activity is discharged and the central nervous system is allowed the opportunity for re-establishing homeostasis.

There are seven meditative exercises:

1. The automatic or spontaneous visualization of colors
2. The visualization of suggested colors
3. The visualization of definable or concrete objects
4. The visualization of certain concepts
5. The experience of a state of feeling
6. Visualization of other people
7. The insight meditation, in which answers to certain questions are explored

Since more detailed explorations of the meditative exercises are beyond the scope of this book, I will only address the processes involved in the first four meditative states. It is my clinical opinion that meditative exercises five, six, and seven should not be attempted without psychotherapeutic support. These exercises may elicit feelings and images that will require exploration and clinical interpretation. Therefore, I will only briefly review these in this section.

Again, the introduction of the meditation is contingent upon the total command over the practice of the standard exercises. Passive concentration plays an even more crucial role here, and if it is not mastered, one should not attempt these advanced techniques. The duration of practice is another important element to keep in mind, as in time it may be required to maintain a state of passive concentration from a few minutes up to an hour. In other words, the exercises should not be rushed.

Meditative Exercise 1: Automatic or Spontaneous Visualization of Colors

The main objective of the first meditative exercise is to promote the spontaneous emergence of fixed colors in the entire visual field. During the practice of the standard exercises, it is likely that the patient might have experienced seeing certain "background" colors from time to time. Here, more direct attention is paid to this visual phenomenon which may serve as an effective method for further deepening the autogenic state. Prior to beginning the first meditative exercise, it is imperative to enter the autogenic state by repeating several of the key formulas.

The following abbreviated sequence may be used for the first meditative exercise. Each formula is repeated five to seven times.

- I am at peace.
- My arms are heavy and warm.
- My shoulders are heavy and warm.
- My legs are heavy and warm.
- My heartbeat is calm and regular.
- My breathing is calm and regular.
- It breathes me.
- My abdomen is pleasantly warm.
- My forehead is pleasantly cool.
- I am at peace.

After repeating these formulas, with eyes closed, patients are asked to allow colors to spontaneously appear in their visual field. Initially they may see total darkness or a "grayish" color. Instruct them to passively observe these colors and emphasize that they should not force themselves to see any particular colors. Gradually, particular uniform or static colors will begin to fill the entire visual field. Once this occurs, they have entered the first meditative state. Keep in mind that at first it may take a while before spontaneous colors begin to emerge. Patients need to be instructed to be patient and allow the process to take shape at its own pace. An important observation by many who have performed this exercise is that in time they begin to see a specific color that appears each time they enter this state. This may be viewed as the patient's "own color" and in time it may be noticed effortlessly as soon as entering the meditative state. It may also serve to signal whether he or she has reached this state. Until this personal color begins to appear spontaneously, one should not look for it. Meanwhile, the ability to maintain a complete level of passivity is extremely crucial. I recommend staying with the first meditative exercise for several weeks prior to progressing to the next level.

When a patient has mastered the autogenic exercises and has been able to visualize his or her color quickly, further abbreviation of the formulas can be used to facilitate the autogenic process in a matter of minutes, with profound benefits. Here is a set of highly abbreviated formulas that can be used by those who have reached advanced levels of training. Again, this approach may be used by those who have been able to generate and visualize their own color after the repetition of general formulas.

- My body is quiet and relaxed.
- I am at peace.
- My arms are heavy and warm.

- My legs are heavy and warm.
- I am at peace.
- My color appears spontaneously.

Meditative Exercise 2: The Visualization of Suggested Colors

The practice of the second meditative exercise can be significantly facilitated with the help of a therapist who can instruct the patient to focus on specific or prescribed colors. However, by following certain instructions and adhering to them, patients can learn to master this state quite effectively in a short while and on their own. As with the first meditative exercise, patients need to begin this exercise by entering the autogenic state and repeating some of the introductory formulas. Please remember that patients should not attempt to enter the mediative state unless they have achieved the basic objectives of each of the standard exercises. After they have completed the repetition of the introductory formulas, I recommend repeating an intentional formula that I have specially developed for the second exercise. This formula is to be repeated for a minute or two before entering the second meditative state and is as follows: "Colors appear naturally and freely." This formula may also serve as an anchor for those occasions when patients find themselves drifting or focusing on unrelated thoughts or sensations. As soon as they become aware of being distracted, instruct them to simply and passively repeat this formula four or five times.

The following introductory and intentional formulas need to be repeated prior to the second meditative exercise:

- I am at peace.
- My arms are heavy and warm.
- My shoulders are heavy and warm.
- My legs are heavy and warm.
- My heartbeat is calm and regular.
- It breathes me.
- My abdomen is pleasantly warm.
- My forehead is pleasantly cool.
- My mind is quiet.
- I am at peace.
- Colors appear naturally and freely.

Prior to starting the second exercise, it is helpful to pre-plan focusing on specific colors. For example, the patient (or as suggested by the therapist) may choose to visualize the color yellow, and then to shift to visualizing a different shade of yellow and then work toward other colors. The patient may use the following helpful suggestion to make the transition to this exercise much smoother. The therapist may read the following statement to the patient:

> Please follow these instructions very closely to avoid the experience of undue tension. As you enter the first meditative state and your color begins to appear, plan to visualize a slightly different shade of your color. It is best, at least initially, not to try to visualize a color that is totally different. For example, if your spontaneous color is dark blue, do not immediately start thinking about bright red or orange. Consider something such as a brighter tone of blue or a darker shade of blue or dark purple. Then gradually begin moving toward visualizing different colors. As a particular color that you have been preplanning begins to appear, allow it to slowly move from one end of your field of vision to the other, very much like moving clouds. In a more advanced state of this exercise, you may begin combining different colors (beginning with different shades), allowing them to merge and move. (I call this the rainbow clouds, which requires a significant amount of practice.)

It is suggested that the initial practice of the second meditative exercise be limited to no longer than twenty minutes. With each subsequent session, the patient may be encouraged to begin adding five to ten minutes to each additional practice period, never exceeding a total of sixty minutes. If performed correctly, the meditative exercises can be restorative and energizing, very much like having a good night's rest.

To fully appreciate the benefits of the second meditative exercise, patients should be instructed to practice several times a week for at least a month, and possibly longer, before proceeding to the next stage of training. It is not prudent to rush the process at any time, or for any reason. Patients are ready to move to the next exercise when they can effortlessly visualize a variety of selected (or predetermined by the therapist) colors with a sense of motion.

Meditative Exercise 3: The Visualization of Definable or Concrete Objects

The third meditative exercise is much more challenging than the previous two exercises and should be practiced with patience and perseverance. Any attempt to hasten the process may result in frustration or may even generate an uncomfortably anxious state. The visualization of specific, concrete, and definable objects is initially rather difficult. Although by now patients might have reported experiencing the transitory appearance of various, shapeless images, the main focus at this point is to visualize specific objects. It is best to start with simple and familiar objects. Such objects may include a box, a comb, a cross, or the Star of David. Objects which evoke a strong emotional response should be avoided. I recall a patient who began experiencing profound guilt while visualizing a crucifix. She reported that the image reminded her that the last time she had gone to confession was over a year ago. She was instructed to choose another image that did not elicit such emotions.

Patients should choose a specific object prior to the first few sessions of practice. The importance of passive concentration cannot be overemphasized. Again, patients should be instructed not to force themselves to see anything. After repeating the introductory formulas and entering the autogenic state, they should allow "their color" to appear. They may then move to the second meditative state by allowing a cloudlike spectrum of colors to emerge in their field of vision. Once this point has been reached, they are ready to begin the third meditative state. Patients may begin this next step by passively thinking about the object they had planned to visualize at the beginning of the exercise. The following instructions may be helpful to share with the patient:

> Allow the object to appear spontaneously. This may take some time initially, and it is quite likely that the images may appear briefly and disappear without a trace. Another common occurrence is that as soon as you begin seeing the object, it begins to drift out of your field of vision. Do not become frustrated! As you continue to maintain a state of passive concentration, the object of choice will begin to materialize and remain in your field of vision for a much longer period. In time, other predetermined objects may be visualized with greater ease and spontaneity.

For those who have some difficulty with this exercise, I have developed a simple intentional formula that can be helpful in promoting a state of passive concentration and in facilitating the process of visualization. In case of persistent distraction, the formula can also be used as a means of refocusing. After repeating the introductory formulas, patients may repeat: "Objects appear spontaneously, effortlessly."

Here is a sequence of formulas that may be used for the third meditative exercise:

- I am at peace.
- My arms are heavy and warm.
- My shoulders are heavy and warm.
- My legs are heavy and warm.
- My heartbeat is calm and regular.
- It breathes me.
- My abdomen is pleasantly warm.
- My forehead is pleasantly cool.

- My mind is quiet.
- I am at peace.
- Objects appear spontaneously.
- Objects appear effortlessly.
- I am at peace.

As with the previous exercise, patients need to be instructed to make sure that they end the exercise session by taking a deep breath and opening and flexing their arms vigorously. Many patients report that as they advance in the meditative exercises, they begin to experience a state of mental clarity and calmness at the conclusion of the period of practice. Nevertheless, it is best to encourage them to take their time and refrain from immediately involving themselves in any form of physically or mentally arduous activity.

Meditative Exercise 4: The Visualization of Certain Concepts

The practice of the fourth meditative exercise will require patience and sensitivity to images, sounds, and possibly certain sensations. The main focus of the exercise is on visualizing certain concepts such as beauty, freedom, peace, and tranquility. It is highly recommended that patients choose a single word (concept) and focus on that particular word during the entire session. If patients have followed the instructions for the previous sessions to the letter, they will find that the fourth exercise can bring their ability for visualization to new heights. Several of my patients discovered that they were quite artistically inclined as a result of using this and the previous meditative exercises. It is critical, however, that patients choose concepts that are pleasant and contain a renewing virtue. At first they may see colors and tones that depict a certain concept (for example, white for freedom). As the meditation process deepens, they may actually begin to see flowing, dreamlike images. Certain sensations may follow these images, and as long as they are positive in nature they should be allowed to emerge. For those who have difficulty visualizing these abstract images, it may be helpful to either visualize the word (the concept) or have them silently repeat it to themselves several times and then quietly watch what happens. As always, it is of therapeutic value for patients to make note of the images that reach their consciousness and observe how they evolve from session to session.

After repeating the sequence of the suggested formulas, patients may either repeat the concept they wish to visualize or see its letters, as if appearing in their visual field. They may, for example, see in bold colors PEACE. Or merely repeat, "Peace ... (Pause) Peace ... (Pause) ... Peace," and then allow images to gradually emerge.

The following sequence of formulas may be used for the third meditative exercise:

- I am at peace.
- My arms are heavy and warm.
- My shoulders are heavy and warm.
- My legs are heavy and warm.
- My heartbeat is calm and regular.
- It breathes me.
- My abdomen is pleasantly warm.
- My forehead is pleasantly cool.
- My mind is quiet.
- I am at peace.

(The predetermined concept may be repeated five to seven times at this juncture prior to its visualization. One may repeat, "Peace ... Peace ... Peace...").

The exercise is concluded by taking a deep breath, flexing the arms and opening the eyes.

About the Next Three Meditative Exercises

As I mentioned earlier, the other three meditative exercises will be briefly discussed in this section because I strongly feel that they should be practiced in the presence of a trained psychotherapist. The fifth exercise, for instance, which focuses on the experience of a selected state of feeling, may require patients to discuss and explore some feelings that emerge during this exercise. This does not mean that they should only worry about experiencing negative feelings. For this exercise to serve its therapeutic purposes, it is extremely helpful to discuss any emerging feelings at the end of the session. Similarly, the visualization of a person (Exercise 6) and the insight-seeking meditation (Exercise 7) require patients to have the opportunity to explore their thoughts and images with someone who can help explore them. The other four meditative exercises require plenty of time and attention and should provide ample therapeutic benefits.

Meditative Exercise 5: The Experience of a State of Feeling

During the fifth meditative exercise, patients are instructed to focus on a selected state of feeling. They may be instructed to passively imagine a beautiful sunset and experience the feelings promoted by this visualization. Because feelings and emotions tend to be dynamic, the patient may spontaneously move from one feeling to another. During this exercise, images may also change and subsequently feelings may reach a certain intensity without warning. Feelings of elation and sadness may be experienced from one moment to the next and these feelings may need to be psychotherapeutically processed. The proper use of this exercise can have many psychological and physiological benefits. In a number of cases, I was surprised to hear my patients use the term "cleansing" as a way of describing their general mental state after the session when this meditative exercise was implemented. A few others used the term "freed" at the end of the exercise. In all of these, a corrective process especially at an emotional level had taken place. The correction, in most cases, brought about improvements in physical symptoms if they were present. After some experience with the fifth meditative exercise in a clinical setting, some patients choose to use it on their own. If this is the case, I recommend that patients keep a journal to record their experiences for the purpose of processing their experiences.

Meditative Exercise 6: Visualization of Other People

The sixth meditative exercise is a significant departure from the other standard and meditative exercises in that its focus is on another person. In other words, there is a shift from self-focus to other-focus. The long-term practice of this exercise can bring about changes in the patient's attitude toward others, such as a deepening of their compassion and empathy. To see the world through the eyes of the other is a very powerful experience that can have profound interpersonal implications. However, Schultz and Luthe (1959) wisely recommend that initially, the patient should focus on "neutral" images of people, for example the mailman, or the custodial staff. The use of neutral images is suggested to avoid any sudden experience of emotionally charged experiences that may dissuade one from further exploring the benefits of this exercise. Almost invariably, my advanced patients report that they begin experiencing a state very similar to dreaming as the images of other people become clearer and unmistakably real. At times such images may shift from one person to another. At other times, while the foreground is focused on the face or the upper torso of the imagined person, the background may change and produce a very different emotional state. Patients' experiences may range from anger and hostility to feelings of love, longing, and compassion. Many patients who suffer from pain due to a motor vehicle accident (especially those with post-traumatic stress disorder), with the subsequent post-traumatic symptoms, find this exercise helpful in resolving their feelings toward the other driver. Because of the potent nature of the imagery that this exercise tends to evoke, I recommend that it is implemented in a clinical setting and under the supervision of a physician or a psychotherapist who can intervene if necessary. As I mentioned above, attitudinal changes are quite common after the practice of this meditative exercise. Some patients have also reported that they felt some deep-seated emotionally charged, interpersonal issues were resolved with its use.

Meditative Exercise 7: The Insight Meditation

I refer to this final meditative exercise as the "insight meditation," instead of answers from the unconscious, in order to take away some of the esoteric images and concepts that patients may conjure up when they hear that they are going to receive "answers" from their unconscious mind. In a sense, this exercise may be viewed as a form of free association with a strong potential for psychotherapeutic benefits. After entering the autogenic state by means of the repetition of the abbreviated formulas, patients are asked to passively focus on answers to questions such as "What are my needs?" or "How can I improve my recovery?" The freely elicited responses should be explored and therapeutically processed at the end of the session. Some patients may experience an anxious state during this exercise because of the "cryptic" nature of their answers. Hence, much like dream interpretation, they may require assistance in deciphering their thoughts and images. I highly recommend journaling after the session as this activity by itself helps with the processing of such mental activities and may reveal their deeper meaning in the process of journaling and passive reflection.

Some Final Thoughts About the Meditative Exercises

An important point about the meditative exercises that cannot be overemphasized is that they are a natural extension of the standard exercises. Remember that the main purpose of autogenic training is to promote a brain-directed state of repair and recuperation. The best word to capture the training is "homeostasis" — a state of balance. Basic autogenic training suggests that exposure to prolonged stress or the experience of trauma may significantly interfere with the body's self-restorative capabilities. With the assistance of specific formulas that reinforce, enhance, and accentuate a process of repair, we can reestablish a state of mind-body balance which accelerates recovery. Some of the theoretical concepts of autogenic training, which evolved into the development of the training formulas, were inspired by observations regarding the various functions of sleep — its physical, psychological, and emotional properties (Luthe, 1973). It has been observed that many of the sensations that occur during a pre-sleep state are almost completely consistent with the objectives of the standard formulas: muscular relaxation, peripheral warmth, changes in breathing, etc. As one enters the various stages of sleep, many psychological and physical phenomena continue to occur, each of which play an important role. As it will be discussed later, during deep or Stage 4 sleep certain biochemicals that promote healing are replenished. During the REM stage of sleep, where much of dreaming takes place, significant changes in the activities of the higher functions of the brain with their concomitant cognitive and physiological effects are made manifest. Pain, stress, worries, and the experience of traumatic events can significantly interfere with some of the natural processes that take place during sleep. With the use of the standard autogenic formulas, patients can be assisted in removing some of the sources of such interference. The meditative exercises foster various recuperative processes, especially those that occur during dreaming. These exercises are similar to the unloading phenomenon in which physical, biochemical, and emotional events that hinder the proper functioning of the nervous system are gradually removed.

Overall, the standard exercises appear to be a key in promoting the entire self-recuperative mechanism. The addition of the meditative exercises, when introduced at the proper time, can further enhance the functioning of such mechanisms. I have observed both in myself and in my patients, very fascinating phenomena as a result of the practice of the meditations that seem to make access to the standard exercises faster and significantly more efficient. Some of those who have been faithfully practicing these techniques report that at one point, by merely thinking about "their (mentally generated) color," they begin to experience an immediate sensation of heaviness and warmth in their extremities. This is followed by a relaxation of their cardiac and respiratory activities, a pleasant sensation of warmth in the abdomen, and finally, the experience of a cooling sensation in the forehead region. Conversely, a deepening in the autogenic state can significantly enhance the visualization of the colors and the objects that are instructed in the meditative exercises.

As indicated earlier in the book, patients ultimately hold the key to allowing these powerful techniques to help with their health maintenance and their ability to cope with chronic conditions. Remind them to be patient, steadfast, and to practice without fail. Always emphasize that they need to make autogenic training a part of their daily activities. As time goes on, they will need mere minutes to reap the benefits of their hard work. In time, they will sleep more restfully and will wake up more refreshed. Ultimately, they will enjoy life more fully despite their chronic conditions.

Case Example

SC was a 42-year-old female who came to see me for pain management. At the age of thirty-five she was diagnosed with rheumatoid arthritis and later with fibromyalgia pain syndrome. Up to the time of her first visit with me, SC's treatment had primarily been based on the trial of different medications, some of which had effectively arrested the progression of her arthritis. She was, however, in some pain and discomfort on a regular basis and did not want to try stronger medications because of a fear of becoming dependent on narcotics. She had also suffered from bouts of depression secondary to her pain as a consequence of feeling helpless about the prognosis of her condition. In addition, she developed some difficulties with her sleep cycles, especially in terms of sleep-onset latency (it took her several hours to fall asleep) and sleep maintenance (she experienced sudden awakenings from deep sleep at least four times a night).

After the initial interview, SC related to me that she was highly motivated to try the autogenic techniques. She had spoken with several patients who were doing well with autogenic training, and I was most impressed with her resolve and determination. She recorded detailed data during her home practice with the standard exercises, which substantially helped with her progress. After completing training in the six exercises, I saw her every four to six weeks and was very pleased with the improvements in her overall functioning. In addition to following a good diet and regular exercise, SC had made autogenic training an important part of her daily activities. Her rheumatologist began reducing the dosage of the arthritis medication, especially as her Sed rate (a general indicator of inflammation) reached the normal range. When I discharged her from my care, SC was, in her own words, "a new person."

Two years after her last session with me, I received a disturbing phone call from SC. She related to me that she had fallen down the stairs while she was washing the windows and was experiencing a significant setback in her condition. Her physicians were closely monitoring her condition and had put her on stronger medication for pain control. Most unsettling to SC was her inability to achieve a deep state of relaxation with the use of the autogenic exercises. After two sessions of reviewing the basic exercises, I decided to take her through the meditative exercises. In approximately six weeks, SC was effectively using the second meditative exercise on a daily basis. Soon she was able to enter a much deeper state of relaxation with greater rapidity. In time, SC was able to enter the autogenic state by simply thinking about "her color" (light blue) for two to three minutes. She is now proficient in all the meditative exercises and from time to time sends me a postcard updating her progress.

15
Autogenic Training and Biofeedback*
(Psychophysiological Feedback)

Long before the term "biofeedback" was coined, the pioneers of autogenic training made use of physiological measures as a way of substantiating the effects and the effectiveness of their technique. However, the information was seldom directly disclosed to the trainee. It was not until the late 1960s that Elmer and Alyce Green successfully combined autogenic formulas with temperature biofeedback to treat a variety of stress-related conditions such as essential hypertension and migraine headaches (Green & Green, 1977). Later on, the first study conducted to treat migraine headaches with the use of autogenic biofeedback was published by Sargent, Green, and Walters (1972).

The combination of autogenic training and biofeedback provide a potent methodology for treating a wide range of medical and psychological complications. For example, as the patient repeats the various autogenic formulas, he or she is provided with verbal (usually early in the treatment) and later with electronic biofeedback about his or her physiological functions (most often peripheral temperature and muscular activity). This strategy can significantly improve the patient's confidence in that the mere repetition and

*Although I will be using the term "biofeedback" frequently in this chapter mainly because of the familiarity of many readers with this term, I need to emphasize that this term is clearly dated and does not do justice to over 50 years of remarkable research in the area of self-regulation. The more appropriate term, indeed the more meaningful term, is that of psychophysiological feedback. That is to say, what is fed back is not merely biological information but psychophysiological information as psychological variables profoundly influence biological processes and vice versa. This is a critical elaboration as it suggests that mental states, thoughts, emotions, and even overt behavior can play a significant role in promoting health and well being. Therefore, we can be active participants in our healthcare as well as much more responsible for it than previously suggested.

visualization of the formulas can bring about instantaneous physical changes, even if they are not readily perceived. This realization is especially important for patients with chronic conditions who often tend to feel helpless and powerless with little or no control over their symptoms. With the appropriate use of autogenic biofeedback, patients will quickly observe how much control they can actually exert over their unconscious physiological functions. This newly acknowledged sense of self-efficacy is perhaps the most important reason why psychophysiological modalities have been so effective in the treatment of a variety of disorders.

What Is Biofeedback?

The term biofeedback literally means to provide individuals with information (that is feedback) about their vital or biological processes (hence, bio from Greek *bios*: life). An oral thermometer, a stethoscope, and a blood pressure unit are instruments used to provide information about biological processes. However, this information is not directly "fed" back to the patient. In the actual biofeedback training, patients are provided with continuous feedback about various biological processes. Depending on the biofeedback modality that is being used, patients may be able to monitor a biological function immediately and for a period of time. Immediate feedback can give patients greater control over the realization of specific functions (e.g., blood flow in the hands) through regular practice and by paying attention to the information that is made available through the instrumentation. Fuller (1977) defined biofeedback as "the use of instrumentation to mirror psychophysiological (mind-body) processes of which the individual is not normally aware and which may be brought under voluntary control. This means giving a person immediate information about his or her own biological conditions such as: muscle tension, skin surface temperatures.... This feedback enables the individual to become an active participant in the process of health maintenance" (p. 3). Similarly, Straub (2007) defined biofeedback as the use of instrumentation that allows a person to become more conscious of psychophysiological processes so that he or she may "...gain awareness of a maladaptive response, such as tense forehead muscles" (p. 146). These definitions cover all the critical facets of biofeedback. Their most important emphasis, however, has to do with patients becoming more active participants in their own health.

During the past few decades, due to advancements in technology, biofeedback instruments have become far more sophisticated. In addition to more accurate digital signal delivery, the data from each session can be recorded and displayed in graphic formats. This will help to keep a very effective visual representation of progress from session to session. With that said, as sophisticated as the feedback technology may appear, it can do nothing more than provide data about psychophysiological processes. What is done with the data as a way of enhancing self-regulation is the true challenge of this approach; a challenge that demands active participation on the part of the patient as well as motivation for ongoing practice.

Even after decades of research and clinical findings, to many the term "biofeedback" continues to conjure up images of mind control and electrodes attached to their head and connected to arcane machines. To help patients better understand and further explore the concept of biofeedback, I often use the following example:

> Imagine that you are driving a car and you are instructed to maintain a speed of 65 miles per hour. You simply comply by first looking at your speedometer (which gives you information or feedback about your speed) and then by working the gas pedal or the brakes to easily adjust your speed so that you are driving at exactly 65 MPH. The speedometer is clearly the key that allows you to gain an accurate sense of your speed. In combination with your knowledge of acceleration or deceleration you can have full control over your speed. Now as you are listening to me, if I ask you to raise the temperature of your right hand, would you be able to comply? Unless you have had some experience with psychophysiological techniques, it is unlikely that you will be able to accomplish such a task because there is no way for you to know whether you are actually raising or decreasing your temperature. If I attach a small digital thermometer to one of your fingers and provide you with instantaneous information about your hand temperature, it will be only a matter of time before you can learn methods of changing the blood flow in your hand. You may spend a few minutes and imagine that you are lying on warm sand at the beach or sitting in a hot tub and enjoying the warmth that relaxes your tired muscles. With the use of a biofeedback thermometer and by focusing on such images, you can quickly discover whether these images accomplish your desired outcome.

Proper returned signal delivery*, that is information that is feed back to the patient, plays a most critical role in the training process. Biofeedback instruments may provide patients information through a variety of sensory modalities. For example, a meter or a graph can immediately show changes in hand temperature, muscle tension, sweat gland activity, etc. Instead of seeing these changes, a biofeedback unit can be set or programmed to provide information via a descending or an ascending tone (i.e., as the hand temper-

---

*In biofeedback instruments, psychophysiological information is captured through highly sensitive sensors. This information is amplified and is then returned to the patients via a variety of means, such as lights, meters, graphs, etc.

ature goes up, the sound may change in tone and volume). Based on the patient's preference, one can adjust the unit so that it produces a tone that gets louder (ascending) as the hand temperature goes up or have it do the opposite (the tone gets softer as the temperature rises). Some biofeedback machines can also provide tactile feedback, which gives the patient a mild vibration as he or she brings about the desired changes. What is most important about signal delivery is that it needs to be as immediate as possible for it to be meaningful. A mirror is a useful tool because it provides us with instantaneous information about our behavior. Any delay may give us the wrong indication as to what is the right, more effective behavior.

What Is Autogenic Biofeedback?

How can we determine whether some mental images have calming or distressing effects on the body? Is it possible that subjective reporting of the effects of such images may not be accurate and subsequently not very helpful in the self-regulation training process?

With the use of biofeedback instruments patients will learn which images are helpful in changing their hand temperature or muscle tension, while at the same time they discover which images generate the opposite effects. For some people, the mere image of being at the beach may be sufficient to promote a state of relaxation as measured by an increase in peripheral temperature; while others may actually notice a decrease in their peripheral temperature because of such images. Hence, education and the subsequent therapeutic implications of a simple biofeedback process can be immensely rewarding.

What if we combine the well-established autogenic formulas with various forms of biofeedback? For example, while practicing the first standard autogenic exercise, heaviness, we provide the patient with information about his or her muscular activity of the right arm. In a short while, the patient can see or hear that the repetition of such formulas can result in a change in the tension levels in specific muscles. The combination of autogenic training and biofeedback can be highly helpful in retraining certain aspects of the nervous system that may be over-functioning due to the prolonged experience of pain and stress. In 1966, Alyce Green developed the following "classic" phrases for autogenic biofeedback. While these phrases have certain components of the standard autogenic exercises, they are also unique and encompass other sensations and experiences. For example, they address quiet thoughts and an inward state of peace and stillness. In my opinion, these should be used only after training in the standard exercises:

- I feel quite quiet.
- I am beginning to feel quite relaxed.
- My feet feel heavy and relaxed.
- My ankles, my knees, and my hips feel heavy, relaxed, and comfortable.
- My solar plexus and the whole central portion of my body feels relaxed and quiet.
- My hands, arms, and my shoulders feel heavy, relaxed, and comfortable.
- My neck, my jaws, and my forehead feel relaxed. They feel comfortable and smooth.
- My whole body feels quite heavy, comfortable, and relaxed.
- I am quite relaxed.
- My arms and hands are heavy and warm.
- I feel quite quiet.
- My whole body is relaxed, and my hands are warm, relaxed and warm.
- My hands are warm.
- Warmth is flowing into my hands. They are warm, warm.
- I can feel the warmth flowing down my arms into my hands.
- My hands are warm, relaxed and warm.
- My whole body feels quiet, comfortable, and relaxed.
- My mind is quiet.
- I withdraw my thoughts from the surroundings and I feel serene and still.
- My thoughts are turned inward and I am at ease.
- Deep within my mind, I can visualize and experience myself as relaxed, comfortable, and still.
- I am alert, but in an easy, quiet, inward-turned way.
- My mind is calm and quiet.
- I feel an inward quietness (in Green and Green, 1977, pp. 337–338).

With the use of the biofeedback instruments, the patient no longer needs to believe that the formulas work; he or she can see a record of progress from moment to moment, and from session to session. After a while, the patient no longer needs the machinery to know whether the desired changes are taking place.

The most common biofeedback units are:

1. *Peripheral Temperature Biofeedback:* A small sensor is attached to a finger to gain information about the blood flow in the hands (or the feet), and to learn to increase blood flow to enhance relaxation and pain control.*

---

*This is a very useful modality to reinforce the changes that take place particularly during the second standard exercise, warmth. Patients need not receive continuous feedback during the early phases of autogenic training. Even pre-post session data is very helpful to educate the patient about the control that he or she is gaining over physiological processes through the practice of the exercises.

2. *Surface Electromyographic Biofeedback:* Small sensors are attached to the surface of a muscle in order to observe the activity of the muscle and to learn to reduce tension in that muscle.*

3. *Electrodermal Response Biofeedback:* Small probes are attached to a hand that allows the monitoring of the activity of the sympathetic nervous system which is involved in the stress response. By reducing this activity, one can significantly enhance the ability to relax.†

Are Biofeedback Instruments Necessary for Autogenic Training?

The most straightforward answer to this question is no. Biofeedback can help patients gain greater knowledge about the functioning of certain aspects of their nervous system but this knowledge can also be achieved through the regular practice of autogenic exercises. I have found autogenic biofeedback to be of special value to those patients who have convinced themselves that nothing they can do will change their pain, their cold hands or feet, etc. In this sense, autogenic biofeedback can initially be used as a way of empowering patients and showing them that they do indeed have some control over their body. This process by itself is highly therapeutic and can significantly diminish the feeling of helplessness that is often experienced when one grapples with chronic conditions. As a rule, I do not immediately introduce biofeedback into my sessions because I do not want patients to experience "performance anxiety." That is to say, I want patients to focus on learning new and more effective responses, instead of merely focusing on changing a certain physiological parameter. A good session is more than just changing the dials or the numbers; it is about becoming aware of the process involved in such changes. In other words, learning is just as important as performance. Initially, I provide patients with some general information about their peripheral temperature or changes in muscle tension and eventually give them more continuous feedback. Some patients are also provided with a small portable biofeedback unit for home practice (especially for the treatment of migraine headaches in which the use of portable temperature units can be extremely helpful).

---

*This is another highly useful form of feedback that can be used during the early phases of autogenic training, especially in the first exercise when the focus of treatment is on the sensation of heaviness.

†This is a powerful form of biofeedback that can be used in conjunction with autogenic exercises in the treatment of anxiety disorders.

16

Sleep, Insomnia, and Pain

That sleep may wearied limbs restore,
And Fit for toil and use once more;
may gently soothe the careworn breast,
And lull our anxieties to rest.
— Ambrose

We spend nearly a third of our lives in nightly slumber. Many of us are not aware of its many functions. Indeed, sleep is that aspect of our existence that we tend to take for granted. Yet more and more scientific studies suggest that sleep plays a significant role in our physical and mental health (Stein et al., 2008). After a long and busy day, people tend to go to bed and expect to close their eyes and enter the realm of forgetfulness and rest. When it does not happen, they hope to find the remedy in a bottle of pills.

Since the dawn of human civilization, in every known culture, speculation has surfaced about the nature of nightly slumber. To some it was quite clear that the renewal of the human spirit relied so heavily on the night journey that without it, sickness and disease were bound to happen. Great poets such as Shakespeare referred to sleep as nature's nurse whose absence signaled the coming of mental anguish and turmoil. To make sure that sleep was not compromised or inadvertently interfered with, different cultures devised certain rituals that were closely observed every night. Perhaps the most common component of such rituals shared cross-culturally was reciting special bedtime prayers (see Foulks, 1992). Researchers are just beginning to appreciate the role of these types of prayers in promoting better sleep. How? It has become quite clear in recent years that one of the worst enemies of sleep is an overactive mind, or, as it was discussed earlier, a mind suffering from cognitive anxiety. Prayer, especially repetitive prayer, tends to quiet the busy mind and bring some semblance of peace.

With the invention of the electroencephalogram (EEG) by Hans Burger in 1929, investigators began to learn a great deal about the complexities and intricacies of sleep. It is now well established that sleep is comprised of a number of overlapping stages that tend to be responsible for a variety of physical and mental changes. There has been substantial literature on the biochemical changes during sleep. Indeed some of the biochemical changes seem to occur during the various stages of sleep. For example, in non-rapid eye movement sleep, there seems to be a significant reduction in stress hormones such as the glucocroticoids, most noticeably cortisol. On the other hand, during the active dream stage of sleep characterized by rapid eye movement, there appears to be a rise in various stress hormones. This suggests a very complex interplay of psychophysiological events during sleep, all of which are important for proper functioning of the various systems in the body. However, in chronic insomnia the body does not seem to have the opportunity to neutralize these hormones. Consequently there is acceleration in "wear and tear" in the body resulting in premature aging and the onset of a variety of diseases (Sapolsky, 2004). Extensive empirical findings during the past few decades suggest that important changes in immune system activity occur during the nightly slumber. Both human and animal studies suggest that even partial awakening can affect the responsiveness of the immune system and may interfere with its effective vigilance (Irwin, Smith, & Gillin, 1992; Rief et al., 2010). All of these suggest that sleep is a very dynamic, active process that accomplishes a variety of tasks critical to our survival. There is nothing passive about sleep!

Karren and colleagues (2010) stated that among the various causes of insomnia there are three factors that may prevent a person from receiving sufficient sleep. These factors may be seen as genetic predispositions, current stressors, and behavioral factors that affect proper sleep hygiene. One or a combination of the above can significantly affect a person's functioning and compromise his or her psychological as well as physical health. We now have ample empirical evidence that mental over-activity can play a significant role in insomnia, particularly as far as sleep onset latency (e.g., how long it takes to fall asleep) is concerned. While for some time in was believed that worry about the future was one of the most important contributors to difficulty falling asleep, a recent study suggested that rumination, that is thoughts focused on the past, tend to play an even greater role. Indeed, the findings of this study call our attention to the role of psychosocial stressors in extended sleep onset latency, particularly if such stressors promote active thinking and processing on what had happened in the past (Zoccolla, Dickerson, & Lam, 2009). Ruminations about the past can be just as potent as worries about the future. In other words our thoughts about what will happen tomorrow or what happened yesterday invariably seem to rob us of our nightly rest.

These and other findings should convince us to pay greater attention to our sleep hygiene and do whatever it takes to enhance its recuperative and restorative functions. To achieve this task, a brief review of the different stages of sleep and its neurophysiology is in order.

The Stages of Sleep

First, let us briefly discuss the various stages of sleep. Generally speaking, sleep is comprised of two distinct stages: non-rapid eye movement (NREM) sleep and REM sleep (or the rapid eye movement sleep, which is often associated with dreaming). The NREM sleep is divided into four overlapping stages.

1. Stage 1 sleep is considered the lightest stage of sleep and can easily be interrupted. During this stage, people may be aware of some events in their immediate environment, such as noise, light, etc. EEG recordings during Stage 1 suggest a gradual slowing of the brain wave activity. While the person may be gradually moving toward the deeper stages of sleep, it is relatively easy to "pull out" of this stage and become fully alert.

2. Stage 2 sleep is characterized by a further slowing down of the electrical activity of the brain and the presence of special wave forms known as the sleep spindle. During this stage awareness of environmental stimuli is significantly lessened, although it is still possible to wake a person with little difficulty. Approximately five minutes into this stage, the person is undeniably asleep as demonstrated by a significant decrease in muscle tone, and changes in breathing patterns.

3. Stage 3 sleep is notable for a significant reduction in the overall metabolic activity. During this stage it is much more difficult to wake a person. The body's core temperature begins to fall gradually. Pulse and breathing rates tend to drop. If awakened, an individual may appear somewhat disoriented and unable to recall thoughts or dreamlike images. Indeed, some people may become very upset that an attempt was made to awaken them from this "deep" stage of sleep. In reality there is even a deeper stage of sleep.

4. Stage 4 sleep is the deepest stage of rest, both physiologically and mentally. Large delta waves dominate the EEG activity. Several studies have documented an increase in the production of the somatotropin, the growth hormone, during this stage of sleep (Luce, 1970; Vgontzas et al., 1999). Many researchers have referred to this stage as restorative sleep,

since many repair processes take place at this stage (Dement, 1999; Rief et al., 2010). If awakened during this stage, an individual may be quite disoriented and momentarily unable to recall even simple information. Stage 4, or delta sleep, has been of significant interest to scientists studying chronic pain, fibromyalgia, and those suffering from PTSD. An inexplicable phenomenon of Stage 4 interruption, known as alpha intrusion has been documented in most fibromyalgia and many chronic pain patients (see Moldofsky et al., 1975). We shall discuss some of the scientific studies that have explored this later in the chapter.

Rapid eye movement (REM) sleep takes place at the conclusion of Stage 4, and as the stages of sleep begin to reverse themselves; that is moving out of Stage 4 to Stage 3, 2 and then instead of Stage 1 we enter REM . Here we see a significant increase in brain wave activity as if the brain is entering a hyperaroused state. During this stage dreaming takes place, and there is an increase in heart rate, blood pressure, respiratory rate, and overall metabolic functioning. Normally, people tend to spend more time in REM sleep when they approach the early hours of the morning. One reason for this may be the brain's attempt at reactivating the higher cognitive functions so as to move toward full wakefulness.

Now that we have some understanding of the different stages of sleep, let us now consider some of the other aspects of this complex and vital process. Sleep onset latency refers to the length of time that is required before entering Stage 1 sleep. Normally, it takes somewhere between ten to twenty minutes to fall asleep. If it takes longer than that, this may suggest that the person is suffering from sleep-onset insomnia. I have worked with many patients who required somewhere between three to five hours to initiate sleep.

An entire sleep cycle, starting with Stage 1 and ending with REM sleep tends to occur within a 90- to 110-minute period. When too much mental activity, or physical discomfort, is present, people are likely to spend more time in the earlier stages of sleep. If this becomes a chronic tendency, we may see significant changes in physical health as well as emotional and psychological changes, most notably changes in memory and a greater sensitivity to pain. As a rule, children tend to spend more time in the deeper stages of sleep, possibly because of the need for replenishing the biochemicals necessary for growth and repair.

While in decades past most Americans used to receive close to nine hours of sleep, things have changed substantially, as on the average we tend to get close to seven hours of sleep, which is an alarming decline. Most sleep researchers suggest that most people require at least eight hours of sleep (see Sapolsky, 2004). Again, based on these same studies, it is safe to say that the

United States is a nation of insomniacs. Most of us tend to get less than eight hours of sleep, and the problem is not going away. At the same time it is important to note that spending too much time in bed can also be problematic. Due to a reduction in respiration rate and metabolic function, those who sleep for more than ten hours tend to wake up tired, disoriented, and may actually suffer from headaches.

Stage 4 Sleep and Fibromyalgia: Is There a Connection?

Almost every publication on fibromyalgia points out that alterations in Stage 4 activity occur in patients suffering from this condition. In 1975, Moldofsky and colleagues published a paper titled, "Musculoskeletal Symptoms and Non-REM Sleep Disturbance in Patients with Fibrositis Syndrome and Healthy Subjects" (Moldofsky et al., 1975). The study's conclusions were twofold. First, it was clearly demonstrated that "fibrositis" (fibromyalgia) patients showed a disruption in Stage 4 sleep as indicated by an intrusion of Alpha waves. Second, healthy subjects who were deprived of Stage 4 sleep (via a loud sound) began experiencing muscle pains and changes in their moods consistent with those observed in fibrositis patients. The study also suggested that since key brain chemicals are produced, metabolized, and synthesized in this stage of sleep, a chronic disruption in deep sleep may be one of the contributing factors in the appearance of symptoms in the fibrositis patients.

Over thirty years have elapsed since the publication of this groundbreaking study. The study itself has been replicated several times with almost identical results. I have looked at hundreds of sleep studies of fibromyalgia patients which supported the findings of the Moldofsky study. But sleep disturbance alone does not seem to be the cause of fibromyalgia (fibrositis) syndrome. The alpha intrusion phenomenon has been seen also in chronic pain patients who do not suffer from fibromyalgia. A study by Leventhal and colleagues (1995) suggested that the disruption of Stage 4 sleep may be more of a "generalized marker for chronic pain rather than a specific anomaly in patients with FM" (p. 110).

From these studies we can conclude that Stage 4 sleep plays a key role in fibromyalgia and chronic pain even though it may not be the primary cause. Therefore, it behooves us to do whatever necessary to enhance the sleep process and the quality of Stage 4 sleep. In my experience, by following certain scientifically supported protocols in conjunction with autogenic training, it is possible to bring about a significant change not only in the overall quality of sleep but also changes in physical and cognitive symptoms.

Reducing Cognitive Anxiety

I have survived more catastrophes than one can possibly imagine ...
only because many of them never came true. — Mark Twain

In almost every case of insomnia that I have treated in a clinical setting, I have observed that excessive thinking, whether it is about the past (rumination) or about the future (worry), seems to be the main reason for people having difficulty falling asleep, staying asleep, or both. This is especially true in those individuals who suffer from chronic pain and stress related disorders. Even when a person has physical discomfort, it appears that it is thinking about the discomfort that tends to interfere with sleep. As it was pointed out in Chapter 3, this phenomenon is often referred to as "cognitive anxiety" and it was illustrated how certain relaxation exercises could potentially reduce the activities of an overactive mind. Some strategies for reducing cognitive anxiety will be discussed later in this chapter. Patients should follow the instructions presented here and incorporate them into their pre-sleep activities every night until these instructions become a natural, regular routine.

No Problem-Solving in Bed

Easier said than done! But this is a key reason that many do not get the quality rest that they need. Sleep is a time for replenishment and people should be encouraged not to cheat themselves of this valuable time by trying to solve problems or address their concerns. They can accomplish these tasks, if they wish, as soon as they get up in the morning. I cannot possibly count the number of my patients and students who reported an improvement in their sleep by merely following this simple rule. I have asked my patients to say the following affirmation to themselves before falling asleep. "I need my sleep to heal. Therefore, I will put aside my worries and concerns and allow myself to rest, refuel, and replenish until morning."

Talk It Out or Write It Down

Now let us consider a patient who goes to sleep with all the right attitudes and preparations but cannot fall asleep because of a certain bothersome topic. In such a case, I suggest that the patient tries to "talk it out." Talking to someone who can listen without offering a thousand suggestions is, in my view, an excellent way of quieting a busy mind. But if a "listening ear" is not available, the next best thing is to write down whatever is interfering with falling asleep. Either approach seems to make an important difference between spending one's sleep time thinking about things that cannot be changed and getting the kind of quality sleep that one deserves.

Relaxing Some of the Expectations about Sleep

After years of developing some bad sleep habits, patients cannot expect to replace them with new habits overnight. All good things happen slowly, so patients need to remain steadfast in their new learning. They also need to let go of certain expectations that may sound very scientific, but have nothing to do with getting good sleep. The best way to illustrate this point is to reflect on a discovery by one of America's most beloved writers, Mark Twain. The following account explains how he discovered some of his irrational beliefs concerning sleep:

> Mark Twain was a cantankerous insomniac. Once the author found himself at a friend's home, unable to sleep. The problem was not a new one to Twain, yet he convinced himself that the reason for his failure to sleep was the poor ventilation in the unfamiliar room. He tossed and turned for some time, cursing the stuffy atmosphere. Finally, in a fit of anger, he picked up his shoe and hurled it through the darkness at the window, which he had been unable to open in the conventional way. He heard the sound of shattering glass, inhaled deeply and thankfully, and fell fast asleep. In the morning the well-rested humorist noticed that the glass-enclosed bookcase had been smashed. The window was still locked and intact [Goldberg & Kaufman, 1978, pp. 38–39].

This story contains a special wisdom which is pertinent to all of us: at times our suffering is largely of our own creation — namely, our expectations. As I have pointed out throughout the book, the prolonged experience of helplessness is perhaps the worst possible source of damage and destruction to one's psyche and soul. Certain things in patients' lives cannot be controlled nor can they be changed. But patients can learn to cope. The first step is to teach them how to let go of self-defeating thoughts and expectations. For example, most chronic pain patients, in my experience, seem to have given up on getting a good night's rest. I often hear them say, "What is the use? I just can't sleep anymore." Obviously after years of disrupted or incomplete sleep, many conclude that they have lost the ability to sleep. This is an irrational conclusion with devastating ramifications. If patients want to gain greater control over their pain and physical symptoms, they need to "relearn" how to sleep. This relearning process requires commitment and steadfastness. In the past, I have worked with patients who used to sleep for a maximum of two to three hours. After weeks of following specific instructions, they were able to sleep, with little interruption, for six to eight hours and began noticing improvements in their pain and overall health.

I am not going to suggest a special pill that will help chronic pain patients recover from insomnia. Sleeping pills often impair certain stages of sleep. Although antidepressants tend to help with achieving deeper sleep, patients can enhance their natural rest and slumber by other means.

Patients need to be encouraged to adhere without fail to the instructions that are stated in pages to come. These instructions are based on some of the most recent scientific studies on insomnia. The only way these instructions can be of help is if they are followed with total determination. There are three points that I often emphasize to those suffering from chronic pain syndrome and any form of stress related disorder.

1. Taking care of one's sleep is a critical step in enhancing pain management as well as stress management.
2. One can do much to improve one's overall health by getting more quality sleep.
3. One must adhere to certain scientific findings and principles that have been shown to improve sleep.

Improving Sleep

Current scientific studies suggest that two of the most helpful methods of improving sleep are stimulus control and sleep restriction.

Stimulus Control

The stimulus control approach to improving sleep was first developed by Richard Bootzin (1972). The main rationale behind this approach suggests that insomnia can be a conditioned response caused by associating (or pairing) the bedroom with certain behaviors that promote arousal instead of sleep. For example, many people do their problem solving or next-day planning while in bed. Such activities promote a state of alertness that can significantly interfere with the ability to fall asleep. Also, many people remain wide awake while lying in their bed waiting for sleep to arrive. Gradually, the unconscious association is made that the bed is a place for alertness and not sleep. This association is why some people tend to fall asleep much more quickly on the couch in the living room than on the comfortable bed in the bedroom.

By following certain specific instructions, individuals can gradually remove or neutralize those associations that tend to keep them alert and awake while in bed. Following is a list of conditions that need to be observed to reestablish healthy sleep patterns.

Make the Bedroom a Place for Sleep

The bedroom should not be used for any other activity (with the exception of intimacy) that will keep one alert. If one tends to do computer work or write letters or balance the checkbook in the bedroom, it is time to find a new spot for such activities. Unfortunately, the television set must go, too.

Do Not Stay in Bed to Force Falling Asleep

If one cannot fall asleep after ten to fifteen minutes of lying in bed, it is time to leave the bedroom and do something else until sleepy. People should be encouraged to read a book or watch a TV show in another room, but return to bed when they become sleepy.

Keep the Bedroom Dark, Quiet, and Cool

Although the stimulus control theory does not emphasize any particularities about the ambiance of the bedroom, it is important to note that certain environmental conditions can also keep people more alert. Reducing environmental stimulation can by itself promote a state of relaxation, which may serve as a prelude to sleep. Adjustments need to be made to keep the bedroom quiet, dark, and pleasantly cool. Blankets and comforters should be used to keep the body warm, but the room should be kept cool (approximately 68° to 70° F).

Sleep Restriction

This approach is based on the total time that is spent in bed. If people are restricted to only a certain number of hours while in bed, they may find themselves trying to get the most out of those hours in terms of sleep. For example, if a person is currently sleeping only six hours, his or her task is to limit the time spent in bed to those six hours. This person should be encouraged not to stay in bed any longer than six hours while trying to get some partial sleep. Gradually, the individual may discover that he or she tends to get a bit more sleep, night after night. Once the person approaches eight to eight-and-one-half hours of sleep, he or she has made the necessary adjustments.

Also, it is imperative that one does not take naps during the day. It is best to restrict one's sleep time to the time spent in bed at night. Although this may be a challenge in the beginning, most people will soon discover an improvement in the quality of their nocturnal sleep. Receiving quality sleep at night, not during the day, is the key to enhancing health, improving coping, and refueling the body for the daily tasks.

Here are some additional suggestions that patients may find very helpful.

1. *Hide the clock.* Looking at the clock throughout the night may actually cause people to become more aroused, which means that they will need more time to unwind before falling asleep.
2. *No laptops or cell phones in bed.* Electronic devices such as cell phone and laptops produce a bright light that will invariably interfere with the process of falling asleep. Such light stimulation may lengthen the sleep onset latency by several minutes and even much longer. As a general rule, exposing oneself to bright lights before or during bedtime means arousing the mind and the body, the very antithesis of sleep. Even though people are very attached to their mobile phone devices, such attachments need to be severed for the duration of sleep.
3. *Take a hot shower before going to bed.* Many chronic pain patients find a hot shower before bedtime is very relaxing and soothing to their tired muscles. However, they should make sure that they do not wash their hair since it takes a while for the hair to dry, and the heat loss may be counterproductive.
4. *Take pain medications before going to bed.* Patients should ask their physicians if they can take their analgesics shortly before bedtime. In order to reduce the sleep-onset latency, it is best to use certain pain medication ten to twenty minutes before bedtime so that one is more pain free while trying to sleep.
5. *As diurnal creatures, we need to be asleep during the night and not during the day.* Many biochemical corrections that are significant for the purpose of pain management are produced at night. For this reason alone, chronic pain patients, particularly, must make sure that they are in bed before midnight. It has been documented that the growth hormone (also known as somatotropin) peaks its production between the hours of 12 A.M. and 4 A.M. (Coleman, 1986). Other studies have suggested that a significant reduction occurs in the growth hormone levels in fibromyalgia and chronic pain patients. Therefore, it is imperative to make every attempt to make sure that patients are doing what is needed to enhance the quality of their sleep at night.
6. *Do not exercise before going to bed at night.* Exercise has many wonderful benefits. Some of these benefits were mentioned in Chapter 1 as far as pain management was concerned. Excessive exercise shortly before going to bed may have an arousing effect making it harder to fall asleep. At

least an hour before bed time one needs to begin the process of "unwinding." Exercise will do the opposite, even if it is for a brief period of time. The best time to exercise is when there is a natural rise in cortisol levels, which occurs early in the morning and in the early hours of evening. Cortisol levels drop rather sharply after 8 P.M.

Autogenic Training and Sleep

In addition to some of the sleep enhancement techniques that were discussed earlier in the chapter, relaxation techniques have been used quite extensively to treat sleep disorders and insomnia. In fact, one of the popular and widely used relaxation techniques, progressive muscle relaxation, was originally developed by Dr. Edmund Jacobson to treat insomnia. Transcendental meditation is another approach to sleep restoration and has been used extensively in clinical studies throughout the world. A study by Miskiman (1977) showed that insomniacs who typically spent over seventy minutes falling asleep reduced this time to approximately fifteen minutes after several months of practice with TM.

Nicassio and Bootzin (1974) compared the efficacy of autogenic training, progressive relaxation, a no-treatment control group, and a self-relaxation control group as treatments for chronic insomnia. Both autogenic training and progressive relaxation were equally effective and superior to the control groups in reducing insomnia. At a six-month follow-up, treatment gains had been maintained over time for falling asleep but not in self-reported, global improvements. The subjects in the control groups, however, showed no spontaneous improvements on either of the two measures.

Simeit, Deck, and Conta-Marx (2004) found a multimodal approach to the treatment of insomnia to be superior to a control group. The multimodal component of the study included relaxation training (autogenic training and progressive relaxation), with some additional cognitive techniques, and general information about stimulus control. One of the treatment groups received autogenic training while the other received progressive relaxation. At the end of the study, both treatment groups showed significant improvements in sleep onset latency, sleep maintenance, and finally sleep efficiency. The control groups did not show any improvements. The study revealed that not only did those receiving relaxation training show improvements in their sleep, they saw an improvement in well-being.

As previously discussed, autogenic training evolved from studies that explored the nature of sleep and its recuperative properties. For this reason alone, the expansive literature on this technique elucidates the causes and the treatments of persistent disorders of sleep (Luthe & Schultz, 1969b; Sadigh & Mierzwa, 1995; Sadigh, 1999). I have found autogenic training a tremendous help to those who suffer from chronic pain, and as a result, tend to suffer from insomnia. Often those who have difficulty with sleep onset latency almost immediately notice an improvement after practicing the techniques for several weeks. With some additional instructions, those with difficulty maintaining their sleep due to frequent waking tend to see improvements by the time they learn the fourth standard exercise.

As patients progress in their daily practice of the autogenic exercises and they proceed to the third and fourth standard exercises, they will be able to tackle some of the most difficult cases of insomnia. Once again it must be emphasized that patients need to follow the instructions on stimulus control and sleep restrictions that were discussed earlier in this chapter to improve their results.

Although patients can use the standard exercises when they go to bed, I recommend an abbreviated version of these exercises for sleep enhancement. There are also several specific formulas that can be used at night as a way of reducing sleep onset latency and improving sleep maintenance. Patients need to memorize these formulas and use them especially if they wake up in the middle of the night and find it difficult to fall back to sleep.

I recommend a total of three sleep exercises which are based on the standard and organ-specific formulas. Patients may use the first sleep exercise as they are mastering the heaviness exercise and the second sleep exercise as they begin working on the warmth exercise. They should not proceed to the third sleep exercise until they have started using the fifth standard exercise (abdominal warmth) during their daily practice. It is imperative that patients use these exercises every night, regardless of how tired or sleepy they might feel. These exercises should become a part of their sleep ritual.

Patients may be instructed to use the following exercises while in bed and as they are about to fall asleep. Each formula is to be repeated approximately ten times.

Sleep Exercise 1

- I am quiet and relaxed.
- I am at peace.
- My right arm is heavy.
- My left arm is heavy.
- I am at peace.
- My shoulders are heavy.
- My jaw is heavy and relaxed.

- I am at peace.
- My right leg is heavy.
- My left leg is heavy.
- I am at peace.
- It sleeps me.

Sleep Exercise 2

- I am quiet and relaxed.
- My right arm is heavy and warm.
- My left arm is heavy and warm.
- I am at peace.
- My shoulders are heavy and warm.
- My jaw is heavy and relaxed.
- I am at peace.
- My right leg is heavy and warm.
- My left leg is heavy and warm.
- I am at peace.
- I am sleepy and relaxed.
- It sleeps me.

Sleep Exercise 3

Patients should use this exercise only after they have begun using the fifth standard exercise.

- I am sleepy and relaxed.
- My arms are heavy and warm.
- My shoulders are heavy and warm.
- My jaw is heavy and warm.
- My legs are heavy and warm.
- My heartbeat is calm and regular.
- It breathes me.
- My abdomen is pleasantly warm.
- Warmth makes me sleepy.
- It sleeps me.

For some patients, it is safe to assume that initially they may have difficulty staying asleep even though they fall asleep more quickly with the help of autogenic formulas. My recommendation is that as soon as patients find themselves wide awake in the middle of the night, they should immediately begin repeating several formulas to themselves, especially those that focus on sensations of heaviness and warmth. The key is to repeat these formulas as soon as one is awakened due to pain or other reasons.

In my experience, the majority of people quickly learn to use the formulas to fall back to sleep. The key is to persevere. Many patients report that by repeating one or two formulas they can fall asleep almost effortlessly. Some, including myself, find "warmth makes me sleepy" to be a very helpful "sleep trigger."

17

Autogenic Neutralization as Psychophysiological Psychotherapy

The systematic approach to psychological therapy by means of verbal expressions of thoughts and feelings was born through the clinical investigations of Sigmund Freud. As a neurologist and researcher interested in the treatment of patients who were exhibiting severe neurological symptoms that were resistant to the medical treatments of his time, Freud constructed an intervention that promised to free his patients of their refractory symptoms; an intervention that, in time, came to be known as psychoanalysis. The two main goals of psychoanalysis are to make the unconscious mind conscious through insight generation, and to strengthen the ego. Insights are considered therapeutic and useful if they are not limited to an intellectual understanding of a certain set of symptoms. That is, they must be an integration of affective and cognitive components.

The strengthening of the ego is a critical aspect of psychoanalysis as it improves coping and enhances adjustment to internal as well as external sources of demand. A fortified ego can better manage intrapsychic as well as interpersonal sources of demand, conflicts, etc. Since the advent of psychoanalysis over a hundred years ago, many other psychotherapeutic interventions have emerged to assist patients with their psychological disorders and psychosocial sources of stress. Depending on specific theoretical formulations, these newer therapies may focus on the restructuring of distorted thinking (as in cognitive therapy), modification of overt behavior (as in behavior therapy), discovery of inner potentialities (as in humanistic approaches), discovery of meaning and purpose in life (as in logotherapy and existential analysis), and scores of other forms of therapy that combine various elements of the above, or those which rely on other formulations of human behavior, some of which may not be well substantiated by any clinical or empirical data.

Autogenic training may be aptly referred to as a form of psychotherapy that purports to achieve the objectives of various forms of psychotherapy. Indeed, it is one approach that very much resembles the basic premises of the original psychoanalytic model as far as the origin of somato-psychic experiences are concerned, without the emphasis on the need for generating insight into the origin of certain symptoms. Very much like psychoanalysis, the early days of autogenic research were primarily focused on the treatment of medical conditions. Again, similar to the early psychoanalytic investigations, some of the early conceptualizations of autogenic training emerged from data that was accumulated through the close investigation of physical and psychological changes that took place in patients during the practice of hypnosis. Finally, in both psychoanalysis (especially in the earlier chapters of its development) and autogenic training we see the importance of certain abreactive experiences.

The literature on the use of autogenic training as a form of psychotherapy is quite impressive. Sadly, the importance of the psychotherapeutic benefits of this approach is not being emphasized enough in the current literature. Regrettably, as I mentioned before, this is mainly due to the fact that many view autogenic training simply as another form of relaxation training. This is most unfortunate as autogenic training contains advanced therapeutic components that surpass any form of cognitive–behavioral modes of meditative-relaxation. It is true that autogenic training may share some of the basic aspects of meditative-relaxation, but such similarities are minor when compared to the depth as well as the diversity of interventions that are generated by the former.

Before we delve into the specifics of autogenic therapy, especially as a form of psychotherapy, I find it necessary to emphasize that often times a variety of psychological improvements are reported by patients as they go through the standard exercises. Once again, a common misconception about autogenic training is that it is limited to the first two exercises: heaviness and warmth. I have met many practitioners who had not even once trained their patients in the third, fourth, fifth, or the sixth standard exercises. They were

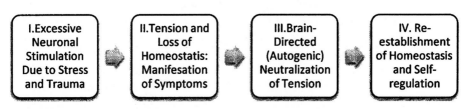

Figure 17.1. The reestablishment of homeostasis through the brain-directed autogenic process.

simply unaware that they constitute the more advanced stages of the training. Again the culprit is the mistaken formulation that suggests autogenic means relaxation. Whereas more accurately put, autogenic means self-generated self-regulation, that is a return to homeostasis through corrective processes.

It is not unusual for patients who are undergoing autogenic training for specific disorders to report that an unrelated disorder, or an unrelated set of symptoms, completely disappeared during the course of treatment, although that was not the focus or purpose of the treatment. Such recognitions are made and divulged by the patient rather spontaneously, chiefly as the patient advances to upper level standard exercises (such as exercises 4, 5, and 6). At other times, the patient reports amelioration of other symptoms after the training is terminated, or during a follow-up visit. It would be interesting to investigate how many such symptom corrections are not reported at all as the patient does not see any connection between the process of training for a specific symptom and disappearance of other symptoms. The example below demonstrates this process.

PS was a 47-year-old woman who began autogenic training for the treatment of her persistent migraine headaches. Patient was making gradual but steady improvements in her headaches, most notably in terms of their frequency, when she had to visit her parents who lived on the west coast. Prior to leaving for the trip, patient related that she did not like to fly as she always experiences panic-like symptoms during the flight. To tolerate the flight, her physician prescribed anxiolytic agents such as Diazepam, which she took prior to the flight. Because of her fear of flying she could not visit her parents very often. Additionally, she could not accompany her husband to various events both within the country and abroad. The patient was away for a month. When she returned from her trip, she reported that she made a most important and pleasant discovery as she did not become anxious during both flights. She went on to say that she also discovered that it was her "claustrophobia" that made her experience panic-like symptoms. The day of her flight, she realized that she did not have her medication with her. With a great deal of apprehension, she decided to practice some autogenic formulas during the flight, hoping that she would avoid a panic attack. The flight went uneventfully even though she only repeated five or six phrases before takeoff, and specific phrases during the flight. On the way back, she held her medication bottle in her hand as the plane took off and again noticed that except for some general apprehension, she did well during the flight. Even though she had received extensive behavior therapy in the past, she had not been able to fly to anywhere in the country without anxiety and panic attacks. During a follow-up meeting six months after the termination of therapy, she reported that she was travelling with her husband almost on a monthly basis without any serious problems with anxiety. Her favorite formula during turbulent flights came to be the key formula in exercise 4, "It breathes me."

The above clinical case may be viewed as an example of corrective psychological and psychophysiological changes in those engaged in the practice of autogenic training. Unlike most forms of psychotherapy, such changes did not need to be scrutinized in terms of what historical events could have contributed to the emergence of claustrophobic experiences. What matters is the fact that such symptoms disappeared, and so far as the clinical data suggest, they did not return even after the termination of treatment. The treatment was discontinued due to the improvement of migraine symptoms.

It needs to be emphasized that the above findings, that is amelioration of symptoms not directly relate to the focus of the treatment, are not uncommon during autogenic training. Had the patient been referred for the treatment of claustrophobia, upon the completion of the standard exercises, organ-specific formulas could have been used to address the symptoms related to that particular condition.

On the other hand, in those cases when the standard exercises do not bring about the desired change, that is symptomatic relief, it may be necessary to use some of the more advanced autogenic interventions that fall under the category of autogenic neutralization. Autogenic neutralization can be best described as a more intensive treatment that has both psychotherapeutic and psychophysiological properties. Nevertheless, it needs to be mentioned here that these advanced treatments are based on the core foundation that is achieved through the proper understanding and practice of the standard exercises. Key to the success of these exercises and the more advanced, adjunctive treatments is the concept of passive concentration, which was discussed in much depth earlier in the book.

The discovery of the phenomenon of autogenic neutralization has a curious story that deserves a basic review. Since the early days of research in the field of autogenic therapy, it was observed that the brain-directed, autogenic, discharges were followed by improvement in patients' symptoms. According to Luthe (1970), "Initial attempts at giving the brain a better opportunity to discharge consisted merely of prolongation of the standard exercises and of a subsequent study of the pattern of autogenic discharges from training protocols which the patient wrote after termination of such prolonged exercises. From pattern analysis of autogenic discharges recorded in this manner, it became evident that the activity of those brain mechanisms which participated in autogenic discharge functions followed certain self-regulatory principles" (p. 3). Hence, one obvious course of action when treating complex disorders was to provide a greater opportunity for sufficient autogenic discharges to take place. This was achieved by lengthening the practice of the formulas. But were the repetition of the standard formulas the sole reason for the therapeutic changes?

Luthe (1970) recounts some of the puzzling observations that he and Schultz were making with regard to a reduction or disappearance of medical symptoms during the practice of standard autogenic exercises. Some of the symptoms, as mentioned above, had nothing to do with the formulas, nor were they the focus of treatment. However, the appearance of certain experiences (e.g., olfactory, visual, tactile, emotional) during the practice of the exercises suggested that something more was taking place within the nervous system. It was as if some "unknown mechanism" in the brain was facilitating the discharge of excessive neuronal loads that were otherwise interfering with proper homeostatic functions. Generally speaking, discharges that unload excessive tension within the nervous system occur during the various stages of sleep. But what if the complete discharge of these disturbing experiences was taking place neither during sleep, nor during the waking hours of a patient's life? In such an example, unreleased tension would no doubt contribute to the emergence of psychological and physical symptoms. Even though the standard exercises often facilitate such releases, there are times when greater release is needed for the nervous system to return to its proper function. The need for the development of more specific treatments that promoted more extensive discharge of internal disturbances led to the development of techniques of autogenic neutralization.

In earlier studies, one of the consistent observations about the neurophysiological effects of autogenic neutralization on the brain had resulted in the hypothesis that due to the experience of a traumatic experience, a lack of hemispheric interaction between the two hemispheres might ensue. Hence, "a functional imbalance or inhibition between the two hemispheres participated in the development of psychodynamic and psychosomatic disorders. One can further hypothesize that [autogenic neutralization through abreaction] facilitates communication between the two cerebral hemispheres and allows repressed, primary process-like, disturbing material (presumably right hemispheric) to become integrated into logical, analytic, verbal awareness (largely left hemispheric). The result is a reduction in the disturbing potency of traumas (neutralization, resolution of intrapsychic conflict)" (Luthe, 1983, p. 176). This is consistent with some of the more recent formulations with regards to a reduction in blood flow (i.e., activity) in the left prefrontal cortex and an increase in blood flow in the right prefrontal cortex, especially in certain forms of anxiety disorders (Wehrenberg & Prinz, 2007). The task of the treatment is henceforth to bring about a balance between the two hemispheres.

De Rivera (1997) offered a more psychoanalytic explanation of the nature of autogenic neutralization. According to him, "the autogenic state is a state of technical 'regression in the service of the ego' characterized by a reversal of the subjective experience of anxiety into a state of psychophysiological relaxation and increased awareness of internal processes. The ego under conditions of reduced anxiety increases its observing function, decreases its defenses, and allows the passage into consciousness of previously represses ideas, memories and impulses.... The therapeutic effect is achieved by (1) the neutralization of traumatic emotional experiences, and (2) the progressive reorganization of the psychic structure to include previously unacceptable mental contents" (p. 181). Here we see a very close connection between psychoanalytic interventions of removing disturbing intrapsychic stimuli through free association and what occurs in autogenic neutralization, although the latter is far more psychophysiologically based. As far as the outcome of treatment is concerned, both are likely to achieve similar goals. Once again, it is necessary to point out that insight generation is not necessarily a required aspect of autogenic training.

In summary, since a psychophysiological disturbance may be brought on by the excessive stimulation of the nervous system (e.g., as when a person is exposed to a traumatic situation), the disturbing load results in neuronal over-excitation. The discharge of such stimulation is necessary through proper outlets of discharge so as to reestablish a state of optimal balance within the nervous system. Again, if the opportunity for the release is not provided, disturbances in physical and psychological health are likely to ensue. The purpose of the techniques of autogenic neutralization is to promote such corrective, unloading discharges. The techniques of autogenic neutralization are: (1) autogenic abreaction and (2) autogenic verbalization. One way of thinking about the process of autogenic neutralization is to think of a valve that allows excessive pressure to be released. Through facilitation of abreactive experiences, and verbalization of internal disturbances, such neutralization of the disturbing material is made possible.

Figure 17.2 captures the essence of autogenic neutralization. The standard exercises form the foundation of the autogenic training and attempt to improve self-regulation and, in turn, the re-establishment of homeostatic mechanisms to their optimal level. This may require the neutralization of disturbing material (physical or psychological) that may be interfering with the proper functioning of the nervous system. If such neutralization cannot be effectively performed due to the intensity of disturbing stimuli, then it may be necessary to use the specific methods of autogenic neutralization, namely autogenic abreaction and autogenic verbalization. Both of these methods are active interventions, which require proper training and supervision of the therapeutic process as far as the patient's progress in treatment is concerned.

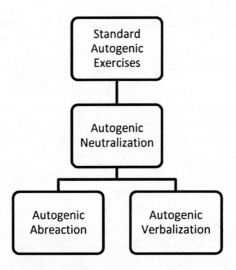

Figure 17.2. Autogenic neutralization.

The Process of Autogenic Abreaction

The process of autogenic abreaction is an active, systematic therapeutic process that consists of well defined steps; all of which need to be closely followed in order to produce the desired effects. Schultz and Luthe (1969) provided the basic information about what the treatment entails. This information was further expanded and elaborated upon by Luthe (1970, 1973). Here is a summary of the guidelines with some additional clinical instructions.

1. In most cases, prior to autogenic abreaction the patient must have achieved a level of mastery of the standard exercises. As it was indicated earlier, these exercises by themselves may bring about the needed neutralization of disturbing stimuli. However, if during the practice of the standard exercises an excessive amount of autogenic discharges are observed and they begin to cause undue stress, it may be necessary to initiate autogenic abreaction earlier. In such cases, at the very least, the patient must be proficient in the first standard exercise, heaviness.

2. During the first stage of autogenic abreaction, the patient practices passive concentration while focusing on the heaviness formulas, such as: "My right (left) arm is heavy." After about 5 minutes of maintaining passive concentration, the patient is asked to shift to a state of passive attitude known as "passive acceptance." This "spectator-like" attitude is the key to promoting abreaction. While maintaining this state, the patient is instructed to describe in detail whatever he or she is experiencing, which may include a variety of sensory (e.g., visual, auditory,

etc.), emotional (i.e., the need to cry), and cognitive (i.e., worries, recollection of certain, often disturbing events) experiences.

3. A cardinal aspect of autogenic abreaction is that of "the principle of non-interference." This principle must be abided by both the patient and the therapist. The psychophysiological events promoted by this intervention must occur at their own pace, in their own direction, and without any prying or active modification. In rare cases, the therapist may intervene if the patient is being overwhelmed by the experience, or if the patient is resisting the process by not properly engaging in the exercise. The latter may happen in the form of paying excessive attention to distractions or by attempting to engage the therapist in an unrelated conversation. In such cases, the therapist may have to prod the patient to return to the exercise.

4. It is not unusual for an autogenic abreaction session to last for 60–90 minutes. It all depends on the amount of discharge and neutralization that may be taking place during the session. It will be improper to bring a session to an abrupt end as this by itself may prove to be disturbing to the patient. Henceforth, it is a good idea to plan ahead and allow extra time for this aspect of treatment. Often a quieting effect is observed after sufficient neutralization has been achieved. A pleasant sensation of warmth that covers the entire body is almost always the "signature" of completion of effective neutralization for the session, which suggests that the session may be concluded.

5. As with the standard exercises, it is imperative that the session is brought to an end in a proper manner. That is done by having the patient take a deep breath, and flex the arms, followed by opening of the eyes. This process may need to be repeated until the patient is fully alert.

6. Schultz and Luthe (1969) and Luthe (1973) suggested that the autogenic abreaction sessions should be recorded, and that the patient should make a transcript of the session (based on the recording) as soon as possible. After the transcript is made, the patient is asked to read the entire transcript out loud for the purpose of integration. These authors also suggested that the patient should practice the technique of autogenic abreaction at home while taping each home session. In my experience, in certain cases when there are indications of severe trauma, it may not be a good idea to have the patient practice autogenic abreaction at home without proper supervision. Also, the processing of the recording material from each session should be done with utmost sensitivity. Some patients may not feel ready to review the tape, especially if what was shared during the session contained significantly disturbing, distressing content. These are matters of therapeutic importance that capable clinicians should be able to address on a case by case basis.

Case Illustration of Autogenic Abreaction

The case example described below is a detailed exploration of the treatment of a young woman who underwent autogenic training and autogenic abreaction. This was a very unusual clinical presentation in which there was sufficient evidence to warrant the incorporation of autogenic abreaction into her treatment.

LC was a 22-year old, adroit violinist who had begun to experience some pain and discomfort in her left arm while playing her instrument. Not only the discomfort prevented her from holding the violin in the proper position, it also interfered with her concentration. A course of physical therapy as well as anti-inflammatory medication had failed to bring about any changes in these symptoms. Her music teacher suggested to her that perhaps she was having these problems because she was trying to be overly perfectionistic. She simply needed to learn to relax. Based on the recommendation of her physical therapist, the patient began to take yoga classes so as to stretch her muscles and quiet her mind. Yoga training helped her improve her posture but did not take away the sporadic pain and tension that she experienced in her left arm. She stopped playing at concerts and gradually became very depressed. Her family physician suggested autogenic training. She learned very quickly how to achieve the goals of the first standard exercise. During the second exercise, warmth, she began to have some unusual sensations. She reported that when we were focusing on her left arm, she felt as if "smoke or steam" was "coming out" of her arm. She had no pain or discomfort in her arm but she found the experience rather frightening. We went over the need to focus on a soothing sensation of warmth and not heat in her arms and legs during the exercise. The experience of seeing steam radiate from her left arm returned during the practice of the 5th exercise, abdominal warmth. During that exercise, she also found herself uncontrollably flexing her left arm during the exercise. She was very disturbed by this. The phenomenon of autogenic discharges was explained to her in great detail, which reassured her and helped her not to interfere with the corrective process should they were to occur again. During the 6th standard exercise, such discharges became more intense and more frequent. Clearly a form of incomplete or ineffective discharge was taking place and it was necessary to promote neutralization of disturbing experiences through the use of autogenic abreaction. Patient received detailed instructions about this approach. During the first session of autogenic abreaction she had several intense, involuntary, flexing of her left arm. Among the various thoughts and emotional surges that she related during the session were the need to run away but she could not move fast enough. During the second session, she could see some smoke, or steam covering her arm to the point that in her mind's eye she could not see her arm. Prior to starting the third session of autogenic abreaction, she reported that she was starting to play the violin and that her pain was almost completely gone. During that session, she had a very vivid and frightening image that she was completely immobilized in front of a fountain which was "throwing off very hot steam" and that she could not get away because her "feet were too small." The session lasted for over an hour and the patient cried during most of it. As the disturbing sensation and images began to disappear, she felt a soothing sensation of warmth all over her body. During the next visit, two weeks later, she reported that she could practice the standard exercises with no physical or mental interference and that the disturbing images had disappeared altogether. In subsequent sessions, she reported that she had started to play at concerts, without experiencing any physical pain or discomfort in her arm. She continued to practice autogenic training several times a week. About a year after the treatment was terminated, patient called to make a follow-up appointment. When we met, she said that she could not wait to share a very interesting story. Apparently, on Christmas day when she was visiting her grandmother, she shared with her some of the "weird" images that she was experiencing during autogenic abreaction sessions. That was when her grandmother conveyed to her that when LC was a toddler, she was sleeping by a radiator when the pipe burst and her left arm was burned due to the steam and hot water that was pouring out of the pipe. Clearly LC had no memory of this experience but the trauma had begun to manifest itself through symptoms in her left arm.

This case illustrates some of the uses of autogenic neutralization when certain symptoms remain unyielding to other forms of treatment. Often times, no immediate insight is generated through the various methods of neutralization, such as autogenic abreaction. What matters most is not necessarily the insight or recall that follows these sessions but the fact that the patient's symptoms disappear or are significantly attenuated in their intensity.

I have had good success with autogenic abreaction particularly in the treatment of symptoms related to Post-Traumatic Stress Disorder (PTSD). In Chapter 19, I have included a case study in which I was able to successfully treat a woman who was suffering from severe and recalcitrant nightmares after a motor vehicle accident, by employing autogenic abreaction. By the end of the treatment, the nightmares had disappeared altogether and remained that way during our follow-up meetings. It is important to note that these methods of neutralization may be used when there is evidence of discernable trauma in the patient's past. The key is to look for persistent, and at times excessive, autogenic discharges during the practice of standard exercises. Methods of autogenic neutralization can then be employed to further assist the nervous system to unload the neuronal tensions that interfere with proper self-regulatory functions.

The Process of Autogenic Verbalization

Autogenic verbalization is another method of autogenic neutralization. This is more of a highly focused, circumscribed approach, which attempts to promote neutralization through the verbalization of issues and concerns that are sources of distress to the patient. These issues may include the treatment of aggressive behaviors, obsessions, excessive worry, etc. Similar to the practice of autogenic abreaction, the patient starts the session by maintaining a state of passive concentration so as to practice about 5 minutes of the standard formulas, particularly the heaviness formulas. After this initial segment the patient is asked to actively focus on a predetermined concern (a source of stress that the patient wants to resolve) and to verbalize everything, thoughts and feelings, about this particular concern. The key is to verbalize thoughts and feelings, from every angle until nothing remains, as if the patient has exhausted, for the moment, all that he or she could express. This brings us to another critical aspect of this method of autogenic neutralization. It is imperative that the session is not stopped until the patient has completed verbalization of the disturbing material. If the sessions are ended abruptly, the patient may experience tension that may manifest itself either physically or psychologically. With that said, in most cases, in my experience, an autogenic verbalization session rarely goes beyond 45 minutes to an hour. Nevertheless, it is important to plan ahead and make sure there is ample time for the patient to benefit from this approach. Upon the completion of each session, the patient is asked to practice a similar procedure at home. I highly recommend at least two office sessions of verbalization prior to assigning such homework assignments. It usually takes several sessions before the required procedures and expectations in this process are well established. Meanwhile, the clinician should pay close attention to the patient's performance during each office session.

Autogenic verbalization is a psychotherapeutic treatment of choice when dealing with acute stressors (Luthe, 1973), or when dealing with definable psychological issues that have become persistent sources of distress. If this treatment is performed properly, patients usually report a noticeable increase in physical energy as well as mental clarity, followed by an improved sense of motivation. As it was discussed earlier, the techniques of autogenic neutralization need to be employed with great care and after successful completion of the standard exercises. Below is a case example in which autogenic verbalization was used effectively in the treatment of excessive fatigue and obsessive thinking.

JY was a 50-year-old man who had suffered an injury to his knee during a skiing accident. Even though he had responded well to physical therapy and the injury had healed as far as the diagnostic tests could reveal, JY constantly felt exhausted and "fatigued." His blood tests did not reveal any abnormalities whatsoever. Generally speaking he slept well, but woke up tired. On certain days he could go to his office, interact with his staff with no difficulty; however, on other days, he felt as if he could not motivate himself to do much because he was tired. Fortunately, his wife was able to manage his business well and he continued to generate a healthy salary. Approximately 6 months after his injury, he was referred for autogenic training for the purpose of improving the quality of his sleep. Although he lacked motivation, he agreed to practice the autogenic exercises with the use of audio recordings of the exercises. Nearly 8 weeks after the start of the treatment, he kept repeating that he was "tired of being tired." He was quite frustrated with his symptoms and his own attitude. Once he was quite comfortable with the standard exercises, it was suggested to him that perhaps it was time to use autogenic verbalization as the next step in his treatment. The requirements for the procedure were described in great detail. After practicing some of the preliminary autogenic formulas (mainly heaviness and warmth), the patient began the process of verbalization. After a period of about 40 minutes, he felt as if his mind was a blank, but "in a very positive way." He felt he was free from all the negative self-talk and the self-incrimination that he was putting himself through on a daily (indeed, hourly) basis. In approximately one week, a second session of autogenic verbalization was conducted, which lasted for about 30 minutes before the patient felt "emptied out." He was then given instruction to practice a similar procedure at home. A week later, the patient reported that his wife was seeing visible changes in his behavior and that he felt "lighter," "freer," and "not as negative." After 4 sessions of autogenic verbalization, the patient had made significant improvements. Hence, additional sessions were not required. During a follow-up meeting, he reported that he was able to maintain his progress, he was back at work, and was planning new additions to his corporation.

Summary

Autogenic psychophysiological psychotherapy can be achieved through the process of autogenic neutralization, a process that is somewhat similar in theory to the early discoveries which led to the development of psychoanalysis.

The entire theory of autogenic therapy (autogenic training and its adjunctive therapies) relies on the premise that the nervous system possesses inborn capabilities that are designed to re-establish homeostasis and optimal functioning after exposure to excessive stimuli, such as excessive stress, trauma, etc. Generally speaking, the brain is equipped to discharge and neutralize such excessive neuronal load during the various phases of sleep, particularly in REM sleep. However, if such neutralization is not sufficient, for example due to interruptions in sleep cycles, it may be necessary to provide the nervous system with opportunities to execute proper neutralization of the neuronal load. This is the goal of autogenic neutralization, which brings about both psychological and psychophysiological corrections. The key methods of autogenic neutralization are autogenic abreaction, which is appropriate for trauma related disorders, and autogenic verbalization, which is appropriate for the treatment of persistent cognitive and behavioral sources of distress. These methods are simply an extension of autogenic training and require proper training in the standard exercises.

In conclusion, it is important to point out that all forms of structured attempts at psychotherapy must meet certain requirements so that the patient receives the most benefit from such practices. The establishment of a safe environment for exploration and treatment is the indispensible criterion in the practice of psychological therapies. Additionally, the psychological interventions require the proper development of a therapeutic alliance between the patient and the clinician. Listening skills are by far the most pertinent requirement for growth and development in any form of therapy. As far as autogenic therapy is concerned, education plays a critical role in the success of this treatment. Hence, the clinician needs to be familiar with the theory and practice of the treatment. No technique alone can assist those in need of help, but a meaningful therapeutic relationship fortified by knowledge and experience can, indeed.

18

Autogenic Training and Autogenic Abreaction as Treatments for Post-Traumatic Nightmares

Nightmares have been the focus of much speculation with regard to their nature and meaning since the dawn of civilization. Throughout the ages various explanations and theories have been offered about the origin of these disturbing dreams by thinkers, philosophers, writers, and artists. One cannot study mythology without coming across the mention of horrifying dreams that served a host of functions in the life of the dreamer, often suggesting an impending doom. Jones (1959) provided a most comprehensive history of nightmares and offered some explanations as to why such a term is used to distinguish frightening dreams from the more common, nocturnal sleep induced images. In nearly every ancient culture there is a reference to evil creatures attacking the vulnerable sleeper. Such fiends often arrived on horses, which would be one explanation as to the use of the words night and "mare." Jones, however, posits that the etymology of the word "mara" comes from "merran," "crusher," which refers to a being who sat on the sleeper's chest so as to exert a crushing force, rendering the sleeper completely helpless. If she were to gain any conscious awareness, what she saw were but grotesque images (Jones, 1959, p. 243).

With the advent of psychoanalysis, new physiological and psychical explanations for the nature of dreams were proposed. Freud (1900) considered dreams as guardians of sleep. Based on this formulation, one may conclude that a nightmare is the result of a serious defect in the dreaming mechanism, as it violently interrupts natural sleep. As Freud remained loyal to his wish-fulfillment theory of dreams, one of his explanations for nightmares was that an aspect of the unconscious was fulfilling its wishes of punishing the person

213

through the experience of frightening dreams (Freud, 1955). But he primarily viewed nightmares as a result of a defect, or a failure in the dreaming mechanism. That is he conceptualized most nightmares as the result of failed psychical mechanisms to properly distort the dream so as to hide the underlying source of distress, hence a manifestation of anxiety in the manifest dream. In his words, "An anxiety-dream occurs only when the censorship is entirely or partially overpowered, and on the other hand, the overpowering of the censorship is facilitated when the actual sensation of anxiety is already present from somatic sources. It thus becomes obvious for what purpose the censorship performs its office and practices dream-distortion; it does so in order to prevent the life development of anxiety or other forms of painful affect" (as quoted in Fodor & Gaynor, p. 54, 2004).

Fenichel (1945) attributed the experience of nightmares to worries and apprehensions that contain such force that cannot be properly repressed, whose energy interferes with the mechanism of sleep resulting in failed dreams, hence, nightmares. In the same vein, Kramer (1991) made a similar point by suggesting that nightmares signify a breakdown in affect regulating properties of dreams with the consequent disruption in REM activity. Usually, intense affective surges are contained within the dreaming process except in those situations that their intensity cannot be contained as in disturbing dreams. Kramer argued that a similar breakdown may be at work in case of recurrent dreams.

Hartmann (1984) asserted that people who suffer from frequent nightmares tend to have certain features that he referred to as "thin boundaries." Individuals with thin boundaries tend to be vulnerable and hypersensitive, which predisposes them to emotional injury, particularly in social situations (Hartmann, Rosen, & Rand, 1998). Pietrowsky and Köthe (2003) in their study of frequent nightmare sufferers found that there was a strong positive correlation between those with thin personal boundaries and the experience of more recurrent nightmare, than those who did not meet the criteria for thin boundaries.

The current description of "Nightmare Disorder" appears in the DSM-IV-TR (APA, 2000): "The essential feature of Nightmare Disorder is the repeated occurrence of frightening dreams that lead to awakenings from sleep (Criterion A). The individual becomes fully alert on awakening (Criterion B). The frightening dreams or sleep interruptions resulting from the awakenings cause the individual significant distress or result in social or occupational dysfunction (Criterion C). This disorder is not diagnosed if the nightmares occur exclusively during the course of another mental disorder or are due to the direct physiological effects of a substance (e.g., a drug of abuse or a medication) or a general medical condition (Criterion D). Nightmares typically occur in a lengthy, elaborate dream sequence that is highly anxiety provoking or terrifying. Dream content most often focuses on imminent physical danger to the individual (e.g., pursuit, attack, injury)" (p. 631). The first two criteria clearly suggest significant levels of sympathetic activation, which if sustained can interrupt sleep and awaken the individual in a state of utter distress. As stated above, it is in criteria C that we see how persistent nightmares can have a considerable effect on social interactions. That is, persistent nightmares are bound to have interpersonal implications, and are not merely nocturnal events that cause distress solely in the sufferer. Once again we see the importance of addressing disorders from a biopsychosocial perspective, without which the patient cannot be properly treated.

Based on clinical experience and empirical findings, I have placed nightmares under 6 categories. These are:

1. Abandonment Nightmares, which are most common in children but can also occur in adults. One of the most effective ways of helping those who suffer from this type of nightmares is by providing them with effective transitional objects, and consistent emotional support. The transitional objects act as reminders of connections to loved ones and may significantly reduce the frequency of nightmares.
2. Existential Anxiety Nightmares, which deal with everyday struggles with uncertainty, making choices, and assuming responsibility for such choices. Such nightmares are most common during significant transition points in life, when important decisions are to be made. Also, when a person is dealing with a situation whose outcome is very uncertain, one expression of such anxiety may be the manifestation of nightmares.
3. Helplessness Nightmares are especially common in those who are experiencing major depression, particularly when it has to do with situations in which they feel there is little or nothing they can do to alter the course of events. A gradual improvement in self-efficacy often causes these nightmares to disappear altogether.
4. Punishment Nightmares, which are consistent with Freud's (1955) observations that some disturbing or anxiety provoking dreams were the result of self-punitive attempts by certain aspects of the psyche. Explorations of guilt and self-destructive tendencies often substantially reduce the frequency of these nightmares.
5. Post-Traumatic Nightmares, which emerge from exposure to a life-threatening situation to the point that a part of the self is seriously injured from such an experience. The healing of the self is the key to stopping such nightmares. By "self," I am referring to the biological, psychological, and social qualities that define the person.
6. Nightmares due to active psychosis, which are particular to those

patients who are experiencing active psychosis and suggest a failure in maintaining ego boundaries and ego integrity. These nightmares need not be interpreted, but often require proper psychiatric interventions.

One of the most challenging forms of nightmares to treat in a clinical setting, without a doubt, must be post-traumatic nightmares. These nightmares may be the result of exposure to motor vehicle accidents, assaults, combat situations, etc. (Blanchard & Hickling, 1997; Norris, 1992). Hartmann (1984) provided a cogent argument that post-traumatic nightmares are not the typical disturbing dreams that are experienced by the majority of people. Current laboratory data, for instance suggest that such dreams are not limited to the rapid eye movement (REM) phase of sleep, and may occur during non–REM (NREM) sleep. This is inconsistent with the DSM-IV-TR's description, which states, "Nightmares arise almost exclusively during rapid eye movement (REM) sleep. Because REM episodes occur periodically throughout nocturnal sleep (approximately every 90–110 minutes), nightmares may also occur at any time during the sleep episode" (APA, 2000, p. 631). Hence, this statement does not include the prevailing characteristics of trauma related nightmares. It simply describes the general types of nightmares that may not have any traumatic components. Most recurrent nightmares may respond to pharmacological interventions that reduce dopamine levels in the brain; however, that is not the case as far as post-traumatic nightmares are concerned as they, at times, respond only to certain antidepressant agents (Hartmann, 1996). In other words, such disturbing dreams are qualitatively and quantitatively different than their more common analogue.

Patients who suffer from Post-Traumatic Stress Disorder (PTSD) almost always report vivid nightmares that are identical in theme and imagery. There is very little symbolic or obscure sense about them. Simply put, they are the exact repetition of the scenes from the trauma with minor, if any, variations. Perhaps that is one reason they bring about such an intense physical and physiological response in the sufferer. They are so "real" that even after the patient awakens, he or she may continue to "relive" the actual event. I once treated a patient who suffered from such nightmares, who confided in me that she tried to avoid falling asleep sometimes for days so as to avoid reliving the assault that she had experienced. Sadly, her attempts at staying awake for prolonged periods had resulted in her experiencing disturbing, intrusive images throughout the day, bringing her closer and closer to a total psychotic break.

Similar to the polysomnographic data from depressed patients, studies suggest that in patients who suffer from PTSD, there is a significant increase in REM activity. This will invariably interfere with proper sleep cycles and is bound to result in unrefreshed sleep that will lead to the emergence of physical and psychosocial symptoms (Dow, Kelsoe, & Gillin, 1996).

The common treatments for PTSD related nightmares are: Pharmacotherapy, psychodynamic therapy, behavior therapy, hypnosis, and cognitive therapy. A variety of anxiolytic and antidepressants have been successfully used to ameliorate the intensity of PTSD related nightmares. A recent study by Raskind and colleagues (2007), which entailed conducting a placebo controlled experiment, reported that Prazosin, an antihypertensive medication, was effective in reducing trauma related nightmares in a group of combat veterans. A general concern about medications has to do with their potential side effects as well as tolerance and withdrawal issues, all of which demand close medical monitoring.

Generally speaking, behavior therapy and hypnosis seem to be helpful in reducing intrusive thoughts that often cause a great deal of distress. They are particularly helpful in reducing the frequency of such thoughts during the waking hours, which may in time have a positive influence on the frequency of disturbing dreams. Exposure therapy as a form of therapy should be done with great care and under close supervision in a clinical setting. Cognitive therapy has a good record of helping PTSD patients better deal with anxiety and depression related to the traumatic experience with potential effects on nightmares. Finally, psychodynamic therapies tend to have a therapeutic effect on avoidant tendencies, a common feature of PTSD (Kellet & Beail, 1997). All the above treatments may have a vicarious, positive influence on the frequency of disturbing dreams (see Solomon, Gerrity, & Muff, 1992).

Hartmann (1996) suggested that the memory of the trauma in PTSD patients is similar to an "encapsulated" abscess that refuses to be integrated, and functions as intrusive memory. Hence, it develops a life of its own and as such creates a state of chaos within the nervous system, which is similar to the early findings that brought about the birth of psychoanalysis. From the psychoanalytic perspective the "abscess," which interfered with neurophysiologic mechanisms, needed to be lanced and drained through either induction of cathartic experiences, or free association, both of which were superior to hypnotic trance as it simply "pushed" the disturbing material deeper into the unconscious. In many cases, it was only a matter of time before the symptoms re-emerged, often with a vengeance and became much more refractory to hypnosis.

From another perspective, Hartmann's description, in particular, underlines the importance of other therapeutic interventions such as autogenic neutralization that address the very nature of such dysfunctions within the nervous system. The operative concepts here are reintegration and normalization, both of which constitute core concepts with the autogenic theory. Luthe (1973) emphasized the importance of autogenic neutralization especially in the treatment of symptoms that emerge from exposure to traumatic events. As it was discussed in great length in Chapter 17, prior to employing any of the advanced autogenic therapy applications, it is critical to make sure that patients have mastered the standard exercises, and that they are able to maintain passive concentration with some ease. In my experience, the mastery of the standard exercises often times is enough to bring about a variety of psychophysiological, therapeutic benefits in trauma patients. However, when symptoms remain refractory to the treatment, it may be necessary to employ some of the more advanced strategies such as autogenic neutralization, which consists of autogenic abreaction and autogenic verbalization. Of these two techniques, the intervention that is most appropriate for the treatment of chronic, trauma-related symptoms is that of autogenic abreaction. On the other hand, autogenic verbalization may be more suitable for the treatment of more acute conditions or concerns that are not of a traumatic nature.

The second part of this chapter consists of an in-depth exploration of a case study in which I was able to effectively treat a patient who suffered from severe and persistent nightmares due to a motor vehicle accident. The patient was referred to me after all psychotropic and psychotherapeutic interventions had failed to produce any significant changes in the frequency and intensity of the nightmares.*

The Treatment of Persistent Post-Traumatic Nightmares with Autogenic Abreaction

KC was a 39-year-old woman who was referred to me as a last resort for the treatment of her frequent, highly disturbing nightmares. Approximately, seven months before I met her, she was in a severe motor vehicle accident, in which a fast moving truck broadsided her while she was stopped at an intersection. The impact could have easily killed her, but fortunately she only sustained some injuries to the neck and shoulders as well as her lower back. She was fully conscious as the truck hit her car and moved it across the street. Initially she was disoriented and experienced some transient loss of balance, but she remained lucid and was able to speak to the paramedics about her symptoms. After a series of diagnostic tests, she was prescribed analgesics and muscle relaxants and was later discharged.

---

*The case example presented here was published in greater detail in the *Journal of Applied Psychophysiology and Biofeedback* (Sadigh, 1999). For those who are interested in the design of the study, data presentation and discussion, I highly recommend reading the actual paper. What appears here is basically a general description of the case with focus on the stages of treatment.

Several weeks after the accident, the patient began experiencing very vivid, detailed, frightening dreams about the accident. She described these dreams as movie-like, very real, in which she saw herself in a state of total helplessness. Once the nightmares began, they started to happen almost every night. Not only had they begun affecting her sleep, they also had noticeable impact on her day to day activities. Perhaps the first set of symptoms that she began to experience had to do with changes in her memory and concentration. She found herself distracted and unable to effectively interact with others. It is important to note that she did not experience any flashbacks while she was awake; at least not as far she was aware. The only time that she relived the experience was when she was asleep, in a state of total helplessness!

She avoided driving, or being in a car. When she had to go to a doctor's visit, she experienced extreme anxiety, especially when she was not the driver. Mild anxiety attacks began to evolve into full blown panic attacks, during which she felt light-headed, unable to breathe, in addition to the experience of a "cold numbness" in her hands. The attacks were very frightening to her as they made her feel as if she was about to die. Prior to the accident, KC viewed herself as a strong, resilient woman who could "handle almost anything." As her anxiety symptoms persisted, she felt extremely vulnerable, easily overwhelmed, and growingly unable to cope with even day to day stressors.

Through the use of anxiolytic agents prescribed by her physicians, she was able to initially manage her anxiety symptoms better. However, these medications did not affect her persistent nightmares. One medication actually worsened her experience of the nightmares as it made it difficult for her to wake up to terminate the disturbing dreams. This loss of control exacerbated her "falling asleep anxiety." Antidepressant agents also produced mixed results. While some symptoms were improved by them (e.g., agoraphobia), other symptoms caused her more distress (e.g., additional difficulties with concentration). In time, she was so fed up with the medications that she gave them up altogether. A course of psychotherapy also did not provide her with any relief from the disturbing dreams, which continued to persist.

After an intensive psychological evaluation, KC was introduced to autogenic training. She was also asked to collect data on the frequency and intensity of her nightmares. After the completion of training in the standard exercises, she received four, one-hour sessions of autogenic abreaction. During the initial phase of the treatment, there was a noticeable improvement in her demeanor as she mastered each exercise. Above all, she seemed to enjoy mastering the fourth standard exercise on breathing. The Organ-Specific formula, "Warmth makes me sleepy," was added to the end of the fifth standard exercise. The relaxing, sleep inducing effects of this formula combined with the potent effects of the previous exercises brought about significant changes in her anxiety and improved her sleep quality. This increased sense of control allowed her to better manage her panic attacks. Indeed, the panic attacks became much more infrequent and ceased altogether. At the end of this phase of treatment, the patient was introduced to another Organ-Specific formula, which has shown to reduce sleep onset latency: "It sleeps me."

As it was mentioned above, the second phase of treatment focused on autogenic abreaction. As it was discussed in Chapter 17, autogenic abreaction builds upon the basic principles of autogenic training, that is the promotion of normalization of the activities of the nervous system. To reach this level of training, the patient is required to have mastered at least the most basic level of autogenic training. I personally prefer to introduce this approach after the patient has completed all the standard exercises. During an autogenic abre-action session, the patient is asked to repeat some of the preliminary phrases followed by assuming a "spectator-like" attitude. This is a critical aspect of the treatment as it is imperative for the patient to observe various thoughts and feelings without interfering with them or looking for explanations or offering any form of interpretation. The purpose of this phase is to promote neutralization of the disturbing experi-ences that may be interfering with the proper functioning of the nervous system.

During the second phase of treatment, KC was informed about the nature and purpose of autogenic abreaction. She was then asked to repeat some of the basic autogenic formulas that focused on the sensations of heaviness and warmth for a few minutes, after which, in a quiet state, she began reporting thoughts, feelings, and sensations from a spectator-like position. Even though KC initially resisted entering this phase by talking about other things, she gradually felt more comfortable and started to allow the process to take shape. At first, she experienced some physical sensations which she reported right away, and noticed that such sensations quickly disappeared. This was followed by brief periods of crying. Then she felt as if she was calm and free of any form of anxiety. She reported a sensation of warmth in her arms and her back. In the next autogenic abreaction as the same procedures were followed, KC experienced some lightheadedness followed by changes in her breathing patterns. At first she attempted to hold her breath but she was able to resume proper breathing, as she on her own volition began repeating the formula "It breathes me." She reported these experiences from a spectator-like perspective with as little interference as possible. At one point some images from the accident emerged for brief moments, which she described in detail. She cried and expressed gratitude that her daughter was not with her in the car as she could have been killed. We ended the session after she entered a state of total peace and tranquility. Her mind was a blank, free of disturbing thoughts.

The next session of autogenic abreaction was filled with moments of clarity as far as her psychological state was concerned. She felt the need to leave the accident and its ensuing, disturbing symptoms behind. She felt cheated of life by all that had ensued after the accident. It was time to move on with her life and to reconnect with her family. She felt "lighter" by the end of the session. Similar thoughts, reflections and insights were reported in the final two sessions of autogenic abreaction.

The data collected by the patient showed that initially the intensity of the nightmares began to drop, particularly during the first phase of treatment. During the autogenic abreaction phase, there was a significant drop in both the frequency and severity of the nightmares altogether. Although during the follow-up phase of the treatment she reported some occasional "bad dreams," these had nothing in common with her trauma-related nightmares. Gradually she reported feeling stronger and rediscovering her "old self" again. Driving became easier, and she stopped minding being a passenger from time to time. The panic attacks disappeared completely and her "anxiety sensations" became less frequent to the point that she was no longer aware of them. Two years after our last session, I spoke with her. She reported that she was finally able to drive on the road where she had her accident. She no longer felt anxious driving on that road, but it was not her "favorite road" in town.

Discussion and Remarks

The successful treatment of the above case has brought greater attention to the powerful applications of autogenic abreaction, chiefly as far as the treatment of post-traumatic nightmares is concerned (although it is not limited to the treatment of PTSD nightmares). Autogenic training has been demonstrated to serve as a method of promoting homeostasis. Often times, as a result of the experience of trauma, the nervous system enters a state of disarray as demonstrated by a variety of physical and psychological symptoms. Initially, the nervous system attempts to discharge such neuronal overload (Luthe, 1973). But if it is not successful at accomplishing this task, dysfunction and dysregulation begin to ensue, at which time interventions such as autogenic training and its adjunctive therapeutic interventions become necessary. The above case supports this explanation and suggests that perhaps one reason KS began to show signs of improvement was because she was allowed to make such psychophysiological correction through enhanced self-regulatory, normalizing processes brought on through the practice of autogenic training and abreaction.

I have used the identical approach as described above to treat some very difficult cases of PTSD with a variety of physical and psychosocial complications. In some cases, it took nearly a year before lasting benefits were observed. However, in all treated cases, there were lasting improvements in symptoms that had remained refractory and resistant to a variety of interventions. Even more importantly, these patients began to resume their social roles and either reconnected with their support system or developed new ones. As many of these patients have stated, they began to "live again." One factor that contributed to this, without a doubt, had to do with an increase in self-efficacy and a growing sense of empowerment that had emerged as a result of properly practicing the exercises and seeing that they brought about changes in the symptoms. I am convinced that this renewed sense of empowerment is at the very core of the process of healing regardless of the method of treatment that is rendered.

I see autogenic training as a piece of the puzzle of treating symptoms of PTSD, particularly traumatic, disturbing dreams. Sadly, in recent years we have seen a growing number of people who present with PTSD symptoms due to the experience of traumatic events. Many of these people are our soldiers who return from combat situations and are unable to effectively control the psychophysiological and psychosocial changes that have been brought on due to their tragic and highly traumatic experiences. It is my hope that more and more practitioners will begin to explore the many benefits of autogenic therapy that can be easily integrated into a variety of medical and psychological interventions.

19

Autogenic Training as Palliative Care

There are times when a disease or condition has resulted in so much deterioration that the focus of treatment can no longer be on curing the condition, such as in advanced and complex forms of chronic pain disorder. In other times, the patient may be considered terminally ill and there is nothing that can be done to change the course of the disease. In these examples, instead of curative approaches, what is needed most is palliative care. Palliative care is often interdisciplinary and focuses on a plethora of interventions that alleviate suffering, while adding quality to the patient's life.

Sepúlveda and colleagues (2002) examined the evolution of the World Health Organizations' (WHO) definition of palliative care. The original definition was rather narrow and simply focused on patients who had reached the terminal stage of the disease. For these patients, therefore, palliative care came to be recognized as basically end-of-life interventions to make the patient as comfortable as possible, or to provide those medical interventions that added greater quality to the remaining days of the patient's life. Pain reduction, primarily became the focus of this approach. But there is so much more that can be included under palliative care. There is now sufficient information to suggest that "the principles of palliative care should be applied as early as possible in the course of any chronic, ultimately fatal illness. This change in thinking emerged from a new understanding that problems at the end of life have their origins at an earlier time in the trajectory of disease. Symptoms not treated at the onset become very difficult to manage in the last days of life. People do not 'get used to' pain; rather, chronic unrelieved pain changes the status of the neural transmission of the pain message within the nervous system, with reinforcement of pain transmission, and activation of previously silent pathways" (Sepúlveda, Marlin, Yoshida, & Ullrich, 2002, p. 92). Once again, while the earlier WHO definition of palliative care stressed its relevance to terminally ill patients who were not responsive to curative therapies, a more expanded understanding of palliative care offers a variety of interventions to help a larger group of patients for the sake of adding tools to their coping repertoire, particularly when dealing with refractory conditions.

Autogenic therapy, that is autogenic training and its adjunctive therapies, can be used as an effective form of palliative care. Treatment of recalcitrant pain would be one example of this, whether this pain is the result of a malignancy or chronic, degenerative, idiopathic conditions. As it was discussed throughout the book, persistent pain is a multifaceted phenomenon that demands multidisciplinary interventions. It quickly becomes a source of stress and anxiety; it changes physiological regulation within the body; it affects sleep; it affects relationships; it distorts cognitive functions, and finally, it, potentially, strips away any semblance of meaning and purpose in the sufferer's life. It is not necessarily pain that has devastating effects on a person's life and its quality, but the helplessness that emerges from the experience of pain, with the hopelessness that ensues, and with a host of maladaptive behaviors that become desperate attempts at coping with pain. Palliative interventions offer a needed dimension to patient care.

I have used the standard autogenic exercises extensively and with much success with cancer patients who were having very adverse reactions to chemotherapy. Although there are many new medications that reduce the gastrointestinal side effects of chemotherapy, some patients do not respond well to them. In some cases, the anxiety of going to the hospital for chemotherapy is sufficient enough to bring about a variety of symptoms. In such cases, anxiolytic mediations may be helpful. Post chemotherapy emesis is another common phenomenon in which anxiety may play a critical role. What if the patient could practice psychophysiological techniques such as autogenic training, before, during, and after her treatment? Would there be a reduction in physical and psychological symptoms? The answer is a resounding yes. There are many studies that have clearly demonstrated that a variety of relaxation and distraction techniques may be used to reduce the side effects of chemotherapy.

In a classic study, Vasterling and colleagues (1993) investigated the effects of cognitive distraction and relaxation training on the side effects of chemotherapy for the treatment of cancer. The results of their study showed that both relaxation and cognitive distraction interventions brought about significant reductions in chemotherapy related nausea and symptoms of distress. Anxiety was found to be a major contributor to post-chemotherapy symptoms.

Phillip and others (2008) stated that women who are diagnosed with breast cancer tend to produce excessive amounts of cortisol, which can contribute to further health complications. These authors studied the effectiveness of a 10-week course of cognitive and behavioral stress management in assisting women who were diagnosed with breast cancer. The course of treatment included relaxation training, cognitive interventions, and other coping skills. When compared to the control group, the treatment group showed a significant reduction in cortisol levels, which was maintained at follow-up observations. Not only did the treatment group show positive physiological changes, they also experienced positive psychological changes such as a greater sense of control as related to their ability to maintain a state of relaxation.

There is a long record of the effectiveness of mind-body interventions that have been successfully used to bring about pain relief in cancer patients. In a review of treatments for cancer pain, Noyes (1981) stated that interventions "such as education, reassurance, and support may have a favorable influence on the patient's experience of pain. The therapeutic relationship may become focused on this critical aspect of the patient's experience and may, in turn, be influenced by it. Consequently pain should be made an object of frank and explicit communication leading to mutually understood and realistic objectives" (p. 63). Often times, providing the patient with tools for controlling anticipatory anxiety prior to a medical intervention can make a significant difference in reducing certain symptoms. These tools fall under the psychological and psychophysiological resources that can be taught and learned in a relatively short span of time. The key is to introduce them as early in the treatment as possible, so as to avoid the formation of powerfully negative associations to medications and even the clinic where they are administered. For example, some patients may become nauseous or experience severe dizziness as they enter the hospital where they receive their chemotherapy. Such associative responses can be quickly and effectively treated through behavioral interventions, including relaxation training, as well as a variety of desensitization strategies.

Specific Autogenic Interventions for Palliative Care

Management of Symptoms Related to Hemodialysis

Many patients who undergo hemodialysis, especially those with end-stage renal disease, experience a variety of symptoms that are often exacerbated by stress and anxiety levels. These symptoms range from nausea, vomiting, and other gastrointestinal symptoms, to dizziness, hypotension, weakness, etc. These symptoms can be brought under control rather quickly with the use of autogenic training. Many of the general symptoms experienced during hemodialysis respond well to the first two standard exercises. I highly recommend at least one week of practice with the first exercise prior to proceeding to the second standard exercise. Once these two exercises have been mastered, the patient is encouraged to practice them while undergoing hemodialysis. Initially, it is recommended that patients listen to an audio version of the exercises during the dialysis sessions. This creates the necessary structure to reduce anxiety and to keep the patient's focus on the exercises rather than on worries and ruminations that can further contribute to the exacerbation of symptoms. Once the appropriate, positive associations have been established and the patient feels that he or she is in control of such symptoms, then the use of audio tapes or CDs may not be necessary, as patients can practice on their own.

To further reduce the adverse effects of dialysis, it is important to proceed to the remaining four standard exercises. One exercise in particular that has a profound effect on nausea and vomiting is the fifth exercise, abdominal warmth. I have come to view this exercise as the "anti-nausea" exercise. Also, since the induction of abdominal warmth tends to produce a deeply tranquil state, most patients notice a significant reduction in their anxiety levels. Some may actually become so relaxed that they may fall asleep while undergoing chemotherapy or dialysis. Above all, the increased sense of self-efficacy helps the patient to better benefit from the medical interventions, while limiting or altogether preventing setbacks. The increase in motivation, adherence to medical advice, and compliance constitute some of the other positive attributes of this training.

Case Example 1

After a failed kidney transplant, Stan was told that he needed to undergo hemodialysis for possibly the rest of his life. Although initially he had not experienced any "seriously" adverse symptoms during or after dialysis, things began to change for him and suddenly he started to have some of the most severe symptoms of nausea, vomiting, shakiness, weakness, and even fatigue. Gradually, Stan began to suffer from insomnia at least several nights before his hospital sessions. He began to feel defeated, depressed, and even started considering not going to his dialysis sessions. Some of his physicians began to refer to his post-session symptoms as "psychogenic." This was an unfortunate comment as he became convinced that he was solely responsible for his adverse reactions. He was referred to me for anxiety management. After a few sessions of psychotherapy, he was introduced to the first autogenic exercise. He was able to achieve the sensation of heaviness in his arms within a matter of days. We then proceeded to the second exercise. During a dialysis session, Stan was asked to listen to an audio CD of the first two standard exercises. He was somewhat nauseous at the beginning of the session, but there was no emesis. In ensuing sessions with me, he learned the third and the fourth standard exercises, all of which helped him to achieve a profound state of relaxation that was helpful in reducing his anxiety levels. He started to sleep better and was able to open up to those meaningful activities that gave him a renewed sense of purpose. It was after the mastery of the fifth autogenic exercise when he noticed that he was not nauseous at all after dialysis. Gradually, he was able to gain full control over his symptoms. Although at one time he was giving up on ever feeling well after his treatments, that sentiment began to change as his sense of control over his symptoms started to grow. In time, he was a more active participant in his dialysis sessions.

Here is a quick summary of formulas that were used for the case example that was described above. For more detailed information, please refer to the 5th autogenic exercise. Also note that to reach this level of training, the patient must first master all the previous exercises.

- I remain peacefully alert during the exercise. (Highly recommended.)
- I am quiet and relaxed.
- I am at peace.
- My right (left) arm is heavy and warm.
- I am at peace.
- My shoulders are heavy and warm.
- I am at peace.
- My jaw is heavy and warm.
- I am at peace.
- My right (left) leg is heavy and warm.
- I am at peace.
- My right (left) foot is heavy and warm.
- I am at peace.
- My heartbeat is calm.
- I am at peace.
- My heartbeat is calm and regular.
- I am at peace.
- My heartbeat is calm and strong.
- I am at peace.
- My breathing is calm.
- I am at peace.
- My breathing is calm and regular.
- It breathes me.

- I am at peace.
- My abdomen is slightly warm.
- I am at peace.
- My abdomen is pleasantly warm.
- I am at peace.
- My abdomen is warm.
- My entire body is comfortably relaxed
- My body is healing. (This is an Intentional Formula and its use is highly recommended.)
- I am at peace

The exercise is ended in the usual manner. However, since the exercise ends prior to the completion of treatments such as hemodialysis, the patient is encouraged to passively focus on his or her breathing until the treatment is over.

Remarks

The above set of formulas for mitigating some of the symptoms of hemodialysis can be effectively applied when, let's says, a cancer patient is receiving chemotherapy. In both cases gastrointestinal symptoms tend to be present, which often cause a great deal of distress, followed by the experience of fatigue. As the gastrointestinal symptoms, such as emesis, begin to subside, the post-treatment fatigue becomes much more manageable or even disappears for the most part (patients may feel tired but not fatigued). Once again, the growing sense of self-efficacy as a result of these or other psychophysiological interventions appears to be the key to reducing the adverse side effects of various medical, pharmacological interventions. Specific Intentional or Organ Specific formulas may be added to deal with persistent, distressing symptoms.

Intensifying the Effects of Autogenic Training in Palliative Care

As it was discussed earlier, chronic conditions, particularly chronic pain, can have a profound effect on interpersonal relationships. For this reason alone, we often see the sufferer struggle with reaching out to others, and on the other hand avoiding them. As the distance between the patient and the family members, friends, colleagues, etc., grows, the illness can potentially begin to develop a new dimension of helplessness, a dimension which if not properly addressed can have devastating effects on everyone involved. Avoiding others, "disconnecting" from the hurting body, will add new layers of complications to the disease process. Cassell (1991) suggested that "Suffering arises in chronic illness because of the conflicts within the person that are generated by the simultaneous need to respond to the demands and limitations of the body and to the forces of society and group life. These struggles to meet opposing needs become internalized, and suffering occurs as the integrity of the person is threatened by dissention. The suffering is exacerbated by conflicts of the self with the body and by dissension within the various parts, or aspects, of the person" (p. 64). Henceforth, suffering is not limited to the set of symptoms that can be measured and medically checked; it is a biopsychosocial, and even spiritual (that is search for meaning) reality that needs to be addressed from a biopsychosocial perspective. Otherwise, maladaptive behaviors are likely to emerge in the disease process with devastating consequences. One such consequence is when the patient turns against him or herself. This may range from engaging in unhealthy behaviors, to incompliance, to disconnecting from friends and family, all of which will lead to a poor prognosis.

For example, from time to time, avoidance appears to be a good option for everyone. The patient removes herself from others, while others disconnect from her to avoid arguments or the experience of additional tension. We often hear statements such as, "I don't call or visit because I don't want to upset her." Other times, family and friends may confess that they feel helpless as there is nothing they can do to assist the patient. Hence, they gradually withdraw. The frequency of personal contacts begins to drop significantly. Phone calls become infrequent, and may drop altogether. Soon, the patient discovers that her physicians, therapists, and nurses are her new family. Even the staff members of the doctors' office bring a sense of comfort and connectedness to the patient. They provide the needed emotional support and concern that the patient yearns. However, as the patient becomes dependant on such attention from clinicians and their staff, new complications may arise, all of which will inevitably result in further misunderstandings, rejections, and a greater tendency for avoidance.

Higginson, Wade, and McCarthy (1990) emphasized the importance of family involvement in palliative care. In their study, they found that both patients and their family began to make more positive reports regarding their management of the symptoms if they were involved in the treatment process. As it was mentioned above, one reason family members may avoid the patient is because they feel helpless. The experience of such helplessness is bound to affect interpersonal relationships, bringing about unnecessary arguments, which may lead to avoidance and neglect. Anger, frustration, and guilt are other emotions that often emerge in such situations. Family therapy is an excellent way of addressing such issues, especially before they become too complex.

In my experience, autogenic training may provide another opportunity for engaging family members in the treatment process. I have treated a number of patients whose family members began to take an active role in the training and as a result not only the effects of the exercises were enhanced, there were also positive interpersonal changes. One way of involving the family, friends, or close relatives, is to train them to go over the autogenic formulas with the patient, whether at home or when they are receiving treatment such as chemotherapy at a clinic. Even though the patient learns the techniques in a therapeutic setting, the practice of the techniques, at least initially, requires listening to an audio version of the exercises. With a few sessions of practice and close supervision, a family member can read the formulas to the patient, hence becoming an active member of the treatment team. The case below is one example of such a process.

Case Example 2

"D" was a 62-year-old woman who was diagnosed with metastatic breast cancer and was receiving chemotherapy. Since she was diagnosed, her children had gradually stopped interacting with her as she was often in pain and they felt that their presence was making her feel worse and often resulted in "D" interacting with them in an angry manner. She was often taken to the clinic for her chemotherapy by a friend, who would drop her off and pick her up later in the day. "D" was having a very hard time with a variety of symptoms related to her chemotherapy. Shortly after the practice of the autogenic exercises, she began to report a noticeable improvement in her post-chemotherapy symptoms. During one of the sessions, she mentioned that she missed seeing her granddaughter, who was in high school. I asked her if she wanted to invite her daughter and her granddaughter to our next session. She initially said that they did not want to have anything to do with her but then she agreed to give them a call. I was pleased to see the three of them at our next meeting. Toward the end of the session I asked her daughter and granddaughter if they wanted to assist "D" with the practice of the exercises when she was at the clinic. Both volunteered. In our next session, I went over some of the structures of each exercise, gave them a recorded version of the exercise, as well as written instructions. In our next session, I supervised them as they read the formulas to "D," and provided them with helpful suggestions. Her daughter started taking "D" to her chemotherapy sessions, while she sat there and softly read the formulas to her. Several times a week, her granddaughter would visit her and guide her through the exercises. In a short while, "D" no longer had any gastrointestinal complications during or after chemotherapy. Her fatigue became much more manageable. Both "D" and her family were empowered as they renewed their love. The helplessness that used to plague the family began to diminish as there was something they could do for her. They visited each other more during the final two years of "D's" life. She passed away as her granddaughter was whispering to her, "I am at peace."

Remarks

The above case is only one example of engaging family members during the practice of autogenic training. I have had very good success with this approach. In each case, both the patient and his or her family members benefited as well. Additionally, I observed that patients began to enter deeper stages of relaxation when they were led by family members who were properly trained to use the formulas. The changes that I saw in family members were striking and truly a pleasure to see.

Another way of intensifying the therapeutic effects of autogenic training in palliative care is to help the patient progress to the more advanced exercises, such as autogenic meditation. The first autogenic meditation exercise, which focuses on the "spontaneous visualization of colors," is a powerful way of facilitating the normalization process that occurs as a result of entering the autogenic state. Autogenic meditation can be properly achieved after the completion of the six standard exercises. Once the patient begins to spontaneously visualize her or his color, and reproduces it almost effortlessly through proper practice, the entire therapeutic process can be achieved with greater rapidity and even depth. Once the color is visualized, one can easily observe the various psychophysiological events occurring in a sequential format, such a decrease in eletromyographic activity in the arms, an increase in peripheral temperature, etc. In other words, the chain of autogenic processes can be activated through the visualization of the person's "color."

A patient of mine who was diagnosed with Parkinson's disease, and was using autogenic exercises to control the tremor in his arms, reported that his spontaneous color was that of a "beautiful brown." This color reminded him of the pews and walls of a chapel where he used to worship. We started calling this his "chapel color." In a little while, during the practice of the first meditative exercise while repeating: "Colors appear spontaneously. Colors appear effortlessly," he could see his color as it filled his field of vision and put him in a state of profound relaxation. At the end of our sessions, he often remarked that he felt refreshed as if he had slept for hours.

What was even more extraordinary was his experience in the MRI unit, a place that used to cause him extreme anxiety and panic. By his own report, one time as he was being moved into the MRI tube, he closed his eyes and simply repeated: "Colors appear spontaneously." The "chapel color" appeared immediately and within a few minutes he felt the sensations of heaviness and warmth in his arms and legs. He had initiated the entire process by simply visualizing his color. He was so proud of this achievement that he had to call me as soon as the scan was over.

To summarize, as seen in Figure 19.1, the entire chain of standard autogenic exercises and their corresponding psychophysiological events can be potentially activated through the use of the first meditative exercise. This requires that, first and foremost, the patient has mastered the standard exercises. Secondly, the patient must be able to easily induce the appearance of his or her color by using the specific Intentional Formulas. In time, the activation of the color may spontaneously lead to the experience of heaviness followed by warmth, etc. This promises to become a powerful tool for promoting profound relaxation and the benefits of the autogenic properties. The process may be especially beneficial before, during, and after stressful procedures as well as other distressing situations.

Summary

In the last few decades we have witnessed a, long overdue, growing interest in palliative care. While traditionally palliative care was a concept used for end of life treatments, today this term is also used to address chronic conditions in which the focus of the treatment in no longer on curing the condition but on its management in a way that brings greater control over the symptoms, by reducing suffering and adding quality to the patient's life. In this vein, Sepúlveda and colleagues (2002) defined palliative care as " ...an approach that improves the quality of life of patients and their families facing the problems associated with life-threatening illness, through the prevention and relief of suffering by means of early identification and impeccable assessment and treatment of pain and other problems, physical, psychosocial and

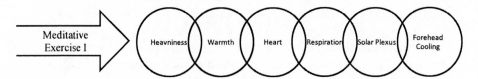

Figure 19.1. Chain of standard autogenic exercises and their corresponding psychophysiological events.

spiritual" (p. 94). Reduction of suffering and enhancement of the life of the patients and even those around them stand at the very core of palliative care.

Autogenic training may be used as an effective, adjunctive form of palliative care. Not only this approach may be used in end of life care of the patient, let's say in the case of pain management, it is also suitable during intensive treatments such as chemotherapy, hemodialysis, etc. In the end, autogenic training has been shown to increase the patient's psychophysiological resources that are critical to the management of long-term, refractory conditions. The case examples provided in this chapter simply highlight a few such interventions. With proper training and supervision, it is possible to engage family members in the process of autogenic training, which may have very meaningful effects on the patient's coping abilities. Such family involvements may actually act as a catalyst to increase patients' motivation for regular practice of the exercises.

20

Questions and Answers

In this section, some of the most commonly asked questions and their answers about autogenic training (and relaxation training in general) will be presented. Clinicians are likely to encounter similar questions while treating patients with autogenic exercises. Hence, a review of the questions and their answers may prove to be of value, especially in a clinical setting. Readers are also encouraged to consult various books and papers that have been written about autogenic techniques that appear in the reference section of this book.

Q: How long does it take to learn autogenic training?

A: The answer to this question varies from person to person. Generally speaking, with regular practice, most people are able to move from one exercise to another by practicing them for at least a week. Some people may initially have a difficult time experiencing the sensations of heaviness and warmth in their extremities, in which case they may have to practice for a longer period of time. In most cases, 6–12 weeks is sufficient to move from the first to the sixth exercise. Motivation and commitment are the critical keys to the success of this treatment. Everything will fall into place if these two ingredients are present. Finally, in my experience, children seem to master the exercises much faster than adults.

Q: I have a very busy schedule. How much time a day should I spend on these exercises? Can I skip some of the exercises and get to the ones that may benefit me most such as the breathing exercise?

A: For best results, you need to practice at least twice a day for a period of several weeks to several months to master these exercises. You should not skip any of the exercises as they build upon each other and form a very dynamic therapeutic process. Think of them as a series of rings that form a chain, a whole that is "greater than the sum of its parts." Specific advanced exercises may be delayed or skipped under special conditions. For example, the only time we may skip exercise 5 is if and when there are indications of the presence of a bleeding stomach ulcer. Exercise 5 in such cases is either skipped, or under close supervision attenuated formulas may be used for this exercise. Schultz and Luthe (1969) also suggested that those who are diagnosed with glaucoma should not use the formulas for exercise six, which focuses on forehead cooling. As it was mentioned, only under rare circumstances do we skip any of the standard exercises. The breathing exercise is the fourth exercise in the series and requires that you have mastered the other three exercises.

Q: Everybody tells me that I should learn to relax. I have bought several books on relaxation techniques but I don't seem to be able to unwind. Is there something wrong with me?

A: First, many people find it difficult to relax and unwind. That is why tranquilizers are so commonly used to promote a relaxed state. Although they give you quick results, unfortunately, tranquilizers are not without side effects, addiction being the most serious one. Some people feel that relaxation is a waste of time and that they have more important things to do. So instead of thinking about relaxation, you should think about replenishing or refueling yourself. Refueling, which is actually the scientifically accurate term for relaxation, should help you with the needed motivation to find the right technique and stay with it.

From this question, I can surmise that you have difficulty quieting your mind and that your inability to relax may not necessarily be a physical problem. Many relaxation techniques focus on relaxing the body; and if you have been trying these techniques, you probably have discovered that they do not particularly help your racing mind. You need to find a technique that preferably quiets both your mind and relaxes your body. Autogenic training may be of great help to you. However, please remember that you should not expect overnight results. If you adhere to the instructions that are provided in this book, it is quite possible that within the first two weeks you should begin noticing some replenishing, rejuvenating results. Keep practicing and you should see results.

Q: Is autogenic training a form of hypnosis?

A: I am often asked this question during the first training session because of the focus on heaviness. The origin of autogenic training was based on certain scientific observations and discoveries from the field of medical hypnosis. However, the field of autogenic training has gone far beyond autosuggestions. Many of the processes that are promoted during autogenic training are based on physiological observations during sleep and when the body enters a repair process similar to what happens in a pre-sleep state. From EEG studies of the hypnotic state we know that hypnosis tends to occur more in an alert state.

In addition, the autogenic formulas are physiologically based. That is, they are not just based on some relaxing suggestions. As the nervous system enters a state of repair and recuperation from stress, the muscles do become more relaxed, the peripheral temperature rises, the heartbeat becomes more steady, etc. The autogenic formulas simply support and enhance the same process. That is why it is called autogenic: it is brain directed or self-generated. With autogenic training there are no posthypnotic suggestions. The formulas are physiologically based and are not based on suggestions about merely inducing a state of relaxation.

Q: I am quite overweight and just the thought of repeating to myself that my arms and legs are heavy is very unsettling. What should I do?

A: The heaviness formulas focus on the *sensation* of heaviness, a tranquil and soothing sensation that we often experience before falling asleep. Keep your focus on that sensation and not on the muscle mass. As you repeat the formula, imagine that your muscles are becoming relaxed and totally free of any tension.

Q: I have been practicing yoga (hatha yoga) for some time but I seem to have stopped benefiting from it. Can I combine yoga with this (autogenic) technique?

A: Hatha yoga is a wonderful technique for stress management, pain management, and overall health enhancement. However, it has been recommended that you do not combine any other techniques, no matter how therapeutically helpful, with autogenic training. The sequence of autogenic formulas has been developed based on decades of intensive research into the dynamics of self-regeneration and a brain-generated process of reestablishing homeostasis (state of balance). It is quite possible that by introducing additional activities into the sequence of formulas, you may inadvertently interfere with the actual autogenic process, and may possibly bring on some paradoxical effects. My recommendation is that you practice the two techniques at different times during the day and refrain from combining them.

Q: I feel that if I say, "My arms and shoulders are light," instead of heavy, I may enter a deeper state of relaxation. Is there any harm in doing that?

A: It is imperative that you do not, at any time, change or alter the autogenic formulas. Remember that these formulas are based on many years of research and they attempt to estimate some of the natural sensations that we experience shortly before falling asleep. In a study by Blizard, Cowings, and Miller (1975), it was decided to change some of the autogenic formulas to see if similar, physiologically corrective phenomena occurred. For example, the subjects in the study were asked to repeat formulas that suggested lighter and cooler extremities. The findings of the study clearly showed that such formulas actually resulted in an increase in the activity of the sympathetic nervous system which is responsible for the stress response. For example, an increase occurred in the heart and respiration rates in those subjects who repeated the light and cool formulas. Meanwhile, it is possible that while people are repeating the heaviness formulas they may initially experience a pleasant sensation which is more similar to the experience of "lightness" in the extremities. However, you should not purposely try to induce such a sensation as far the practice of autogenic exercises is concerned.

Q: I became very excited when I learned that the autogenic meditative exercises can be used to further add depth to my ability to relax. There is, however, a big problem for me. I don't think I can visualize colors, even my dreams are in black and white. Does this mean that I am not a good candidate for the advanced, meditative exercises?

A: Not at all. I recall that I personally had the same concerns when I was studying advanced autogenic training. So allow me to share some of my own experiences with you. First, the color gray has many shades — a color that is most easily observed shortly after we close our eyes. Your autogenic color may be a shade of gray that in time, and with some practice, you will learn to recognize and generate during the practice of the autogenic-meditative exercises. I recall that during the practice of the first meditative exercise, I spontaneously began to visualize a dark shade of blue and gradually other colors began to enter my visual field. I also noticed that I gradually began to dream in color which has persisted to this day. So, my recommendation is that you focus on different shades of gray and be open to visualizing other colors.

Q: What if a persistent thought keeps showing up during the practice of the autogenic phrases? What if ignoring the thought does not seem to do the trick?

A: This is a very common question that requires deeper exploration as to the cause of such distractions. I can only provide some general guidelines to remedy this problem. Perhaps the most expedient way of addressing the problem of distraction is to initially shorten the period of training, such as starting with only two to three minutes of practice. Then, as you become more comfortable with letting go of your mental distractions, you may add a few more minutes to each training (practice) session. In a clinical setting, patients can effectively overcome persistent mental distractions by talking about their thoughts, worries, and concerns. If you don't have access to your therapist while practicing at home, I recommend writing down your thoughts. This practice often has a profound effect on reducing mental or cognitive anxiety. Finally, my patients find the following affirmation very helpful: "I need to replenish my resources by relaxing my body and mind. I will therefore allow myself to put aside my thoughts and worries for the next ten (fifteen, twenty) minutes and will return to my concerns much more refreshed at the end of the exercise." Incidentally, many patients report that by the end of the exercise they have no desire to entertain troublesome thoughts and ideas.

Q: I am very interested in this technique and have read much about it. However, each time I try to practice, I fall asleep. Do you have a suggestion?

A: You can do several things to reduce the chances of falling asleep during your training sessions. First, choose a training posture other than the "Horizontal Posture" (Chapter 6). You may instead choose the sitting position or the reclined position. Second, you may want to reconsider the period that you put aside for your practice. Some people do much better in the early afternoon, while some prefer the early morning to practice. Finally, there are several formulas that you may wish to repeat to yourself prior to repeating the standard formulas. These appear in Chapter 12.

Q: How long does it usually take before one begins to see some results from practicing this technique?

A: This is a difficult question to answer. In my experience, almost everyone masters the technique at their own pace. Those who have been in pain or exposed to prolonged stress may need more time to benefit from the therapeutic effects of this approach. As a general rule, two to three weeks after practicing the technique, most people begin to report positive changes in their symptoms. The pioneers of autogenic training stated that it may take as long as six months before positive effects are experienced. However, with daily practice, I have seen steady results in some of the most difficult cases in as early as six to eight weeks.

Q: How often should I practice and what are the best times for daily practice?

A: At least initially, you should make sure to practice twice a day for approximately twenty minutes. The autogenic literature recommends practicing around 12 P.M. or 1 P.M. and also every evening (about an hour after or before you eat your dinner). You may have to discover on your own the best time for your practice of these exercises. In time, you will be able to enter the autogenic state in minutes, but meanwhile you should keep practicing until you reach that point.

Q: I came across autogenic training in a book on stress management. They had a list of warm and heaviness phrases and you were told to repeat

them to yourself. I repeated the phrases on the list but it really did not do much for me.

A: It is unfortunate that there is such a limited and poor presentation of autogenic training in general books on pain and stress management. Your statement that there were warm and heaviness phrases suggests that there simply combined bits and pieces of autogenic phrases without any regard or understanding of the process involved in this training. First and foremost, you must not proceed to the warmth exercise unless you have been able to achieve the objectives of the first standard exercise, which is the sensation of heaviness in the extremities. If this objective has not been achieved and one simply moves to the second exercise, warmth, chances are that either nothing will happen or paradoxical experiences may be induced through improper attempts at inducing these critical sensations. With the advent of the Internet, I often hear people telling me that they were practicing autogenic by going to websites that purported to teach them about the technique. Such instructions based on what I read and saw had nothing to do with autogenic training. Autogenic technique, as I have emphasized time and again, throughout the book, is a powerful therapeutic technique that needs to be implemented with proper education as well as initial supervision of a knowledgeable clinician.

Q: Many years ago I used autogenic training to control my headaches and I had very good results. I was recently diagnosed with FMS but I don't seem to be able to warm up my hands or calm my breathing the way I used to. What do you think is the problem?

A: First make sure that you remain under medical supervision while practicing the autogenic exercises. It is possible that changes in your health have resulted in overactivation of the stress response — a condition which is often observed with chronic pain and fibromyalgia patients. Next, you may need to begin with the first standard exercise for a while and then move to the warmth, heart, and breathing exercises. It may take a while before you can warm your hands but it is worth it. Above all, do not try to force yourself to warm your hands and/or calm your breathing. Such attempts may result in paradoxical responses. That is, you may actually feel more anxious while relaxing.

Q: What do you mean by the formula "It breathes me?"

A: What happens to your respiration when you fall asleep? What happens to your cardiac and digestive activities? Do they cease to function because you are asleep? One hopes not! Most of the life-sustaining functions of the body are not under our conscious control. The brain contains an elaborate network of self-regulating mechanisms that constantly monitor and attempt to balance the activities of these functions. Your respiratory mechanism knows how to breathe effectively without your assistance — it knows how to breathe. So the word "it" refers to unconscious physiological mechanisms that are constantly working to maintain a state of vitality and balance within the body.

Q: From time to time I suffer from restless leg syndrome. I don't want to be on any more medications than I am already taking. Can autogenic training help me with this condition?

A: The first standard autogenic training exercise, heaviness, often brings up significant positive, therapeutic changes in those patients who suffer from restless legs syndrome. This condition can disrupt sleep and bring about many physical and psychological complications. There are very effective medications that can help you with this annoying condition and you may use them in conjunction with autogenic training while you are mastering the exercises.

Q: My husband is a combat veteran and was diagnosed with PTSD about a year ago. He cannot sleep at night because of bad dreams about the war. The only way he can fall asleep is by having a few drinks. But I am very concerned that he is changing because of his drinking. A friend of mine suggested this technique. Can it be of help to my husband?

A: Disturbing dreams are very common among those who suffer from PTSD. Also, while alcohol may help some people to fall asleep, it actually fragments the various stages of sleep and reduces the overall quality of sleep. It is imperative to make sure that he receives proper psychological counseling about his drinking so as to avoid becoming dependent on alcohol. As far as autogenic techniques and nightmares are concerned, I highly recommend reviewing Chapter 18, which addresses post-traumatic nightmares. I have had good success using the autogenic technique to assist those who were suffering from a variety of PTSD related symptoms, particularly disturbing dreams. I always recommend a multidisciplinary approach to the treatment of various disorders. A multidisciplinary team may include internists, psychiatrists, psychologists, social workers, nurses, etc. PTSD is a very complex condition that requires the contributions of a variety of specialists to make the treatments as effective as possible, with the hope to ultimately reduce the patient's suffering.

Appendix A: The Autogenic Pain and Tension Checklists (Forms A and B)

These checklists were developed to provide patients with information about their pain or tension levels before and after each training session.

The Autogenic Pain Checklist

Form A

NAME_____ EXERCISE: I. II. III. IV. V. VI. (CIRCLE ONE)

INSTRUCTIONS: Complete this form before your autogenic training session. Simply rate your pain levels by circling the number on a scale of 0 to 10. A score of 0 indicates the absence of pain, whereas a score of 10 indicates severe pain in that body part.

1. My right arm is

0	1	2	3	4	5	6	7	8	9	10

2. My left arm is

0	1	2	3	4	5	6	7	8	9	10

3. My shoulders are

0	1	2	3	4	5	6	7	8	9	10

4. My neck is

0	1	2	3	4	5	6	7	8	9	10

5. My forehead is

0	1	2	3	4	5	6	7	8	9	10

6. My jaw is

0	1	2	3	4	5	6	7	8	9	10

7. My chest is

0	1	2	3	4	5	6	7	8	9	10

8. My abdomen is

0	1	2	3	4	5	6	7	8	9	10

9. My lower back is

0	1	2	3	4	5	6	7	8	9	10

10. My right leg is

0	1	2	3	4	5	6	7	8	9	10

11. My left leg is

0	1	2	3	4	5	6	7	8	9	10

12. Overall my body is

0	1	2	3	4	5	6	7	8	9	10

The Autogenic Pain Checklist

Form B

NAME_____EXERCISE: I. II. III. IV. V. VI. (CIRCLE ONE)

INSTRUCTIONS: Complete this form after your autogenic training session. Simply rate your pain levels by circling the number on a scale of 0 to 10. A score of 0 indicates the absence of pain, whereas a score of 10 indicates severe pain in that body part.

1. My right arm is

0	1	2	3	4	5	6	7	8	9	10

2. My left arm is

0	1	2	3	4	5	6	7	8	9	10

3. My shoulders are

0	1	2	3	4	5	6	7	8	9	10

4. My neck is

0	1	2	3	4	5	6	7	8	9	10

5. My forehead is

0	1	2	3	4	5	6	7	8	9	10

6. My jaw is

0	1	2	3	4	5	6	7	8	9	10

7. My chest is

0	1	2	3	4	5	6	7	8	9	10

8. My abdomen is

0	1	2	3	4	5	6	7	8	9	10

9. My lower back is

0	1	2	3	4	5	6	7	8	9	10

10. My right leg is

0	1	2	3	4	5	6	7	8	9	10

11. My left leg is

0	1	2	3	4	5	6	7	8	9	10

12. Overall my body is

0	1	2	3	4	5	6	7	8	9	10

The Autogenic Tension Checklist

Form A

NAME_____EXERCISE: I. II. III. IV. V. VI. (CIRCLE ONE)

INSTRUCTIONS: Complete this form before your autogenic training session. Simply rate your tension levels by circling the number on a scale of 0 to 10. A score of 0 indicates the absence of tension, whereas a score of 10 indicates extreme tension in that body part.

1. My right arm is

0	1	2	3	4	5	6	7	8	9	10

2. My left arm is

0	1	2	3	4	5	6	7	8	9	10

3. My shoulders are

0	1	2	3	4	5	6	7	8	9	10

4. My neck is

0	1	2	3	4	5	6	7	8	9	10

5. My forehead is

0	1	2	3	4	5	6	7	8	9	10

6. My jaw is

0	1	2	3	4	5	6	7	8	9	10

7. My chest is

0	1	2	3	4	5	6	7	8	9	10

8. My abdomen is

0	1	2	3	4	5	6	7	8	9	10

9. My lower back is

0	1	2	3	4	5	6	7	8	9	10

10. My right leg is

0	1	2	3	4	5	6	7	8	9	10

11. My left leg is

0	1	2	3	4	5	6	7	8	9	10

12. Overall my body is

0	1	2	3	4	5	6	7	8	9	10

The Autogenic Tension Checklist

Form B

NAME_____EXERCISE: I. II. III. IV. V. VI. (CIRCLE ONE)

INSTRUCTIONS: Complete this form after your autogenic training session. Simply rate your tension levels by circling the number on a scale of 0 to 10. A score of 0 indicates the absence of tension, whereas a score of 10 indicates extreme tension in that body part.

1. My right arm is

0	1	2	3	4	5	6	7	8	9	10

2. My left arm is

0	1	2	3	4	5	6	7	8	9	10

3. My shoulders are

0	1	2	3	4	5	6	7	8	9	10

4. My neck is

0	1	2	3	4	5	6	7	8	9	10

5. My forehead is

0	1	2	3	4	5	6	7	8	9	10

6. My jaw is

0	1	2	3	4	5	6	7	8	9	10

7. My chest is

0	1	2	3	4	5	6	7	8	9	10

8. My abdomen is

0	1	2	3	4	5	6	7	8	9	10

9. My lower back is

0	1	2	3	4	5	6	7	8	9	10

10. My right leg is

0	1	2	3	4	5	6	7	8	9	10

11. My left leg is

0	1	2	3	4	5	6	7	8	9	10

12. Overall my body is

0	1	2	3	4	5	6	7	8	9	10

Appendix B: The Autogenic Training Progress Index

This index was developed to provide patients with information about their mastery of the different standard exercises. It is completed at the end of training in each of the standard exercises.

The First Standard Exercise: Heaviness

MILD SENSATION OF HEAVINESS							PROFOUND HEAVINESS		
1	2	3	4	5	6	7	8	9	10

The Second Standard Exercise: Warmth

MILD SENSATION OF WARMTH							PROFOUND WARMTH		
1	2	3	4	5	6	7	8	9	10

The Third Standard Exercise: Heart

TENSE CARDIAC ACTIVITY							CALM CARDIAC ACTIVITY		
1	2	3	4	5	6	7	8	9	10

The Fourth Standard Exercise: Respiration

TENSE RESPIRATION							CALM RESPIRATION		
1	2	3	4	5	6	7	8	9	10

The Fifth Standard Exercise: Abdominal Warmth

LITTLE WARMTH							PLEASANT WARMTH		
1	2	3	4	5	6	7	8	9	10

The Sixth Standard Exercise: Forehead Cooling

LITTLE COOLING SENSATION							PLEASANT COOLING		
1	2	3	4	5	6	7	8	9	10

References

Achterberg, J. (1985). *Imagery in healing: Shamanism and modern medicine*. Boston: New Science Library.

Adams, N., and Sim, J. (1998). An overview of fibromyalgia syndrome: Mechanisms, differential diagnosis and treatment approaches. *Physiotherapy*, 84, 304–318.

Alexander, F. (1950). *Psychosomatic medicine*. New York: W.W. Norton.

American Psychiatric Association (2000). *The diagnostic and statistical manual of mental disorders* (4th ed., text rev.). Washington, DC: American Psychiatric Association.

Arnold, L. M. (2008). Management of fibromyalgia and comorbid psychiatric disorders. *Journal of Clinical Psychiatry*, 69, 14–19.

_____, Clauw, D. J., Wohlreich, M. M., Wang, F., Ahl, J., Gaynor, P. J., and Chappell, A. S. (2009). Efficacy of Duloxetine in patients with fibromyalgia: Pooled analysis of 4 placebo-controlled clinical trials. *Primary Care Companion to Journal of Clinical Psychiatry*, 11, 237–244.

_____, Keck, P. E., and Welge, J. A. (2000). Antidepressant treatment of fibromyalgia: A meta-analysis and review. *Psychosomatics*, 41, 104–113.

Aronoff, G. M. (1992). *Evaluation and treatment of chronic pain*. Baltimore: Williams & Wilkins.

_____, and Rutrick, D. (1992). Psychodynamics and psychotherapy of the chronic pain syndrome. In G. F. Aronoff (ed.), *Evaluation and treatment of chronic pain* (pp. 394-398). Baltimore: Williams & Wilkins.

Banks, S., Jacobs, D. W., Gevirtz, R., and Hubbard, D. R. (1998). The effects of autogenic relaxation training on electromyographic activity in active myofascial trigger points. *Journal of Musculoskeletal Pain*, 6, 23–32.

Banner, C. N., and Meadows, W. M. (1983). Examination of the effectiveness of various treatment techniques for reducing tension. *British Journal of Clinical Psychology*, 22, 183–186.

Beard, G. (1869). Neurasthenia or nervous exhaustion. *Boston Medicine and Surgery Journal*, 3, 217–221.

Beck, A. T., and Alford, B. A. (2009). *Depression: Causes and treatment* (2d ed.). Philadelphia: University of Pennsylvania Press.

Bendtsen, L., and Fernandez-de-la-Penas, C. (2011). The role of muscles in tension-type headaches. Current Pain Headache Reports. Doi: 10.1007/s11916-011-0216-0.

Bennett, R. M., Clark, S. R., Campbell, S. M., and Burckhart, C. S. (1992). Low levels of somatomedian C in patients with the fibromyalgia syndrome. A possible link between sleep and muscle pain. *Arthritis and Rheumatology*, 35, 1113–1116.

Benson, H. (2000). *The relaxation response*. New York: Harper.

_____, Beary, J. F., and Carol, M. P. (1974). The relaxation response. *Journal of Psychiatry*, 39, 37–46.

_____, and Friedman, R. (1985). Meditation and somatic arousal reduction. *American Psychologist*, 40, 725–727.

Berman, B. M. (1997). The NIH format for achieving the integration of behavioral and relaxation techniques into medical practice: A review and critique. *Mind-Body Medicine, 2*, 169–175.

Blacker, H. M. (1980). Volitional sympathetic control. *Anesthesia and Analgesia, 59*, 785–788.

Blanchard, E. B., and Hickling, E. J. (1997). *After the crash: Assessment and treatment of motor vehicle accident survivors.* Washington, DC: American Psychological Association.

Blanks, S. M., and Kerns, R. D. (1996). Explaining high rates of depression in chronic pain: A diathesis-stress framework. *Psychological Bulletin, 119*, 95–110.

Blizard, D., Cowings, P., and Miller, N. E. (1975). Visceral responses to opposite types of autogenic training imagery. *Biological Psychology, 3*, 49–55.

Boomershine, C. S., and Crofford, L. J. (2009). A symptom-based approach to pharmacological management of fibromyalgia. *National Review of Rheumatology, 5*, 154–159.

Bootzin, R. R. (1972). Stimulus control treatment of insomnia. *Proceedings of the American Psychological Association, 7*, 395–396.

Brannon, L., and Feist, J. (2010). *Health psychology: An introduction to behavior and health* (7th ed.). Delmont, CA: Wadsworth.

Budzynski, T. H., Stoyva, J. M., Adler, C. S., and Mullaney, D. J. (1973). EMG bio-feedback and tension headaches: A controlled outcome study. *Psychosomatic Medicine, 6*, 509–514.

Campbell, S. M., Clark, S., Tindall, E. A., Forehand, M. E., and Bennett, R. M. (1983). Clinical characteristics of fibrositis: A "blinded," controlled study of symptoms and tender points. *Arthritis and Rheumatism, 26*, 817–824.

Cannon, W. B. (1932). *Wisdom of the body.* New York: Norton.

Carette, S., McCain, G. A., Bell, D. A., and Fam, A. G. (1986). Evaluation of amitriptyline in primary fibrositis: A double-blind, placebo-controlled study. *Arthritis and Rheumatism, 29*, 655–659.

Carrington, P. (1977). *Freedom in meditation.* New York: Doubleday.

Carson, M. A., Hathaway, A., Tuohey, J. P., and McKay, B. M. (1988). The effect of relaxation techniques on coronary risk factor. *Behavioral Medicine, 14*, 71–77.

Cassell, E. (1991). *The nature of suffering.* New York: Oxford University Press.

Chou, R., and Huffman, L. H. (2007). Nonpharmacologic therapies for acute chronic low back pain: A review of the evidence for an American Pain Society/American College of Physicians clinical practice guideline. *Annals of Internal Medicine, 147*, 492–504.

Clauw, D. J. (1995). Fibromyalgia: More than just a musculoskeletal disease. *American Family Physician, 52*, 843–851.

_____. (2008). Pharmacotherapy for patients with fibromyalgia. *Journal of Clinical Psychiatry, 69*, 25–29.

Cohen, S. (1980). Aftereffects of stress on human performance and social behavior: A review of research and theory. *Psychological Bulletin, 88*, 82–108.

Coleman, R. M. (1986). *Wide awake at 3:00 a.m.* New York: W. H. Freeman.

Cooper, C. L., and Dewe, P. (2004). *Stress: A brief history.* Malden, MA: Blackwell.

Courmel, K. (1996). *A companion volume to Dr. Jay A. Goldstein's betrayal by the brain: A guide for patients and their physicians.* Binghamton, NY: The Haworth Press.

Coursey, R. D., Frankel, B. L., Gaarder, K. R., and Mott, D. E. (1980). A comparison of relaxation techniques with electrosleep therapy for chronic, sleep-onset insomnia: A sleep EEG study. *Biofeedback and Self-Regulation, 5*, 57–73.

Cox, I. M., Campbell, M. J., and Dowson, D. (1991). Red blood cell magnesium and chronic fatigue syndrome. *Lancet, 337*, 757–760.

Crider, A. B., and Glaros, A. G. (1999). A meta-analysis of EMG biofeedback treatment of temporomandibular disorders. *Journal of Orofacial Pain, 13*, 29–37.

Danish, D. (1997). *Fibromyalgia: A comprehensive approach to evaluation and treatment.* Bethlehem, PA: Core Physical Therapy Publications.

Davidson, R. J., and Schwartz, G. E. (1976). The psychobiology of relaxation and related states: A multiprocess theory. In D. Mastofsky (ed.), *Behavior control and motivation of psychological activity* (pp. 399–442). New York: Prentice Hall.

_____, and _____. (1984). Matching relaxation therapies to types of anxiety: A patterning approach. In D. H. Shapiro and R. N. Walsh (eds.), *Meditation: Classic and contemporary perspectives* (pp. 622–631). New York: Aldine.

Del Paso, G. A. R., Garrido, S., Pulgar, A., and Martin-Vazquez, M. (2010). Aberrances in autonomic cardiovascular regulation in fibromyalgia syndrome and their relevance for clinical pain reports. *Psychosomatic Medicine, 72,* 462–470.

Dement, W. C. (1999). *The promise of sleep.* New York: Delacorte.

De Rivera, J. L. G. (1997). Autogenic psychotherapy and psychoanalysis. In J. Guimon (ed.), *The body in psychotherapy* (pp. 176–181). Basel: Krager.

Derogatis, L. R. (1983). *The SCL-90-R Manual II.* Baltimore: Clinical Psychometric Research.

Dow, B. M., Kelsoe, J. R., and Gillin, J. C. (1994). Sleep and dreams in Vietnam PTSD and depression. *Biological Psychiatry, 39,* 42–50.

Eisinger, J., Plantamura, A., Marie, P. A., and Ayavou, T. (1994). Selenium and magnesium status of fibromyalgia. *Magnesium Research, 7,* 285–288.

Elliot, G. R., and Eisdorfer, C. (1982). *Stress and human health.* New York: Springer.

Engel, G. L. (1977). The need for a new medical model: A challenge for biomedical science. *Science, 196,* 129–136.

_____. (1980). The clinical application of the biopsychosocial model. *The American Journal of Psychiatry, 137,* 535–544.

English, E. H., and Baker, T. B. (1983). Relaxation training and cardiovascular response to experimental stressor. *Health Psychology, 2,* 239–259.

Fenichel, O. (1945). *The psychoanalytic theory of neurosis.* New York: W.W. Norton.

Ferraccioli, G., Ghirelli, L., and Scita, F. (1987). EMG biofeedback training in fibromyalgia syndrome. *Journal of Rheumatology, 14,* 820–825.

Fodor, N., and Gaynor, F. (2004). *Freud: Dictionary of psychoanalysis.* New York: Barnes & Noble.

Fosshage, J. (1983). The psychological function of dreams: A revised psychoanalytic perspective. *Contemporary Psychoanalytic Thought, 6,* 641-669.

Foulks, E. F. (1992). Reflections on dream material from Arctic native people. *The Journal of the American Academy of Psychoanalysis, 20,* 193–203.

Frankl, V. E. (2006). *Man's search for meaning.* Boston: Beacon Press.

Freedman, R. R., Ianni, P., and Weing, P. (1983). Behavioral treatment of Raynaud's disease. *Journal of Consulting and Clinical Psychology, 51,* 539–549.

Freud, S. (1955). *Beyond the pleasure principle.* Standard ed., 18: 7–64. London: Hogarth Press.

_____. (1900/1994). *The interpretation of dreams.* New York: Barnes & Noble.

Fuller, G. (1977). *Biofeedback: Methods and procedures in clinical practice.* San Francisco: Biofeedback Institute of San Francisco.

_____. (1986). Biofeedback. In I. L. Kutash and A. Wolf (eds.), *Psychotherapist's casebook* (pp. 228–296). San Francisco: Jossey-Bass.

Gallagher, R. M. (1997). Behavioral and biobehavioral treatment of pain: Perspectives on the evidence of effectiveness. *Mind-Body Medicine, 2,* 176–186.

Gerster, J. C., and Hadj-Djilani, A. *(1984).* Hearing and vestibular abnormalities in primary fibrositis syndrome. *Journal of Rheumatology, 11,* 678-680.

Girdano, D. A., Everly, G. S., and Dusek, D. E. (1997). *Controlling stress and tension.* Boston: Allyn & Bacon.

Goldberg, P., and Kaufman, D. (1978). *Natural sleep.* Emmaus, PA: Rodale Press.

Goldenberg D. L. (1989). An overview of psychologic studies in fibromyalgia. *Journal of Rheumatology, 16,* 12-14.

_____. (1989a). An overview of psychologic studies in fibromyalgia. *Journal of Rheumatology, 16,* 12–14.

_____. (1989b). Psychological symptoms and psychiatric diagnosis in patients with fibromyalgia. *Journal of Rheumatology, 16,* 127–130.

_____. (1992). Controversies in fibromyalgia and myofascial pain syndrome. In G. M. Aronoff (ed.), *Evaluation and treatment of chronic pain* (pp. 164–175). Baltimore: Williams and Wilkins.

_____, Burckhardt, C., and Crofford, L. (2004). Management of fibromyalgia syndrome. *JAMA, 292,* 2388–2395.

Goldstein, D. S. *(1998).* The sympathetic and the adrenomedullary hormonal systems: Differential responses to stressors. *Journal of Musculoskeletal Pain, 6,* 63-68.

Goto, F., Nakai, K., Ogawa, K. (2011). Application of autogenic training in patients with Meniere disease. European Archive of Otorhinolaryngology. Doi: 10.1007/s00405-011-1530-1.

Gowers, W. R. (1904). Lumbago: Its lessons and analogues. *British Medical Journal, 1,* 117–121.

Graber, A. V. (2004). *Viktor Frankl's logotherapy* (2d ed.). Lima, OH: Wyndham Hall Press.

Gray, M. (1978). *Neuroses: A comprehensive and critical review.* New York: Van Nostrand Reinhold.

Green, E., and Green, A. M. (1977). *Beyond biofeedback.* New York: Delacorte Press.

Griep, E. N., Boersma, J. W., and de Kloet, E. R. (1993). Altered reactivity of the hypo-thalamic-pituitary-adrenal axis in the primary fibromyalgia syndrome. *Journal of Rheumatology, 20,* 469–474.

Grossman, P., Tiefenthaler-Gimer, U., Raysz, A., and Kesper, U. (2007). Mindfulness training as an intervention for fibromyalgia: Evidence of postintervention and 3-year follow-up benefits in well-being. *Psychotherapy and Psychosomatics.* Doi:10.1159/000

Hartmann, E. (1984). *The Nightmare: The psychology and biology of terrifying dreams.* New York: Basic Books.

_____. (1996). Who develops PTSD nightmares and who doesn't. In D. Barrett (ed.), *Trauma and dreams* (pp. 100–113). Cambridge, MA: Harvard University Press.

_____, Rosen, G., and Rand, W. (1998). Personality and dreaming: Boundary structure and dream content. *Dreaming, 8,* 31–39.

Hauser, W., Eich, W., Hermann, M, Nutzinger, D. O., Schiltenwolf, M., and Henningsen, P. (2009). Fibromyalgia syndrome: Classification, diagnosis, and treatment. *Deutsches Arzteblatt International, 106,* 383–391.

Heide, F. J., and Borkovec, T. D. (1984). Relaxation-induced anxiety: Mechanisms and theoretical implications. *Behaviour Research and Therapy, 22,* 1–12.

Hench, P. K., and Mitler, M. M. (1986). Fibromyalgia. II: Management guidelines and research findings. *Postgraduate Medicine, 80,* 57–64.

Herring, M. P., O'Connor, P. J., and Dishman, R.K. (2010). The effects if exercise training on anxiety symptoms among patients: A systematic review. *Archives of Internal Medicine, 170,* 321–331.

Higginson, I., Wade, A. and McCarthy, M. (1990). Palliative care: Views of patients and their families. *British Medical Journal, 301,* 227–281.

Hobfoll, S. E. (1989). Conservation of resources; A new attempt at conceptualizing stress. *American Psychologist, 44,* 513–524.

Holmes, G. P., Kaplan, J. E., and Gantz, N. M. et al. (1988). Chronic fatigue syndrome: A working case definition. *Annals of Internal Medicine, 108,* 387–389.

Holmes, T. H., and Rahe, R. H. (1967). The social readjustment rating scale. *Journal of Psychosomatic Research,* 11, 213–218.

Hudson, J. I., Hudson, M. S., and Pliner, L. F. (1985). Fibrositis and major affective disorders: A controlled phenomenology and family history study. *Journal of Psychiatry, 142,* 441–446.

Institute of Medicine of the National Academies. (2011). *Relieving pain in America: A blueprint for treatment prevention, care, education, and research.* Washington, DC: The national Academies Press.

Irwin, M., Smith, T., and Gillin, J. C. (1992). Electroencephalographic sleep and natural killer activity in depressed patients and control subjects. *Psychosomatic Medicine, 54,* 10–21.

Iyengar, B. K. S. (1972). *Light on yoga.* New York: Schocken.

Jacobson, E. (1938). *Progressive relaxation.* Chicago: University of Chicago Press.

Janssen, K., and Neutgens, J. (1986). Autogenic training and progressive relaxation in the treatment of three kinds of headache. *Behaviour Research and Therapy, 24,* 199–208.

Jencks, B. (1977). *Your body: Biofeedback at its best.* Chicago: Nelson-Hall.

_____. (1979). *Exercise manual for J. H. Schutlz's standard autogenic training and special formulas.* Salt Lake City, UT: Author.

Jones, E. (1957). *The life and works of Sigmund Freud: The last phase* (Vol. 3). New York: Basic Books.

_____. (1959). *On the nightmare.* New York: Evergreen.

Jones, F., and Bright, J. (2001). *Stress: Myth, theory and research.* New York: Pearson.

Jouvet, M. (1969). Biogenic amines and the states of sleep. *Science, 163,* 32–41.

Jus, A., and Jus, K. (1965). The structure and reactivity of the electroencephalogram during autogenic training. In W. Luthe (ed.), *Autogenic training: Correlationes psychosomaticae* (pp. 12–14). New York: Grune and Stratton.

Karren, K. J., Smith, N. L., Hafen, B. Q., and Jenkins, K. J. (2010). *Mind-body health: The effects of attitudes, emotions and relationships.* New York: Pearson.

Kazdin, A. E. (1982). Single-case research design: Methods for clinical and applied settings. New York: Oxford.

Keefe, F. J. and Van Horn, Y. (1993). Cognitive-behavioral treatment of rheumatoid arthritis pain: Maintaining treatment gains. *Arthritis Care Research, 6,* 213–222.

Kellett, S., and Beail, N. (1997). The treatment of chronic post-traumatic nightmares using psychodynamic-interpersonal psychotherapy: A single-case study. *British Journal of Medical Psychology, 70,* 35–49

Kramer, M. (1991). The nightmare: A failure in dream function. *Dreaming, 1,* 277–285.

Kulich, R., and Loeser, J. D. (2011). The business of pain medicine: The present mirrors antiquity. *Pain Medicine, 12,* 1063–1075.

Labbe, E. L., and Williamson, D. A. (1984). The treatment of childhood migraine using autogenic feedback training. *Journal of Consulting and Clinical Psychology, 52,* 968–976.

Lavey, R. S., and Taylor, C. B. (1985). The nature of relaxation therapy. In Burchfield (ed.), *Stress: Psychological and physiological interactions* (pp. 329–358). Washington, DC: Hemisphere Publishing.

Lazarus, A. A. (1985). *Casebook of multimodal therapy.* New York: Guilford.

_____, and Mayne, T. J. (1990). Relaxation: Some limitations, side effects, and proposed solutions. *Psychotherapy, 27,* 261–266.

Lazarus, R. S. (2006). *Stress an emotion: A new synthesis.* New York: Springer.

_____, DeLongis, A., Folkman, S., and Gruen, R. (1985). Stress and psychological coping. *American Psychologist, 40,* 770–779.

_____, and Folkman, S. (1984). *Stress, appraisal, and coping.* New York: Springer.

Leavitt, F., Kantz, C., and Golden, M. (1986). Comparison of pain properties of fibromyalgia patients and rheumatoid arthritis. *Arthritis and Rheumatology, 29,* 775–781.

Lehrer, P. M., Woolfolk, R. L., and Sime, W. E. (2008). *Principles and practice of stress management.* New York: Guilford.

Leshan, L. (1964). The world of the patient in severe pain of long duration. *Journal of Chronic Diseases, 17,* 119–126.

Leventhal, L., Freundlich, B., Lewis, J., Gillen, K., Henry, J., and Dinges, D. (1995). Controlled study of sleep parameters in patients with fibromyalgia. *Journal of Clinical Rheumatology, 1,* 110–113.

Lichstein, K. L. (1989). *Clinical relaxation training.* New York: Wiley.

Lilly, J. C. (1977). *The deep self: Profound relaxation and the tank isolation technique.* New York: Simon & Schuster.

Lindemann, H. (1973). *Relieve tension the autogenic way.* New York: Peter H. Wyden.

Loeser, J. D. (1982). Concepts of pain. In M. Stantin and R. Boas (eds.), *Chronic low back pain.* Raven Press: New York.

Lolas, F., and Von Rad, M. (1989). Alexithymia. In S. Cheren (ed.), *Psychosomatic Medicine* (Vol. 1, pp. 189-237). Madison, CT: International Universities Press.

Low, C . A., Salomon, K., and Mathews, K. A. (2009). Chronic life stress, cardiovascular reactivity, and subclinical cardiovascular disease in adolescents. *Psychosomatic Medicine, 71,* 927, 931.

Luce, G. G. (1970). *Biological rhythms in psychiatry and medicine.* Rockville, MD: National Institute of Mental Health.

Luthe, W. (1965). Autogenic training: Method, research, and application in medicine. *American Journal of Psychotherapy, 17,* 174–195.

_____. (1970a). *Autogenic therapy: Research and theory* (Vol. IV). New York: Grune and Stratton.

_____. (1970b). *Autogenic therapy: Dynamics of autogenic neutralization* (Vol. V). New York: Grune and Stratton.

_____. (1973). *Autogenic therapy: Treatment with autogenic neutralization* (Vol. VI). New York: Grune and Stratton.

_____. (1977). *A training workshop for professionals: Introduction to the methods of autogenic therapy.* Orlando: The Biofeedback Society of America.

_____. (1979). About the methods of autogenic therapy. In E. Peper, S. Ancoli, and M. Quinn (Eds.), *Mind/body integration: Essential papers in biofeedback* (pp. 167–186). New York: Plenum Press.

_____. (1983). About the method of autogenic therapy. In E. Pepper, S. Ancoli, and M. Quinn (eds.), *Mind/body integration: Essential papers in biofeedback* (pp. 167- 186). New York: Plenum.

_____, and Blumberger, S. R. (1977). Autogenic therapy. In E. D. Wittkower and H. Warnes (eds.), *Psychosomatic medicine: Its clinical applications* (pp. 146–165). New York: Harper & Row.

_____, Jus, A., and Geissman, P. (1965). Autogenic state and autogenic shift: Psychophysiologic and neurophysiologic aspects. In W. Luthe (ed.), *Autogenic training: Correlationes psychosomaticae* (pp. 3–11). New York: Grune and Stratton.

_____, and Schultz, J. H. (1969a). *Autogenic therapy: Medical applications* (Vol. II). New York: Grune and Stratton.

_____, and _____. (1969b). *Autogenic therapy: Applications in psychotherapy* (Vol. III). New York: Grune and Stratton.

Mannerkorpi, K., and Iversen, M. D. (2003). Physical exercise in fibromyalgia and related syndromes. *Best Practice Research in Clinical Rheumatology, 17,* 629–647.

Marquardt, M. (1951). *Paul Ehrlich.* New York: Henry Schuman.

McEwen, B. C., and Stellar, E. (1993). Stress and the individual: Mechanisms leading to disease. *Archives of Internal Medicine, 153,* 2093-2101.

McLean, A. A. (1979). *Work stress.* Reading, MA: Addison-Wesley.

McIwain, H. H., and Bruce, D. F. (1996). *The fibromyalgia handbook.* New York: Owl Books.

Meichenbaum, D. (1977). *Cognitive-behavior modification: An integrated approach*. New York: Plenum.

_____. (2007). Stress inoculation training: A preventative and treatment approach. In P. M. Lehrer, R. L Woolfolk, and W. E. Sime (eds.), *Principles and practice of stress management* (pp. 497–516). New York: Guilford.

_____, and Turk, D. C. (1976). The cognitive behavioral management of anxiety, anger, and pain. In P. O. Davidson (ed.), *The behavioral management of anxiety, depression, and pain*. New York: Brunner and Mazel.

Milling, L. S., Kirsch, I., Meunier, S. A., and Levine, M. R. (2002). Hypnotic analgesia and stress inoculation training: Individual and combined effect in analog treatment of experimental pain. *Cognitive Therapy and Research, 26*, 355-371.

Miskiman, D. E. (1977). The treatment of insomnia by transcendental meditation program. In D. W. Orne-Johnson and J. T. Farrow (eds.), *Scientific research on the transcendental meditation program* (Vol. 1, pp. 296–298). Livingston Manor, NY: Maharishi European Research University Press.

Moldofsky, H. (1989). Sleep and fibrositis. *Rheumatic Diseases Clinics of North America, 15*, 91-103.

_____. (1995). Sleep, wakefulness, neuroendocrine and immune function in fibromyalgia and chronic fatigue syndrome. *Journal of Musculoskeletal Pain, 3*, 75-79.

_____, and Lue, F. A. (1980). The relationship of alpha and delta EEG frequencies to pain and mood in fibrositis patients treated with chlorpromazine and L-tryptophan. *Electro-Encephalography and Clinical Neurophysiology, 50*, 71–80.

_____, and Scarisbrick, P. (1976). Induction of neurasthenic musculoskeletal pain syndrome by selective sleep stage deprivation. *Psychosomatic Medicine, 38*, 35-44.

_____, _____, and England, R., and Smythe, H. (1975). Musculoskeletal symptoms and non-REM sleep disturbance in patients with 'fibrositic syndrome' and healthy subjects. *Psychosomatic Medicine, 37*, 341-351.

Neiss, R. (1988). Reconceptualizing relaxation treatments: Psychobiological states in sports. *Clinical Psychology Review, 8*, 139–159.

Nicassio, P., and Bootzin, R. (1974). A comparison of progressive relaxation and autogenic training as treatments for insomnia. *Journal of Abnormal Psychology, 83*, 253–260.

Norris, F. H. (1992). Epidemiology of trauma: Frequency and impact of different potentially traumatic events on different demographic groups. *Journal of Consulting and Clinical Psychology, 60*, 409–418.

Norris, P. A., Fahrion, S. L., and Oikawa, L. O. (2007). Autogenic biofeedback training in psychophysiological therapy and stress management. In P. M. Lehrer, R. L Woolfolk, and W. E. Sime (eds.), *Principles and practice of stress management* (pp. 175–205). New York: Guilford Press.

Noyes, R. (1981). Treatment of pain. *Psychosomatic Medicine, 43*, 57–70.

Olpin, M., and Hesson, M. (2010). *Stress management for life: A research based experiential approach* (2d ed.). Delmont, CA: Wadsworth.

O'Moore, A. M., O'Moore, R. R., Harrison, R. F., Murphy, G., and Garruthers, M. E. (1983). Psychosomatic aspects of idiopathic infertility: Effects of treatment with autogenic training. *Journal of Psychosomatic Research, 27*, 145–151.

Oringel, S. E. (1983). Somatic versus cognitive processes in relaxation training: A comparison of effects of three types of training on somatic versus cognitive anxiety subjects. *Dissertation Abstracts International, 43*, 3713B.

Patel, C. (1984). Yogic therapy. In R. L. Woolfolk and P. M. Lehrer (eds.), *Principles and practice of stress management* (pp. 70–103). New York: Guilford Press.

Pellegrino, M. J., Van Fossen, D., Gordon C., Ryan J. M., and Waylonis, G. W. (1989) Prevalence of mitral valve prolapse in primary fibromyalgia: A pilot investigation. *Archives of Physical Medicine and Rehabilitation, 70*, 541–543.

Pelletier, K. P. (1977). *Mind as healer, mind as slayer:* New York: Delta/Seymour Lawrence.
_____. (1979). *Holistic medicine: From stress to optimum health.* New York: Delta/Seymour Lawrence.
Phillips, K. M., Antoni, M. H., Lechner, S. C. et al. (2008). Stress management intervention reduces serum cortisol and increases relaxation during treatment for nonmetastatic breast cancer. *Psychosomatic Medicine, 70,* 1044–1049.
Pietrowsky, R., and Köthe, M. (2003). Personal boundaries and nightmare consequences in frequent nightmare sufferers. *Dreams, 13,* 245–254.
Pitman, R. K., Altman, B., and Greenwald, E., Longpre, R. E., Macklin, M. L., Poire, R. E., and Steketee, G. (1991). Psychiatric complications during flooding therapy for post-traumatic stress disorder. *Journal of Clinical Psychiatry, 52,* 17–20.
Polatin, P. B., Kinney, R. K., Gatchel, R. J., Lillo, E., and Mayer, T. G. (1993). Psychiatric illness and chronic pain. *Spine, 18,* 66–71.
Pretzer, J. L., and Beck, A. T. (2007). Cognitive approaches to stress. In P. M. Lehrer, R. L. Woolfolk, and W. E. Sime (eds.), *Principles and practice of stress management* (pp. 465–496). New York: Guilford Press.
Rama, S. (1985). *Perennial psychology of the Bhagavad Gita.* Honesdale, PA: The Himalayan International Institute.
Raskind, M. A., Peskind, E. R., Hoff, D. J., Hart, K. L., et al. (2007). A parallel group placebo controlled study of Prazosin for trauma nightmares and sleep disturbance in combat veterans with post-traumatic stress disorder. *Biological Psychiatry, 61,* 928–934.
Rief, W., Mills, P. J., Ancoli-Israel, S., Zigler, M. G., Pung, M. A., and Dimsadale, J. E. (2010). Overnight changes of immune parameters and catecholamines are associated with mood and stress. *Psychosomatic Medicine, 72,* 755–762.
Russell, I. J. (1989). Neurohormonal aspects of fibromyalgia syndrome. *Rheumatic Diseases Clinics of North America, 15,* 149–168.
_____, Fletcher, E. M., Michalek, J. E., McBroom, P. C., and Hester, G. G. (1991). Treatment of primary fibrositis (fibromyalgia) syndrome with ibuprofen and alprazolam: A double-blind placebo-controlled study. *Arthritis and Rheumatology, 34,* 552–560.
_____, Mease, P. J., Smith, T. R., Kajdasz, D. K., Wohlreich, M. M., Detke, M. J., Walker, D. J., Chappell, A. S., and Arnold, L. M. (2008). Efficacy and safety of duloxetine for treatment of fibromyalgia in patients with or without major depressive disorder: Results from a 6-month, randomized, double-blind, placebo-controlled, fixed-dose trial. *Pain, 136,* 432–444.
Sadigh, M. R. (1997). Psychological treatment of the fibromyalgia pain disorder. *Proceedings from the Spring Conference of the Pennsylvania Society of Behavioral Medicine and Biofeedback* (pp. 3–11), Philadelphia, April.
_____. (1998). Chronic pain and personality disorders: Implications for rehabilitation. *Journal of Rehabilitation, 64,* 4–8.
_____. (1999). The treatment of recalcitrant post-traumatic nightmares with autogenic training and autogenic abreaction. *Journal of Applied Psychophysiology and Biofeedback, 24,* 203–210.
_____. (2003). The fibromyalgia pain disorder and psycho-biological disregulation: A theoretical formulation. *Advances in Medical Psychotherapy and Psychodiagnosis, 11,* 45–58.
_____. (2006). The use of logotherapy in unraveling the noölogical dimension of psychosomatic symptoms. *The International Forum for Logotherapy, 29,* 46–53.
_____, and Mierzwa, J. A. (1995). The treatment of persistent night terrors with autogenic training: A case study. *Biofeedback and Self-Regulation, 20,* 205–209.
Sadler, W. S. (1929). *The truth about mind cure.* Chicago: A. C. McClurg.
Sakai, M. (1997). Application of autogenic training for anxiety disorders: A clinical study in psychiatric setting. *Fukuoka Igaku Zasshi, 88,* 56–64.

Sapolsky, R. M. (2004). Why Zebras don't get ulcers (3d ed.). New York: Holt.

Sargent, J. D., Green, E. E., and Walters, E. D. (1972). The use of autogenic feedback in a pilot study of migraine and tension headaches. *Headache, 12*, 120–125.

Schneiderman, N., and Tapp, J. T. (1985). *Behavioral medicine: The biopsychosocial approach.* Hillside, NJ: Earlbaum Associates.

Schultz, J. H. (1932). *Das autogene training.* Leipzig, Germany: Verlag.

_____. (1950). *Das autogene training: Konzentrative selbstentspannung.* Stuttgart, Germany: Verlag.

_____, and Luthe, W. (1959). *Autogenic training: A psychophysiological approach in psychotherapy.* New York: Grune and Stratton.

_____, and _____. (1965). Autogenic training. A psychophysiological approach in psychotherapy. New York: Grune and Stratton.

_____, and _____. (1969). *Autogenic therapy* (Vol. 1). New York: Grune and Stratton.

_____, and _____. (1969). *Autogenic therapy: Autogenic methods* (Vol. I). New York: Grune and Stratton.

Schwartz, D. P. (1984). A chronic emergency room visitor with chest pain: Successful treatment by stress management training and biofeedback. *Pain, 18*, 315–319.

Schwartz, G. E. (1979). Disregulation and system theory: A biobehavioral framework for biofeedback and behavioral medicine. In N. Birbaumer and H. D. Kimmel (Eds.), *Biofeedback and Self-Regulation* (pp. 19–48). Hillside, NJ: Earlbaum.

_____. (1989). Disregulation theory and disease: Toward a general model of psychosomatic medicine. In S. Cheren (Ed.), *Psychosomatic medicine: Theory, physiology and practice* (pp. 91–117). Madison, CT: International Universities Press.

_____, Davidson, R. J., and Goleman, D. T. (1978). Patterning of cognitive and somatic processes in self-regulation of anxiety: Effects of meditation versus exercise. *Psychosomatic Medicine, 40*, 321–328.

Seaward, B. L. (2011). Essentials of managing stress (2d ed.). Sudbury, MA: Jones and Bartlett.

Seligman, M. E. P. (1975). *Helplessness: On depression, development and death.* San Francisco: W.H. Freeman.

Selye, H. (1950). *The physiology and pathology of exposure to stress.* Montreal: Acta.

_____. (1976). *The stress of life.* New York: McGraw-Hill.

_____. (1982). History and present status of the stress concept. In L. Goldberger and S. Breznitz (eds.), *Handbook of stress: Theoretical and clinical aspects* (pp. 7–17). New York: Free Press.

_____. (1984). *The stress of life,* (3d ed.). New York: McGraw-Hill.

Semble, E. L., and Wise, C. M. (1988). Fibrositis. *American Family Physician, 38*, 129–139.

Sepúlveda, C., Marlin, A., Yoshida, T., and Ullrich, A. (2002). Palliative care: The World Health Organization's global perspective. *Journal of Pain and Symptom Management, 24*, 91–96.

Shinozaki, M., Kanazawa, K., Endo, Nakaya, H., and Fukudo, S. (2010). Effects of autogenic training on general improvements in patients with irritable bowel syndrome: A randomized controlled trial. *Applied Psychophysiology and Biofeedback, 35*, 189–198.

Simeit, R., Deck, R., and Conta-Marx, B. (2004). Sleep management training for cancer patients with insomnia. *Supportive Care in Cancer, 12*, 176–183.

Simons, D. G. (1975). Special review, muscle pain syndrome: Part I. *American Journal of Physical Medicine, 54*, 289–311.

_____. (1976). Muscle pain syndrome: Part II. *American Journal of Physical Medicine, 55*, 15–42.

Sklar, L. S., and Anisman, H. (1981). Stress and cancer. *Psychological Bulletin, 89*, 369–406.

Smith, J. C. (1989). *Relaxation dynamics: A cognitive-behavioral approach to relaxation.* Champaign, IL: Research Press.

Solomon, S. D., Gerrity, E. T., and Muff, A. M. (1992). Efficacy of treatments for post-traumatic disorder: An empirical review. *The Journal of American Medical Association, 268,* 633–638.

Stein, D., Peri, T., Edelstein, E., Elizur, A., and Floman, Y. (1996). The efficacy of amitriptyline and acetaminophen in the management of acute low back pain. *Psychosomatics, 37,* 36–70.

Stein, M. B., Belik, S. L, Jacobi, F., and Sareen, J. (2008). Impairment associated with sleep problems in the community; Relationship to physical and mental health co-morbidity. *Psychosomatic Medicine, 70,* 913–919.

Sternbach, R. A. (1983). Acute versus chronic pain. In P. D. Walls and R. Melzack (eds.), *Textbook of Pain* (pp. 173–177). London: Churchill Livingstone.

Stoyva, J., and Anderson, C. (1982). A coping-rest model of relaxation and stress management. In L. Goldberger and S. Breznitz (eds.), *Handbook of stress: Theoretical and clinical aspects* (pp. 745–763). New York: Free Press.

Straub, R. O. (2007). *Health psychology: A biopsychosocial approach.* New York: Worth.

Suedfeld, P. (1980). *Restricted environmental stimulation.* New York: Wiley.

Syrjala, K. L., Donaldson, G. W., Davis, M. W., Kippes, M. E., and Carr, J. E. (1995). Relaxation and imagery and cognitive-behavioral training reduce pain during cancer treatment: A controlled clinical trial. *Pain, 63,* 189–198.

Taylor, S. E. (2012). *Health psychology* (8th ed.). New York: McGraw-Hill

Thieme, K., Turk, D. C., and Flor, H. (2004). Comorbid depression and anxiety in fibromyalgia syndrome: Relationship to somatic and psychosocial variables. *Psychosomatic Medicine, 66,* 837–844.

Thomas, K. (1967). *Praxis der selbsthypnose des autogenen training.* Stuttgart, Germany: George Thieme Verlag.

Tollison, C. D. (1998). Pain and its magnitude. In R. S. Weiner (ed.), *Pain management: A practical guide for clinicians* (pp. 3–6). Boca Raton: St. Lucie Press.

Travell, J. (1952). Referred pain from skeletal muscles. *New York State Journal of Medicine, 55,* 331–339.

_____, and Simons, D. G. (1983). *Myofascial pain and dysfunction: The trigger point manual.* Baltimore: Williams and Wilkins.

Treadwell, B. J. (1981). Fibromyalgia. *New Zealand Medical Journal, 94,* 157–158.

Turner, J. A. (1982). Comparison of group progressive relaxation training and cognitive behavioral group therapy for chronic low back pain. *Journal of Consulting and Clinical Psychology, 50,* 757–765.

Turner, J. W., and Fine, T. H. (1983). Effects of relaxation associated with brief restricted environmental stimulation therapy (REST) on plasma cortisol, ACTH, and LH. *Biofeedback and Self-Regulation, 8,* 115–126.

Vahia, N. S., and Doongaji, D. R. (1977). Yoga. In E. D. Wittkower and H. Warnes (eds.), *Psychosomatic medicine: Its clinical applications* (pp. 190–198). New York: Harper and Row.

van Diest, R., and Apples, W. P. M. (1994). Sleep characteristics of exhausted men. *Psychosomatic Medicine, 56,* 28–35.

Vgontzas, A. N., Mastorakos, G., Bixler, E. O., Kales, A., Gold, P. W., and Chrousos, G. P. (1999). Sleep deprivation effects on the hypothalamic-pituitary-adrenal and growth axes: Potential clinical implications. *Clinical Endocrinology, 51,* 205–215.

Wallace, D. J. (1990). Genitourinary manifestations of fibrositis: An association with the female urethral syndrome. *Journal of Rheumatology, 17,* 238–239.

Wehrenberg, M., and Prinz, S. M. (2007). *The anxious brain: A neurobiological basis of anxiety disorders and how to effectively treat them.* New York: Norton.

Weiner, H. (1977). *Psychobiology and human disease.* New York: Elsevier-North Holland.

_____. (1982). The prospect for psychosomatic medicine. *Psychosomatic Medicine, 44,* 491-517.

Weiss, R. J. (1973). *Loneliness: The experience of emotional and social isolation.* Cambridge: MIT Press.

Weitz, R. (2007). *The sociology of health, illness, and health care: A critical approach* (4th ed.). Belmont, CA: Wadsworth.

Wilke, W. S. (2009). New developments in the diagnosis of fibromyalgia syndrome: Say goodbye to tender points? *Cleveland Clinical Journal of Medicine, 76,* 345-352.

Winnicott, C., Shepherd, R., and Davis, M. (1989). *Psychonalytic explorations: D. W. Winnicott.* Cambridge, MA: Harvard University Press.

Winnicott, D. W. (1966). Psychosomatic illness in its positive and negative aspects. *International Journal of Psychoanalysis, 47,* 510-516.

Wolfe, F. (1986). The clinical syndrome of fibrositis. *American Journal of Medicine, 81,* 7-14.

_____. (1995). The future of fibromyalgia: Some critical issues. *Journal of Musculoskeletal Pain, 3,* 3-15.

_____, Cathey, M. A., and Klienheskel, S. M. (1984). Psychological status in primary fibrositis and fibrositis associated with rheumatoid arthritis. *Journal of Rheumatology, 11,* 500-506.

_____, Clauw, D. J., Fitzcharles, M. A., Goldenberg, D. L., Katz, R. S., Mease, P., Russell, A. S., Russell, I. J., Winfield, J. B., and Yunus, M. B. (2010). The American College of Rheumatology preliminary diagnostic criteria for fibromyalgia and measurement of symptom severity. *Arthritis Care and Research, 62,* 600-610.

_____, Smythe, H. A., and Yunus, M. B. (1990). The American College of Rheumatology 1990 criteria for the classification of fibromyalgia: Report of the Multicenter Criteria Committee. *Arthritis and Rheumatism, 33,* 160-172.

Wolpe, J. (1958). *Psychotherapy by reciprocal inhibition.* Stanford: Stanford University Press.

Yunus, M. B. (1994). Psychological aspects of fibromyalgia syndrome: A component of the dysfunctional spectrum syndrome. *Bailliere's Clinical Rheumatology, 8,* 811-837.

_____. (1994a). Fibromyalgia syndrome: Clinical features and spectrum. *Journal of Musculoskeletal Pain, 2,* 5-21.

_____, Masi, A. T., and Aldag, J. C. (1989). A controlled study of primary fibromyalgia syndrome: Clinical features and association with other functional syndromes. *Journal of Rheumatology, 13,* 183-186.

_____, _____, and Calabro, J. J. (1981). Primary fibromyalgia: Clinical study of 5 patients with matched normal controls. *Seminars in Arthritis and Rheumatology, 11,* 151-171.

Zoccola, P. M., Dickerson, S. S., and Lam, S. (2009). Rumination predicts longer sleep onset latency after acute psychosocial stressor. *Psychosomatic Medicine, 71,* 771-775.

Index